D1571021

THE GREEN AGES

THE GREEN AGES

Medieval Innovations in Sustainability

ANNETTE KEHNEL

Translated from the German by Gesche Ipsen

Brandeis University Press | Waltham, Massachusetts

First published in North America in 2024 by Brandeis University Press

Published in Great Britain in 2024 by Profile Books Ltd

Originally published in German, entitled
Wir konnten auch anders by Karl Blessing Verlag, 2021

The translation of this work was supported by a grant from the Goethe-Institut

Brandeis University Press

Manufactured in the United States of America

Library of Congress Cataloging-in-Publication Data

Names: Kehnel, Annette, author.
Title: The green ages : medieval innovations in sustainability /
Annette Kehnel ; translated from the German by Gesche Ipsen .
Other titles: Wir konnten auch anders. English
Description: Waltham, MA : Brandeis University Press, 2024. |
Includes index. | Summary: "In this fascinating meld of history and
ecological economics, the author uncovers the medieval precedents for
modern concepts of sustainable living"—Provided by publisher.
Identifiers: LCCN 2024017885 (print) | LCCN 2024017886 (ebook) |
ISBN 9781684582433 (cloth) | ISBN 9781684582426 (ebook)
Subjects: LCSH: Human ecology—Europe—History—To 1500. |
Sustainable living. | Ecological economics. | Environmentalism. | Middle Ages. |
BISAC: HISTORY / Europe / Medieval | NATURE / Environmental Conservation & Protection
Classification: LCC GF540 .K4513 2024 (print) | LCC GF540 (ebook) |
DDC 338.94/070902—dc23/eng/20240514
LC record available at https://lccn.loc.gov/2024017885
LC ebook record available at https://lccn.loc.gov/2024017886

To my children and grandchildren –
thank you for your infectious yen for the future
and for wanting to do things differently

Sustainable development (n.): Development that meets the needs of the present without compromising the ability of future generations to meet their own needs

UN Brundtland Report, 1987

Contents

INTRODUCTION

We are facing a watershed moment. Limited resources, the end of the consumer society, increasing injustice, globalisation, accelerated digitalisation, climate change and, finally, growing political uncertainty – particularly in the world's major economies – have thrown humanity into a state of collective bewilderment. While politicians and economists are trying to come up with solutions, populists everywhere are preaching radical change and seeking salvation in a world neatly parcelled into sovereign nations; here and there, some people are tentatively criticising capitalism, while others are putting their hopes in medical and digital advances. What to do, though, in the face of these developments, none of which currently offer any real prospect of a solution, even less a viable future? Something has to change: that much is clear.

Modern Strategies Have Had Their Day

Why is it that, despite our frantic search for solutions to the challenges of the twenty-first century, we find ourselves gradually running out of ideas? The trouble is that we're attempting to fix the problems of the future using 'modern' strategies. The term 'modern' may evoke progress and innovation, but this 'modern age' of ours is, historically speaking, already more than two centuries old; it means that we are endeavouring to solve twenty-first-century issues using frameworks developed in the late eighteenth and nineteenth centuries – the same frameworks that facilitated the rise of the modern era.

Back then, the three magic words were 'progress', 'growth' and 'wealth'. They guided our political, social and economic actions, and brought about considerable advances. Industrialisation, the French Revolution, nation states and democracy were what made nineteenth- and early twentieth-century Europe 'modern'; and then the second half of the twentieth century unexpectedly dished out a second helping: while people were still suffering from the deep wounds inflicted by two world wars, modernity served up an economic boom on the back of a sharp spike in consumption and the birth of the throwaway society. Ever since the Western industrialised nations embarked on the dizzying ascent that was the 'economic miracle', we have tried, like junkies, to maintain our high, or at any rate to recapture it again and again. The last few decades might have worked out quite well for us, but we've lost our taste for it for some time now, having been presented with the final bill: microplastics in the oceans, glyphosate in our food, and CO_2 in the atmosphere; all irreversible and with serious consequences for the entire planet. Yet rather than face reality, we yearn for the good old days, lock, stock and barrel. 'Life used to be so nice!' we cry, and sit there like grumpy toddlers with an empty bag of sweets, whining for more. We're simply out of ideas – unless the idea is to have even more growth and even more wealth.

We are still stuck in the nineteenth century, approaching problem-solving using a system of coordinates that is nearly two hundred years old. Admittedly, that system was perfect for devising things like revenue optimisation models, returns on investment and ways to squeeze the last drop out of our resources, but when it comes to matters not related to profit maximisation it is getting us nowhere.

Homo Economicus – Modernity's Desperate Hero

Homo economicus plays a key role in this narrative. He is a rational agent and 'maximiser of utility', and the embodiment of the notion that people are always, and first and foremost, concerned with how useful something is to them. Granted, economic man is merely a model, a fictional operator in formulas used to explain economic relationships; and the 'maximiser of utility' is a fairly recent invention of modern economics, elevated to dogma only with the introduction of rational choice theory in the 1970s. However, this canonisation of 'personal gain' has its roots in the nineteenth century, when the popular mind misinterpreted it as one of the 'selective advantages' mentioned in Charles Darwin and Herbert Spencer's theory of evolution. People mistakenly thought that being able to assimilate, cleverly exploit available resources and beat the competition were evolutionary success factors. All of a sudden, competition and the fight for survival were biological facts, and if you didn't keep up, nature left you out in the cold. What evolutionary biologists called natural selection, economic theorists turned into the market's invisible hand: the intangible force that regulates everything and thus renders the old-fashioned moral baggage of pre-modern societies superfluous. The two concepts seamlessly combined into a modern whole, promoting the rational maximiser of utility to the position of a much-lauded (usually male) employee – no, more than that: to the boss, the CEO, of the modern era.

The only problem is that the nineteenth century is long over. Modernity has doubtless achieved great things, and we shouldn't diminish them; but after 200 years of growth, progress and wealth, what we urgently need now is a reality check. We must rise to the challenge, and put our modern-age strategies to the test: are they still relevant? Most importantly, can they help us solve twenty-first-century problems?

Fear of Change

We could also call it a collective refusal to evolve. What we need to do is work out a way to loosen the ties that bind us to outdated notions and principles. Ideally, it would be enough for us to realise that they – though valuable during a particular phase in human history, perhaps even key to our survival – have outlived their usefulness. Generally speaking, what holds us fast is an intricate network of diffuse phobias, particularly the fear of change. What can we do about it? The first step is self-awareness, fresh insights and a change in perspective – and then, at some point, the desire for change will emerge. The new magic words are 'expanding our horizon': deploying our collective imagination for a better future.

The situation we find ourselves in is similar to that of an artist: over the past 200 years humanity has worked hard on the modern era, showing admirable focus and a willingness to make considerable sacrifices. At some point, though, every artist has to look up from their labours, step back and regard the work of art they are creating. We must now do the same. Only then can we see how all those individual little details combine into a whole, and determine where next to place the paintbrush. If we can develop a vision for the future, we will know what to do next. And then our urge to keep painting will return.

Create distance, take a step back, detach, put the paintbrush down for once and choose a new perspective – these are the steps we must take if we want to come up with fresh, future-proof ideas fit for the twenty-first century.

Navel-gazing vs the Historical View

As a historian, I can't help but notice how short-sighted we are these days. It is one of the main reasons why we can't create the distance we need in order to properly assess our prospects. Our collective consciousness is haunted by countless images of the past, and the unspoken law of linear progression hovers in our minds like a cloud.

What springs to mind when we picture life in the old days? We immediately think of humans advancing from Stone Age cave to Renaissance palace, and thence straight into today's comfortable abodes with bathrooms and wi-fi. Much the same happens when we consider economics. We think of economics as having only got going recently, with the dawn of industrialisation. Of course, people have always swapped and traded goods, but things didn't really take off until we invented capitalism and the Industrial Revolution arrived. Moreover – the logic goes – there is no alternative to capitalism. As we know, the 'managed economies' of both socialism and fascism have failed, and it appears that non-European economic models are not up to much either. For the next few centuries, then, we'll have no choice but to somehow come to terms with capitalism.

If we take the historical view, however, such statements turn out to be symptoms of an extreme case of myopia and a fixation with the present; perhaps also of a decent dose of hubris, a lack of imagination and a fear of venturing beyond our comfort zone and considering the possibility that somewhere else – whether earlier, i.e. in the past, or later, i.e. in the future – things were, or could be, very different. Different, but good nevertheless.

What we need is a new vision of the future. The strategies of the past 200 years, the period we call 'modernity', were excellent, and we have enjoyed a great degree of success. Much of what the advent of the modern era promised has indeed come to pass. But what now? As everyone knows, there is a reason why fairy tales end the moment the enchanted prince marries the princess and everyone lives happily ever after; for what kind of life can you live in a world where all your dreams have come true? A world of washing machines, a global literacy rate of close to 90 per cent, and seemingly unlimited mobility, where you can cross the Alps in an hour and a half and fly from Frankfurt to Milan for as little as ten euros? What do we do now, with all those magnificent achievements of the modern era? What do we do now, in a world that suddenly seems to spin faster than it did even ten years ago, which has become much smaller but also more fragile, which is groaning under the burden of modernity's successes but also bursting with young humans, hungry for the future?

Broadening the Horizons

In order to have a clear view of the future, let us turn to the past. The aim is to grasp the bigger picture and thereby give ourselves greater scope for action. To do that, though, we must go back further than just two centuries. We modern *Homines sapientes* have no less than 300,000 years behind us; about 100,000 years ago, we set out from Africa and managed to gradually populate five continents before surviving the Great Ice Age as well as the period of global warming that followed – unlike the woolly mammoth, for instance, which died out in 12,000 BC. How did we do it? How did we manage our resources? How did we survive calamities and disasters?

In what follows, I shall concentrate on the pre-modern era, the period immediately preceding the eighteenth-century Industrial Revolution. 'Pre-modern' is a tricky concept, because it divides history into the modern – i.e. 'us' – and all that went before – i.e. 'them'. This is not a particularly helpful distinction, especially when you consider that 'pre-modern' is supposed to encompass more than 300,000 years of human history; so we'll try to avoid the term. Our focus will be on the more than two millennia that preceded industrialisation, stretching from Greek antiquity (the fifth century BC) to the Enlightenment (the eighteenth century). Most of my examples come from the high to late Middle Ages, that is, roughly from the 1000s to the 1500s, and from societies and economies based in Europe, the Middle East and North

Africa – because the Mediterranean was an economic nerve centre in those days, they were to an extent considered a cultural and economic whole. The advantage of this is that the people who lived in that region during this period left behind a comparatively large volume of written material, granting us unexpectedly detailed insights into their lives and conceptual world, which allow us to reconstruct pre-modern takes on economic norms, theories and practices.

At this point, I should make it clear that the aim of this book is not to propose concrete solutions, such as a return to medieval forms of economy. Far from it. No one who knows even a little about the Middle Ages will want to go back there. Rather, it is designed to inspire, to awaken our sense of the possibilities out there, and to help us to think outside now defunct thought patterns.

There is much disagreement about whether or not we can learn from history. In my experience, this much is clear: the past may not be able to provide tailor-made solutions for the future – because each epoch has to work things out for itself – but what it can do is expand our imaginative horizon and provide fresh stimuli as we search for sustainable economic models and attempt to reinterpret the status quo through the prism of new ideas. What does the future look like if we stop staring at it through the lens of musty modernity, which is nothing if not normative and standardised? What happens if, for once, we take off this much-too-tight and old-fashioned corset? What happens if we – inspired by the diversity of the past – make room for alternative views of the present and the future? What if it turns out that we can do things completely differently?

Reassessing the Framework

People are already trying all sorts of things. There are attempts to make corporate governance more holistic and sustainable, such as the OECD's non-profit initiative to establish new accounting standards for listed companies. The disadvantages of property – the associated responsibilities and costs – and the allure of living an unencumbered life – make collective-use models seem appealing. More and more people are opting out of the hamster wheel of maximum productivity and rapid promotion, choosing to work less and instead spend more time with their children. Or travelling the world with little to no money in their pocket, deliberately eschewing a steady income. Not that this is the belated legacy of superannuated hippies: the new minimalism movement is very much postmodern and digitised. You'll bump into its adherents at TED conferences and book fairs, and they are winning prestigious awards for designing microhomes and suchlike.

Swap sites are flourishing everywhere, as are start-ups such as the one that repurposes old truck tarpaulins into bags (with hefty price tags). Market sectors related to shared use and collaborative consumption are growing at a remarkable rate, as are vintage sites selling anything up to and including haute couture. An increasing number of us, too, are pondering the possibilities of a 'post-growth economy' under the banner of slogans like 'From bigger to better', and there's a growing demand for pluralism in economic studies – see, for instance, the UK-based NGO Promoting Economic Pluralism and the International Student Initiative for Pluralism in Economics. You don't have to agree with all these movements, but they are concerned with pressing issues. These people are active in the markets; they are market participants, and want to do their share to help shape the future – but in a way that runs counter to the conventional, decrepit economic approaches of a decaying modernity.

The aim of this book is to help increase our scope for action. I hope that it will spark your curiosity, dispel some fears and whet your appetite for the future. It is also a plea for us to reassess our economic abilities: the problem is not economics but our simplistic idea of what it entails.

A Tour Through the Book

The first chapter examines some current (mis)conceptions regarding what life was like in the past, explains how grand narratives work and argues that we need new stories for the twenty-first century. We will analyse the familiar narrative of human progress that grew out of the nineteenth century, when it seemed that things were continuously getting better – and when, to allow the present to shine, we forced the past to retreat into the shadows. It seems obvious to us, even inevitable, that more or less everyone was poor and miserable before the 1800s, a thought that still shapes our view of the past. But did our progenitors really have to toil from dawn till dusk? Was everyone as poor as the proverbial church mice, living in miserable, dirty conditions? To help us orient ourselves, this chapter, in place of the usual myths and legends, contains some solid data that we have on Europe during the high and late Middle Ages.

Thus equipped, we will set out on our journey into the past, where we'll encounter Europe's pre-industrial economies – in all their rich diversity.

Sharing: medieval monasteries and convents ended up with 1,500 years' worth of experience in sharing economies. They are proof that it is actually possible to use resources collectively, and manage valuable assets profitably as well as sustainably. In this chapter we will also look at the centuries-long history of the commons, where people managed communal resources in a way that ensured their lasting survival. How did they do that? How did they factor external costs into their decision-making, or 'internalise externalities'? The publication in 1713 of Hans Carl von Carlowitz's *Sylvicultura oeconomica* is generally considered the date when sustainability was born – but the concept existed long before that, as evidenced, for example, by the fishing industry on Lake Constance and transhumance economies in southern France. Another success story was that of the female residents of Flanders's economic centres, who, beginning in the thirteenth century, chose to live together in lay communities called 'beguinages'; they pursued all kinds of work, and it is to them that cities like Antwerp and Bruges owe their beautiful green spaces.

Recycling: this chapter is about ecological sustainability, i.e. the sparing use of our planet's resources. The modern definition of 'waste' as useless leftovers did not enter European dictionaries until the twentieth century. Before then, we couldn't conceive of such a thing. Every economy was circular, things were routinely reused, second-hand goods dominated the market and recycled products were the norm. We will look at the 'repair professions' in medieval Frankfurt am Main, where the stalls of menders who sold second-hand goods and fixed everything from shoes to knives shaped the city's streetscape and were omnipresent at trade fairs. Next, contemporary accounts of second-hand markets in Paris suggest that fashion was more or less dictated by upcycling and hand-me-downs. We'll also examine the history of paper, a recycled product from China that won over the world, and learn how experts who regard themselves as guardians of tradition – and are therefore inclined to be sceptical of new techniques and materials – can put obstacles in the way of innovation. The final section reveals the popularity of recycled building materials during the Middle Ages, for instance in the construction of Aachen's cathedral. Back then, builders would reuse bits of ancient edifices as a matter of course; not only was it the pragmatic choice, but they took pleasure in assemblage and bricolage as such, and in the value they could add to something simply by injecting a little of the past into it.

Microfinance: the fourth chapter tackles the matter of socio-economic sustainability, starting with microfinance institutions in fifteenth-century Italian towns and cities. The aim of the *monti di pietà*, a form of communal pawnbroker, was to give the less well-off – especially poor craftsmen, peasants, day labourers and so on – access to investment capital. The money came from the wealthier urban citizens, and meant that a farmer could pledge his winter coat in the spring for a loan to buy seeds and redeem it again in the autumn with his earnings from the harvest. This model quickly spread across Europe, where lending money to your peers was everyday practice during the Middle Ages. Both creditors and debtors came from all walks of life, as illustrated by the city of Basel, which safeguarded every single loan by registering it in a public debt ledger called the *Vergichtbücher*, which can still be viewed in the city archive. These books give us an insight into contemporary credit practices, and how debt could act as the glue that held urban communities together. Next, we learn how rural and urban economies were sustainably intertwined, for example via 'livestock leasing', whereby town residents issued loans to regional farmers in the form of cattle, which the farmer would raise, care for and use. The crucial point here is that both parties shared the risks as well as the profits (i.e. the calves, foals, piglets, etc. born during the loan period).

Minimalism: the fifth chapter offers frugality as one possible solution to our problems. For centuries, people who eschewed money and even the idea of 'making a living' altogether were a familiar sight in every city, and played an important part in shaping Europe's political and social life. This chapter takes us back to ancient Greece during the fourth century BC and to Diogenes the Cynic in his *pithos*, who argued that the path to freedom and the good life was paved with a pragmatic sort of abstinence. The next example comes from the late Middle Ages: beginning in the late twelfth century, thanks to climate change and the resulting population increase, Europe became progressively urbanised; at the same time there was a boom in minimalist communities – that is, mendicant orders that lived by the motto 'Less is more'. They left a permanent mark on society and economics and produced the most original economic theorists of the age. One such radical minimalist was Pierre de Jean Olivi, from Sérignan in southern France, who – 500 years before Karl Marx – not only published a groundbreaking analysis of market processes but defined the concept of 'capital'.

The book's final chapter suggests ways in which the past can help us reshape the future. There is more than one way to skin an economy, and we have proved that we can do things differently. We are capable of change. We desire so much more than merely to gratify our self-interest, and there is no reason why we can't. To achieve our individual as well as our collective goals, though, we have to work together. We also need guidelines to ensure that we don't end up acting even more foolishly than usual. Finally, the book concludes with ideas for how to silence the sound of inevitability: as history teaches us, people are capable of far more than acting selfishly. It shows that we can, in fact, do things differently – all we have to do is want to.

1

WAS EVERYONE POOR UNTIL WE INVENTED CAPITALISM?

The History of Progress: Modern Grand Narratives and their Pitfalls

We find it hard these days not to present human history as a story of progress and advancement. It was not always thus. Throughout the past, there have been periods when history was seen differently, perhaps as a cycle of constantly recurring rhythms, as proceeding towards a Judgement Day or as a story of decline. It was only in the course of the eighteenth century that we first put progress on a pedestal, during the so-called Enlightenment, when Europe was illuminated by the light of reason and Immanuel Kant told the story of how we 'emerged from self-imposed immaturity' (1784), giving the modern era its very own creation myth.

The myth bore fruit for science, politics and economics in the nineteenth century, and Darwin's *On the Origin of Species* (1859) extended the idea to the realm of nature. His 'tree of life', which conceptualised the biological advancement of species, shows *Homo sapiens* at the very pinnacle, the victor, so to speak, in the biological battle for survival. Karl Marx and Friedrich Engels urged the proletariat to finally emerge from oppression and evolve into a classless society, even as capitalism proclaimed that technology and economics would propel us into a world where every need was satisfied.

Another, particularly egregious, chapter in the enlightened

story of our ascent was the division of mankind into 'us' and 'them'. White Western man was naturally the driver of all progress, because he was superior to the rest of the world – because it was his story; and with the invention of races (which also happened in the eighteenth century), the notion that he had risen to the top thanks to his hard work, efficiency and reason was underwritten by supposedly scientific arguments. The consequences are well known, and remain a burden: slavery, racism, colonialism and the exploitation of man and nature across vast swathes of the planet have cemented global injustices that are anything but easy to undo.

The same goes for the lasting damage and destruction caused by the myth that self-interest is the mainspring of progress. This myth is perhaps one of the most resilient narratives of the past two centuries. Adam Smith is said to have devised it when, in a chapter on the division of labour in his classic work *The Wealth of Nations* (1776), he argued that, although it goes without saying that bakers sell bread out of self-interest rather than altruism, they nonetheless contribute to the well-being of society.[1] People inferred from this that an individual's desire for profit benefits everyone and is good for innovation and progress; and that, consequently, humanity owes its ascent to capitalism, whose roots, prototypes and precursors could be traced back deep into antiquity.

The future blew in with the birth of European modernity more than two hundred years ago, and the tale of progress not only suited the age but endured for a remarkably long time, surviving in our collective memory to this day. This phenomenon is called a 'metanarrative' or 'grand narrative': it isn't history in the literal sense – you don't read about it in journals or hear about it from teachers; no, it is history that simply exists, that doesn't need to be explicitly told. It is a narrative, a story, which plays out as if below the surface of history itself. It makes us feel safe and gives meaning to things. Grand narratives store up generations' worth of empirical knowledge and affect how we see ourselves. They are important, and they are useful.[2]

But only insofar as they accord with the reality they are supposed to explain. The question is, do we still need a story that explains the rise of the Western world? It suited the age of accelerated industrialisation and colonialism; it accompanied our increasing domination of nature via new methods and technologies, from the invention of the steam engine in the 1700s and the first public steam railway – the Stockton and Darlington – in September 1825, to the first nuclear power station in Obninsk, Russia in summer 1954, and the Moon landings in July 1969. But does that old narrative still suit the twenty-first century? The world has kept turning. Nature has handed us the bill for those two centuries of merciless exploitation and our division of the planet into 'us' and 'them' has caused wholesale destruction – so there is every reason in the world for us to put these metanarratives to the test. Which are still useful? Which can we do without?

Romantics vs modernists: the good old days or the bad old days?

'Once upon a time we were poor, then capitalism flourished, and now as a result we are rich.'[3] With this pithy statement, Deirdre McCloskey, an economist at the University of Illinois in Chicago, exposes what she calls the naive world view of many of her colleagues, for whom capitalism is still key to our salvation. They believe that wherever there is poverty, capitalism simply hasn't had a chance to properly take hold yet. They quietly take it for granted that the day will come when capitalism, and with it progress, wins out in Africa, Southeast Asia and South America too.

The idea that life was worse in the old days – be it in the Middle Ages or the nineteenth century or the years following the Second World War – runs like a red thread through our collective historical imagination. As does, incidentally, the counter-narrative that things used to be better, simpler, more natural, less complicated and somehow more human. They are two oddly contradictory narratives, which our brains have somehow managed to store simultaneously, to be recalled as required, without ever really getting in each other's way.

The debate pitches modernists against romantics, and while the former praise the blessings of our age, the latter grieve for a lost world. The two camps have one thing in common, though: both exoticise the world of those who came before us. The romantics lament the disappearance of simplicity, of extended families and family solidarity, of life lived in harmony with nature, without alienation and consumerism. The modernists are delighted that we have overcome the primitive living conditions of the past. Both arguments follow the same pattern, really. People used to be different; depending on your world view and the topic under discussion, they were either more violent or more peaceful and either better or worse off – but whatever the case, they were 'different'.

Whether we see ourselves as romantic victims or modernist victors, we make strangers of our ancestors, distance ourselves from them and draw comparisons, so that we can feel superior. You could call it a form of 'othering', a term used in social psychology to describe our tendency to distinguish between 'us' and 'them'.[4] This mechanism plays a significant part in the construction of modern myths: it is the engine that powers our self-assurance.

Of lice, doctors' saws and boredom

Take, for example, the following passage from Steven Pinker's *The Better Angels of Our Nature*, a book in which he argues that humanity emerged from a dark and violent past into a peaceful and much less violent present:

> Our ancestors [...] were infested with lice and parasites and lived above cellars heaped with their own feces. Food was bland, monotonous, and intermittent. Health care consisted of the doctor's saw and the dentist's pliers. Both sexes labored from sunrise to sundown, whereupon they were plunged into darkness. Winter meant months of hunger, boredom and gnawing loneliness in snowbound farmhouses. [...] [They also did without] the higher and nobler things in life, such as knowledge, beauty, and human connection. Until recently most people never traveled more than a few miles from their place of birth. Everyone was ignorant of the vastness of the cosmos [...]. When children emigrated, their parents might never see them again, or hear their voices, or meet their grandchildren. And then there are modernity's gifts of life itself: the additional decades of existence, the mothers who live to see their newborns, the children who survive their first years on earth. When I stroll through old New England graveyards, I am always struck by the abundance of tiny plots and poignant epitaphs: 'Elvina Maria, died July 12, 1845; aged 4 years, and 9 months. *Forgive this tear, a parent weeps. 'Tis here, the faded floweret sleeps.*'[5]

By the time we have witnessed this moving scene at the grave of a four-year-old girl who died in 1845, Pinker has brought us firmly on side. The old days must have been awful. Surely few would disagree that life was tough, least of all anyone who knows anything about history. Still, it's worth noting that, what with all the drama, Pinker never actually tells us which past he is talking about. When exactly, and where, did our ancestors reside on top of their faeces? In which century were there physicians whose only treatment plan was the bone saw? When did those people live who never once left their place of birth, and does this tally with the medieval duty of every good Christian to undertake a pilgrimage?

Does it tally with the countless migrations in history – the Great Migration of the 400s and 500s, the Anglo-Saxon migration to Britain in the 400s and the Normans who, from the 700s onwards, settled throughout Europe, from the Atlantic coast to Kyiv and from Scotland to Sicily? Does it tally with the overbooked ships, and the numerous people who, ever since the twelfth century, have regularly set off for the Holy Land? Finally, you wonder quite how our poor ancestors' experience of oppressive paralysis can be reconciled with the terrible experiences they had when they emigrated.

What is being served up here is a light, colourful summer salad of pseudo-knowledge across the centuries, a well-nigh comprehensive summary of all the supposed truisms about 'the old days' to be found in our collective subconscious. But is any of it true?

Did Our Forebears Toil from Dawn till Dusk?

Take Pinker's notion, for instance, that our forebears worked tirelessly 'from sunrise to sundown', and that they would afterwards sit around in the dark knowing neither art nor beauty nor 'human connection'. What do we know about people's working lives in centuries past? How many hours a week did they work? How many days off did they have in a given year?

We instinctively assume that Pinker is right in what he says. We automatically surmise that capitalism alleviated the wretchedness of work. We compare today's forty-hour week to the nineteenth-century's eighty-hour week, and expect that things were the same before that. We recall the hard life of medieval peasants forced to work the fields day in and day out, and the poor craftsmen and craftswomen who often sat up late into the night in a cold, damp workshop to fulfil their customers' orders. These visions are reverse projections, imposed by us in the present on to a putative past – and they are wrong. It isn't true that people used to work extremely long hours until we came up with the idea of capitalism. Life had a different rhythm and pace back then. People probably had less money than now, but they had a lot more spare time.

Five-day weeks, 'Saint Monday' and plenty of holidays

For workers in England, half a day's work once counted as 'one day's labour', and if you worked a whole day it counted as two. The economist and sociologist Juliet B. Schor has studied the evolution of twentieth-century working hours, and compared them to pre-modern hours using metadata from studies of various medieval English towns and regions.[6] She found that craftsmen, builders, carpenters and joiners worked an average of eight to nine hours a day, and the number of holidays varied from region to region and diocese to diocese: in 1222, for example, workers in the diocese of Oxford had forty days off in addition to the usual fifty-two Sundays, including five days for Christmas and three days each at Easter and Whitsun. In some regions in France people had more than ninety days off, and Spanish workers are reported to have had close to five months off a year. Workers also had a certain degree of autonomy, and sometimes set their own hours – not that their employers were always pleased about them. For example, they sometimes stretched their weekend out a little and skipped work on Mondays. These became known as 'Saint Mondays', and they survived largely unscathed until the sixteenth century.[7] As the economic historian Gerhard Fouquet once drily remarked, it was the Reformation that put a stop to 'the medieval idler's five-day week'.[8] We can thus say with reasonable certainty that the average person spent around 2,000 hours a year working, which is comparable to today's average. It wasn't until the nineteenth century that working hours rose sharply, children entered the workforce and the inhumane conditions we recall with a pang from Dickens's novels came into

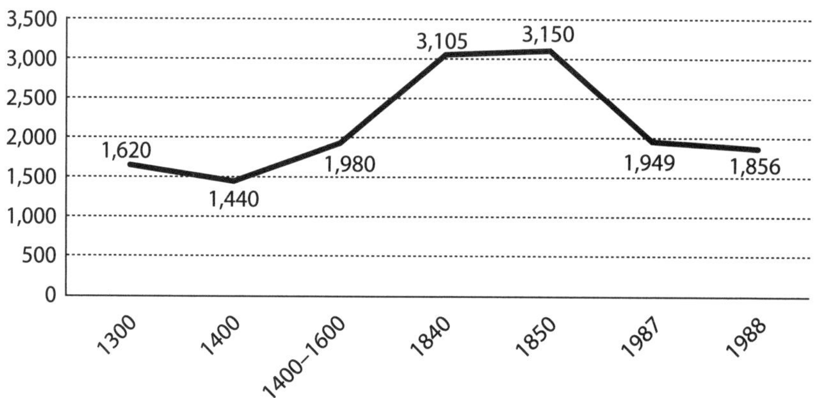

1. How average annual working hours evolved from the Middle Ages to the twentieth century

effect. Nonetheless, we seem to have completely forgotten that the nineteenth century didn't mark the end of the Middle Ages, but ushered in the first golden age of modernity.

Is life without a washing machine worth living?

As regards working hours, then, there has been no improvement since the Middle Ages. Neither the five-day week nor the 2,000 hours we work on average per year can be credited to modernity. In fact, the opposite is true: with the advent of the modern era and the Industrial Revolution, both were abolished for the time being.

But what about living standards? There, the matter seems clear-cut. In the fourteenth century, there was definitely more uncertainty: food supplies were often unreliable, and the age was prone to crises and instability. Yet we'd be wrong to paint life as universally miserable, because it was when living standards were at their lowest that people were best provided for, comparatively speaking.[9] Still, from today's perspective it is difficult not to describe people back then as desperately poor. At least, they lacked the amenities that we take for granted – living without washing machines, fridges, telephones and all those other blessings of technology. Quite inconceivable, isn't it? Clearly, there is a risk of hindsight bias: it is tempting to evaluate past societies from today's perspective, and it never once occurs to us to ask the one crucial question: might life without a washing machine still be a life worth living?

This somewhat provocative question isn't meant to suggest that the past was rosy – on the contrary: it should prompt us to stop arguing about whether things used to be better or worse, and consider instead that they might simply have been different.

Food and living standards

How about nutrition? Well, people rarely ate meat. On Fridays and Saturdays, the weekly 'fast days', they generally ate none, and in some places meat-eating days were even limited to three a week; add to that the six-week fast before Easter and, in some regions, another four-week (Advent) fast in the run-up to Christmas, and it means that, in total, people ate meat only 138–230 days a year. This was true for all social strata: we know from the bishop of Arles's meticulous fifteenth-century household ledgers that his (doubtless anything but ascetic) household served meat 214 days a year; Nuremberg's rations records for 1449–50 reveal that the city's Swiss mercenaries – much sought after and highly paid specialist soldiers – received 109 kg of meat a year, Eger infantrymen 54.3 kg, and prisoners of war (who were of course fed as cheaply as possible) 32.7 kg. In his 1527 chronicle, the Strasbourg burgher Heinrich Hug notes that the price of meat has gone up, and tersely blames the Reformation for converting his fellow residents to meat-eating on Fridays and Saturdays too.[10] In the nineteenth century, average meat consumption if anything decreased slightly, down to 37.7 kg in 1890. By comparison, Germans today consume an average of around 78.7 kg a year (as compared to India, for instance, with an average of 4.5 kg).[11]

Apprenticeship premiums paid to masters are perhaps not an ideal yardstick for measuring living standards, given that they include compensation for the master's investment in the apprentice. Still, they show up in various account ledgers: for instance, in 1472 the Nuremberg merchant Hans Praun apprenticed his daughter to a silk embroiderer, whom he paid seven and a half guilders per annum for 'board and training'. In 1496, Heidelberg's municipal stipend for poor but gifted pupils amounted to 8.75 guilders (fl.) a year; and although it can hardly have covered their living costs, we can estimate that it at least provided them with a modest living. Around the same time, in 1482, fostering a Strasbourg orphan cost 5.7 fl. to 7.6 fl.; and in Nuremberg in 1496, one man paid an innkeeper 14.5 fl. a year pro rata to put up a relative, while the annual expenditure of an ordinary family living a modest lifestyle was estimated at somewhere between 29 fl. and 31 fl. According to the Strasbourg merchants' exchange accounts of 1450, a scribe employed by the man in charge of the exchange earned 19.4 fl., and the parish ledger of St Lorenz in Nuremberg recorded that an organ builder engaged in 1448–9 received 31.5 fl. for 'food and wine',[12] on which sum a craftsman could easily live a moderately comfortable life. Regional differences and variations in exchange rates mean that it is difficult for us to convert those amounts into today's money – but these numbers and case studies suffice to show that the myth of the lice-infested, bored and lonely medieval European is questionable at best.

Europe in the High to Late Middle Ages: Some Useful Data

Climate change, population growth and urbanisation

Most examples in this book are drawn from the high to late Middle Ages, i.e. AD 1000–1600. To aid our understanding, therefore, I will now list some data concerning the period's social, economic and climatic conditions; because we don't have access to the kind of solid data available for the twentieth century, they are in the main scholarly estimates.[13]

Roughly at the turn of the second millennium AD, we can discern a – first slight and then more distinct – population increase. In the year 1000, around 20 million people lived on the European continent; by 1200, the population had risen to about 60 million, and by 1300 to around 73 million. In the mid-fourteenth century, the number dropped off dramatically, stabilising again only in the mid-1400s at 53–5 million, nearly 10 million less than in 1200. One reason – perhaps the most significant reason – for this development was that the region experienced a period of climate change. Average annual temperatures had increased slightly since the turn of the millennium, and the climate had become milder and more congenial; some have called it (somewhat misleadingly) the 'medieval climatic optimum', and it lasted until the end of the thirteenth century. Temperatures subsequently fell again, the weather worsened significantly and crops were damaged by major meteorological events and plagues. The year 1342 marked the beginning of a series of extremely wet and cold summers, and the summer freeze of 1347 was the worst in 700 years of climate history. Before that, during the 1320s and 1330s, summers had been warm – but largely dry too, leading to food shortages. This weakened the health of the European population to such an extent that when the Black Death arrived in Europe in the late 1340s, it had an easy time of it: it had been our constant companion for thousands of years, but this time people could put up only scant resistance and it was able to rage across the continent, killing nearly a third of the population. The Little Ice Age of the late Middle Ages was thus the reason for a dramatic drop in Europe's population.

The climate change was felt most keenly in the Alps and along northern coastlines. Mountain passes were blocked by snow

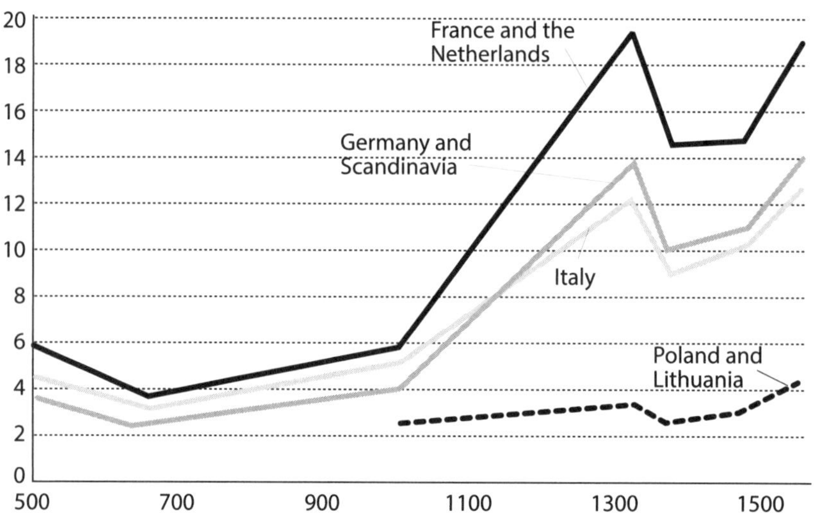

2. Population changes in medieval Europe, 500 to 1500

and ice, and in the middle of the twelfth century, ice tongues began to push into the valleys. In the thirteenth century, sea levels started rising sharply, large tracts of land were lost, and storm surges such as St Marcellus's flood – which hit the British Isles, northern Germany, Denmark and the Netherlands in 1362 – broke coastal areas up into islands and wiped out entire towns. One response to the encroaching sea was to build dykes, which people had been doing increasingly since the early tenth century. In Flanders, for instance, people formed cooperatives and constructed closed dyke systems with locks along the coast, and in the thirteenth and fourteenth centuries the Netherlands reclaimed more than 70,000 hectares of land. Canal systems were also increasingly used; in Bristol, for example, the Great Ditch dug in 1247–8 connected the city directly to the sea, making it England's second most important harbour. In Lombardy, the Milanese created the Ticinello to carry water diverted from a

Po tributary to Milan, later expanding it into a shipping canal. Countless bridges were built too: the one across the Rhône at Avignon was begun in the late twelfth century, and in 1357 Peter Parler started construction on the famous Charles Bridge across the Vltava in Prague. In the mountains, too, gorges were bridged – for example the Schöllenen, near the Gotthard Pass – and along the Brenner Route a merchant from Bolzano called Heinrich Kunter cut a trail to Chiusa through the Eisack Gorge. Across Europe, land was cultivated and forests cleared. People began to settle in hitherto inaccessible and reasonably infertile areas, such as France's Massif Central, and others moved from the regions north of the Alps into the sparsely populated eastern territories, with the newly founded city of Lübeck becoming the focus of eastward migration.

One consequence of this population growth was that Europe became progressively urbanised. New towns sprang up in the wealthier agricultural regions, and the mid-eleventh century saw a growing number of urban centres being sustained by the surrounding farming economy. In the 1200s, Konrad von Megenberg wrote that no farmer returned voluntarily to the countryside once he had seen the 'urbanitas': towns promised higher wages and better food, and we were evidently as attracted to city life then as we are now. Close to 25 per cent of rural settlements were abandoned during this time, and hamlets and villages lay deserted as residents departed en masse for urban centres.

In the thirteenth century, town-founding reached a climax. So-called 'chartered towns' created by local sovereigns – including Kiel (1242), Rostock (1218), Stralsund (1234) and Berlin (1230) – dominated until 1250 or so; from the 1250s onwards, charters were also conveyed on existing settlements already in the process of expanding, which resulted in numerous small and even miniature towns, often with no more than 800 inhabitants. Towards the end of the thirteenth century, the boom subsided. At this

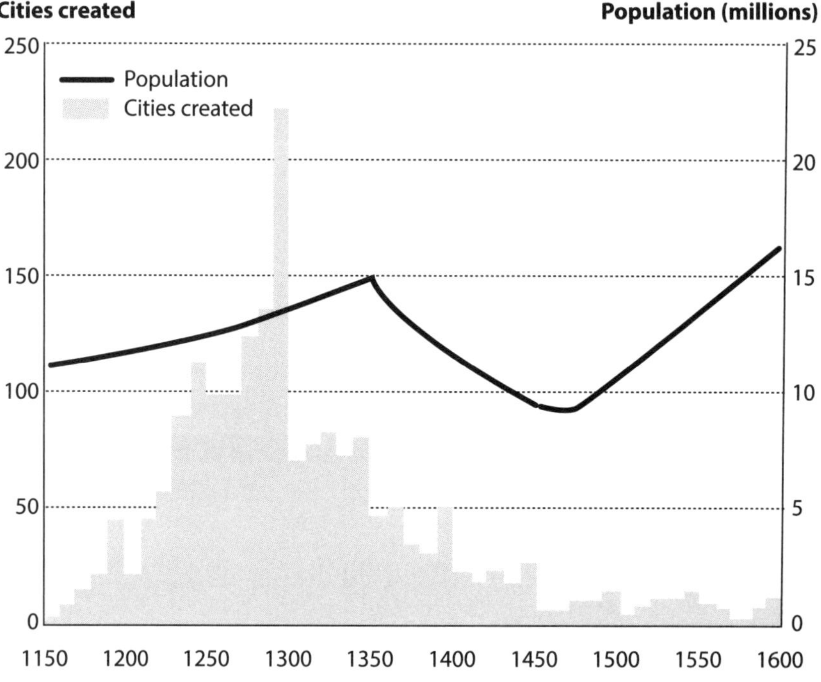

3. New cities and population change in Central Europe, 1150–1600

point, miniature towns made up about 18.5 per cent of urban areas across Europe, large towns only 1.5 per cent. Cologne was Germany's largest metropolis, with an estimated population of 35,000 at the start of the 1300s; about 50,000 people lived in Ghent and Bruges; and northern Italian cities occupied the top spots, with Milan, Florence and Venice numbering close to 100,000 inhabitants each.

The bigger the city, the more marked its class differences. Separating urban populations into classes is not straightforward, but we can distinguish three social strata: the upper classes, which included both the patrician municipal elite and the politically less privileged category of the rich; the middle classes, wealthy merchants and craftsmen; and the lower classes, estimated to have made up half the urban population of the Middle Ages – people who either earned too little to show up on municipal tax registers at all, or paid the lowest tax rate (in Augsburg this was called the *Habnit-Steuer*, the 'have-not tax'). The latter were not, however, vegetating away on the poverty line: they usually worked for small manufacturing establishments, ran little shops or workshops, or were hired hands. Only few were actually poor and dependent on municipal charity or church alms. Yet social classes were amorphous, with fluid boundaries: then, as now, you could move both up and down the social ladder.

'Foreigners' – that is, anyone who came from elsewhere to settle in a town, either short-term or permanently – were an integral part of the medieval urban tapestry. Trade as well as manufacturing depended on international business, and for that you obviously needed relationships with people from other towns and countries. Europeans were geographically mobile, and it was perfectly normal for a merchant from Prato in Italy to spend ten years or more in Avignon, before moving on to Florence. It was also perfectly normal for any young man to leave his home town to study in Bologna, Paris or Oxford, or for a father in twelfth-century Normandy to send his daughter to her Parisian uncle for her education. Jewish communities represented the largest ethno-religious minority in almost every big or medium-sized town in Europe. In 1300 around 1,000 Jews lived in Erfurt and Nuremberg, making up between 5 and 10 per cent of the towns' population. In most places, however, they numbered somewhere between several dozen and a few hundred, or 0.5–0.8 per cent of the population. In total, an estimated 100,000 lived in the medieval German empire in 1300, but the crisis-ridden fourteenth century witnessed a rise in conspiracy theories, most of them directed at Jews, whom many blamed for the Black Death. Brutal mass expulsions and mass murders in the course of the fourteenth century resulted in a rapid decline in the Jewish population; according to latest estimates, it shrank to as little as 40,000 people.[14]

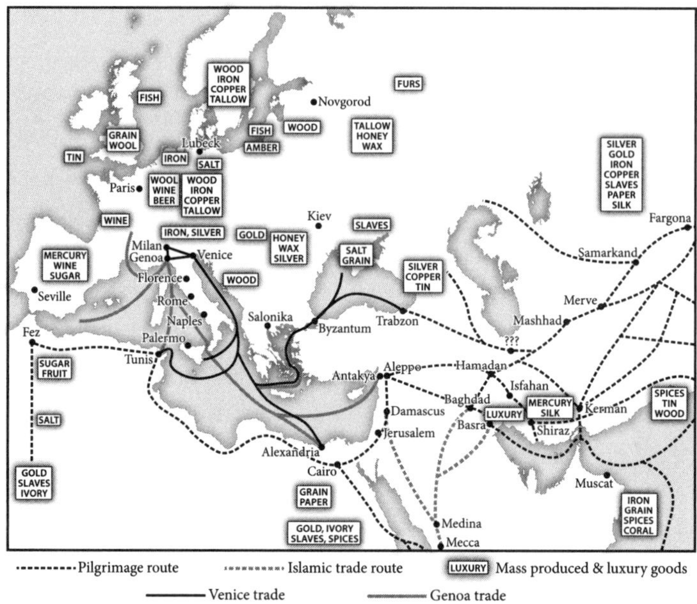

4. Twelfth- and thirteenth-century trade and caravan routes to Asia

Finally, trade and financial activities expanded significantly during this period, a phenomenon that the historian Roberto S. Lopez has called 'the Commercial Revolution', arguing that the emergence of a trade-based economy was one of the greatest achievements of the 'European' Middle Ages. The revolution started in the Byzantine eastern Mediterranean in the eleventh century, and over the course of the next few centuries engulfed first Italy and then the rest of Europe. According to Lopez, the arrival of the Renaissance in the fifteenth century then inaugurated a period of economic decline.

The twenty-first century needs new grand narratives

So: was everyone poor until we invented capitalism? Did our ancestors, beset by lice and parasites, live above cellars in which their own faeces lay piled high after all? The answer is definitely no. Or, to be more precise: it is true that some people were forced to live in such conditions, but certainly no more than today. Such notions belong in the realm of the mythology of modernity. They reassure us, and confirm that unless we want to relapse into a primitive, pre-capitalist past, we should carry on as we are. Those tales of the rational decision-maker, of our ascent from demeaning barter economies to our present-day heights, of the virtue of self-interest ... well, somehow they still seem to hold weight. They aren't entirely wrong. And yet they occupy the very space where something new has to emerge.

What we need are stories that help us to overcome the challenges of the twenty-first century, not the nineteenth. It is high time that *Homo economicus* passed the baton to Planet Earth. It is time for nature to re-enter our grand narratives, time for flesh-and-blood humans instead of models. We need markets where not only supply and demand can meet, but people too; we need ideas that do more than reduce shortages and distribute goods. It's time we took all that we have learnt from dealing with crises and challenges in the past and used it to shape the future. The history of sustainability is at heart a story of resilience. Perhaps more than anything else, it is about our capacity to learn from our mistakes.

The chapters that follow will hopefully prompt some creative thinking. Perhaps not everything you'll read in them will quite do the trick; perhaps you won't believe everything you read, either – and you don't have to: if it arouses your curiosity and makes you think, that's enough. We will encounter people who used to tell each other very different kinds of stories, managed their economies in their own way and overcame all manner of crises. Some ended up amassing great riches; others declared that 'wealth is the vomit of fortune', lived in voluntary poverty, travelled to all four corners of the world, set up communities, ate vegetarian food and lent each other money. We'll meet people for whom recycling was second nature, and people who set great store by the common good, for whom self-denial was a type of economy – without growth, without mass consumption, without rational choice theory. Were they primitive? Poor? Glad when capitalism finally put an end to their misery? Maybe they weren't all that miserable. Maybe they were entirely content, and maybe, if they could see us now, they'd cry with laughter. It wasn't until the modern era dawned that economics became the sad, grey science it is today, beholden to its phobia of shortages and addicted to constant growth. And who knows: as we look back at the diversity of economies we once knew, we might just discover new strategies for the future.

2

SHARING

Sharing Makes Things Easier

> Now the multitude of those who believed were of one heart and one soul; neither did anyone say that any of the things he possessed was his own, but they had all things in common. [...] Nor was there anyone among them who lacked; for all who were possessors of lands or houses sold them, and brought the proceeds of the things that were sold and laid them at the apostles' feet; and they distributed to each as anyone had need. (Acts 4:32–5)

> [B]reaking bread from house to house, they ate their food with gladness and simplicity of heart. (Acts 2:46)

It sounds like a fairy tale, doesn't it. 'And they lived happily ever after.' In Acts, communal Christian life appears rather cosy: lots of good people sharing food and drink by candlelight, and being nice to each other day and night. Everything belongs to everyone; it sounds as tempting as it does unworldly. Then, too, socialism has shown us where it can lead; humans, not to mention economies, need private property. At any rate, that's how most people instinctively react to the early Christian idyll, where all property was communal: a dose of scepticism is surely warranted.

Or is it?

From a historical perspective, the human capacity to share is anything but a fairy tale. Sharing has been key to *Homo sapiens'* success. The comparative psychologist Michael Tomasello has conducted numerous studies of humans and other apes, and discovered that the ability to share a valuable resource with the group, even if there is no prospect of any direct benefit to us personally, is a sophisticated 'cultural technique' that distinguishes humans from great apes. We are born to share. It isn't something we have to be taught. True, apes can recognise others as intentional agents and respond to them – but sharing requires a common intentionality, i.e. shared intentions and communal goals. Only humans communicate in order to share information and agree goals, which creates a high degree of cooperation and togetherness, resulting in a significant selective advantage.[1] Humans who shared their soup – or their catch, their fire, their hunting grounds, their tools, the place where they slept – found it easier to access not only food, but sex. They had more children too, and teamwork helped raise those children.

Another invaluable side effect was that when we shared the kill, cooked it and ate together, we gossiped. It is through our conversations that we communicated and established our shared rules and norms. The psychologist Robin Dunbar argues that the process of sharing our food resources allowed us to reduce the heat of group conflicts to a more socially palatable temperature, which increased the group's chance of survival.[2] And that is why the positive aspects of sharing became firmly lodged in our collective memory.

Homo economicus vs Homo cooperans

Our short-sighted modern age often conveys the impression that sharing is alien to humans, that it may be a socially desirable virtue (and one preached by the Church and other moral authorities) but runs counter to human nature. In reality, the opposite is true; yet we forgot all about it during the age of the 'maximiser of self-interest'. How about focusing our attention on *Homo cooperans*, as we once did with *Homo economicus*? We have a lot of catching up to do: for too long, academics – including historians – have focused purely on the rise of capitalism; we have lost sight of the crucial role played by the sharing economy and forgotten that cooperative economies, collective provision and the communal use of resources have always existed alongside private-sector market systems.[3] There are good reasons for this, not least that, in our collective memory, the traumatic failure of managed economies – whether communist, fascist or idealistic – has overshadowed any positive experiences we've had of sharing economies, and the knowledge that there used to be a range of coexisting economic systems has given way to the belief that, realistically, there are only two: managed ones and capitalism. Since the former haven't worked out, the logic goes, the latter is the only viable option.[4]

In some ways, the new sharing economy seems to have been swallowed up by this logic too: the Silicon Valley success stories of Airbnb, Uber and other global leaders in the sharing economy have, a mere decade and a half or so later, been unmasked as no more than a nightmare born of neoliberal capitalism, whose free-market forces have been left to run riot, unencumbered by employee rights or state regulation.[5] If you consider the matter with a dose of realism, you quickly understand it as further proof that 'there is no other way'. However, as Robert Musil once said, where there's realism there must also be a sense of the possible. Anyone who argues on the basis of inevitability is already in trouble, defensive, averse to change; but if we broaden our horizons, we may stop being so afraid of the alternatives. And in that regard, the past has a lot to offer.

Sharing Brings Riches: The Monastic Economy

The collective use of resources makes us rich. The best way to understand how this works is to look at the history of the monasteries, with their tradition of sharing and of shunning private property. Monasteries are sharing communities with thousands of years of experience in the collective use of resources, and a way of life that appears in various guises – both temporary and permanent – in Buddhism, Hinduism, Christianity and other religions, and has done so throughout history. There were probably never as many religious communes as in the twentieth century, which saw ashrams, Hare Krishna communities and Zen monasteries multiply around the world.[6]

The Rule of St Benedict: don't own – use

There was to be no such thing as private property: 'This vice especially is to be cut out of the monastery by the roots,' wrote Benedict of Nursia in *c.* 540, in a book of precepts he composed for his community on Monte Cassino, south of Rome. The *Rule of St Benedict* deals with the various spiritual and practical aspects of communal life in seventy-three short paragraphs,[7] and in Chapter 33 states that no one must 'have anything as his own – anything whatever, whether book or tablets or pen or whatever it may be'. In return, the brothers could expect the abbot to provide them with what they needed, according to their individual needs (Chapter 34).

This did not mean that monks who enjoyed a certain eminence could expect preferential treatment; instead, special consideration would be shown to individual weaknesses: 'He who needs less should thank God and not be discontented; but he who needs more should be humbled by the thought of his infirmity rather than feeling important on account of the kindness shown him.' Grumbling was forbidden. In addition, all practical everyday tasks would be shared, including serving in the kitchen. None were excused, except the ill or those otherwise engaged in essential tasks, 'for this service brings increase of reward and of charity' (Chapter 35). If a monk couldn't get to grips with the domestic chores, the others were supposed to help him, to avoid distress. A 'week of service' ran from Saturday to Saturday, and at the end the monks on duty had to clean all the utensils and wash the cloths the brothers used to dry their hands and feet. They would then hand everything, 'clean and in good condition', to the cellarer (sometimes called the 'treasurer' or 'bursar'), who was responsible for the monastery's staff and provisions. The cellarer then passed everything on to 'the incoming server, in order that he may know what he gives out and what he receives back'.

It is quite astonishing how rigorously the Benedictine monasteries' sharing economy was organised. Compared to the older *Rule of the Master* that served as his model, St Benedict's version had the great advantage that it covered the essentials in brief and clear instructions.[8] It is why it became a seminal text in monastic history. And rightly so, because the way of life and economic system it proposes are wholly innovative. There had been nothing like this before: a meticulously structured life of communal property and division of labour, with clearly allocated responsibilities, to which everyone had to contribute their share, without recourse to slavery.

From the ninth century onwards, Benedict's model established itself across Europe, evolving into one of the most stable forms of sharing community. The monasteries were also highly successful in financial terms and in terms of their longevity; we can even describe them as far superior to private enterprises of the day, because the process of handing them on to the next generation was only rarely hampered by squabbling between heirs. Then, following the French Revolution in the late eighteenth and early nineteenth centuries, Europe underwent a process of secularisation, and the wholesale expropriation of churches and monasteries ensued. Chief among the reasons was the wealth and superior economic power that these institutions, as consumption and production communities, had amassed down the centuries. Their economic prowess was a key reason for their dissolution; that they had acquired that prowess not least by virtue of being successful sharing communities is a fact that often remains unacknowledged.

Depop, monastery-style

As regards private property, the rules were consistent and strict. There was none of any kind; instead, everyone was collectively equipped with clothes, food and bedding. Augustine, the founding father of another monastic order, wrote the following to his community in Milan: 'Do not call anything your own; but possess everything in common. Your superior ought to provide each of you with food and clothing, not on an equal basis to all, because all do not enjoy the same health, but to each one in proportion to his need.'[9] These words make it clear that the communes' social make-up was heterogeneous – today, we would call it diverse. In his treatise Augustine explains that some were used to a lavish lifestyle before they took orders, and might therefore be given a little more food and clothing at first, as well as a better bed or more blankets. Others, who were hardier and thus more fortunate – because they needed less, and were further along the road to frugality – had no need for such consideration.

The question of clothes comes up again and again: Augustine even seems to suggest a sort of Depop for monasteries, arguing in his *Rule* that the monks should stand out in a crowd for their exemplary behaviour, not their expensive clothes. All items of clothing should be common property, and be looked after by one or more people whose job it was to shake out and air them to prevent moth damage: 'Just as a single storeroom furnishes your food, so a single wardrobe should supply your clothing. Pay as little attention as possible to the clothes you receive as the season requires. Whether each of you receives what he had turned in or what was worn by someone else is of little concern.'[10] And whenever a fellow brother received, for instance, clothing or other necessaries from his parents or other relatives, he must not secretly keep them for himself but hand them over to the community, i.e. give them to his superior; and once something became communal property, the superior had to give the clothes (or whatever it might be) to whoever needed it. Furthermore, monks who were given the responsibility of doing the laundry, working in the kitchen or looking after the books in the library should do their job without complaining. Those in charge of books would distribute them at a prearranged time each day, and only then; however, those in charge of distributing clothing or shoes should not hesitate to do so whenever someone needed them. Good and bad times were shared equally by all. Finally, every single rule included a reminder to be considerate of the sick, who were allowed to eat meat and excused from fasting, and who received medical treatment and were looked after in the infirmary – which was perhaps more than many people who lived outside monastery walls could expect.

Benedict's *Rule* is essentially a wonderfully succinct summary of his predecessors' work. Its recipe for success was its brevity and clarity: clear-cut responsibilities, unambiguous allocation of duties, straightforward parameters – while always taking the monks' individual needs into consideration. Not everyone had to do everything, and one man took overall responsibility for the community's needs: the abbot. If there were arguments, his word was final and his decision binding. As we can see, these communes were far removed from the grass-roots democracy of our time, but it nevertheless is worth engaging with their texts. Their struggle to balance individual well-being and the well-being of the group offers up a wealth of experiences for us to draw on, providing us with valuable contextual knowledge and practical know-how.[11]

From self-sufficiency to economic success

Chapter 66 of Benedict's *Rule* states that a monastery should, if possible, be arranged in such a way that it contains everything it needs – water, mills, a garden and so on – within its walls, and so that the various crafts could be carried out on-site. The monks will thus avoid wasting valuable time with a lot of unnecessary walking about. Then, too, they should not live off charity, but support themselves with their own two hands, plant their own vegetables, bake their own bread and wear shoes they have made themselves. Gardens for vegetables, grain for bread, vineyards for altar wine, flax for clothes, animals for wool and leather ... to have all this they needed land, arable fields, pastures, workshops, tools – in short, the means of production. And these belonged to everyone. This form of property was permissible, because the ideal of dispossession applied only to the individual monk or nun, not to the commune as a whole.

This distinction between individual and collective property is found in many religious communities all over the world. Others took a different approach, however. In the early thirteenth century, for instance, communities that chose voluntary collective dispossession were being set up all over Europe: these were the so-called mendicant orders. St Francis is perhaps the most extreme proponent of their attitude: when the citizens of Assisi offered him and his followers a house to live in, he personally climbed on to the roof and started ripping off the tiles. It was a protest action against all ownership, including communal property.[12] He was motivated by the enormous profits posted by the Benedictine monasteries; their way of life, based on the principles of a monastic sharing economy, worked extremely well for them, so well, in fact, that their wealth grew and grew. Prayer and work truly paid off – in part because they shared not only everyday things like clothes and tools, but the daily routine, with communal rhythms, rituals and habits deeply embedded in the traditional eight daily prayer periods known as the Liturgy of the Hours or Divine Offices.

The 'rhythmification' of work made it easier to get tasks done, and played an important part in stabilising the monastic economy. Some researchers claim that the monasteries' routine of hourly prayers (which were sung) prepared humans for the idea of 'clocking on and off', and thus for the rhythm of the modern factory.[13] This is arguable, but what we do know is that monastic communities rigorously organised their shared life and work, including structuring their various pursuits according to the monks' and nuns' needs.

To illustrate this, we have an early ninth-century drawing showing the layout of an ideal abbey – a proper 'monastic town', with the cloisters as the focal point of all communication and movement. The blueprint is orientated east–west, with the church, the locus of the monks' spiritual needs, situated north of the cloisters; and the refectory or dining hall, which provided for their physical needs, south of the cloisters. There is a dormitory, common room (chapter house), writing room (scriptorium) and library – the latter was often known as a monastery's *armarium*, or armoury, because the books and the wisdom they contained constituted the monks' spiritual weapons. These were followed by kitchens, privies, the warming house (calefactory), a room for clothes (vestiary), as well as a bath house and laundry. At the heart of the monastery was the conclave, reserved for the monks and nuns; anyone who didn't belong to the monastery was excluded. To the south were outbuildings, stables and workshops, and to the north the servants' quarters and accommodation for guests. Kitchens and breweries are scattered throughout the site, as are the infirmary and physic garden, schoolhouse, vegetable garden, orchard and cemetery.[14]

The monastic economy became optimised with the Cistercians. The order, one of whose most prominent members was Bernard of Clairvaux, was founded at the end of the eleventh century. Cistercians subscribed to extreme modesty, a return to manual labour and a focus on spiritual duties. In addition, they retreated from the

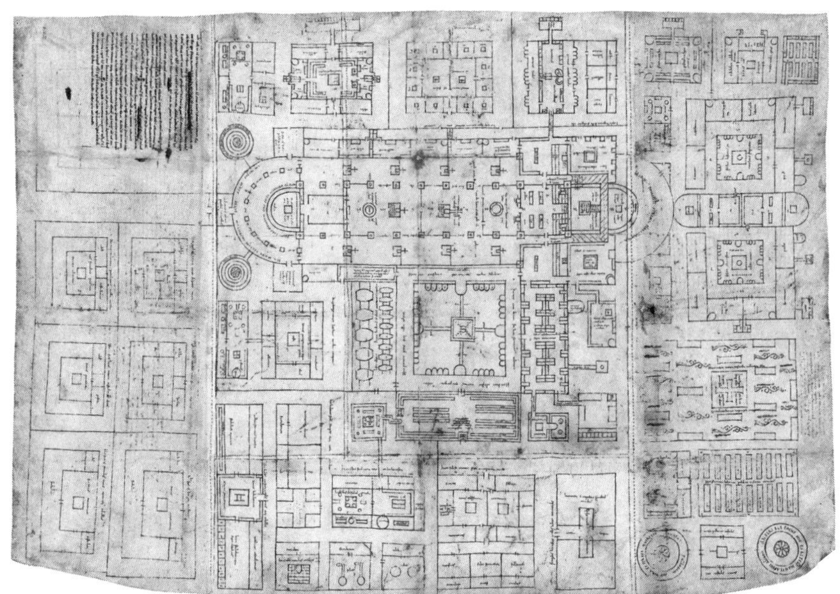

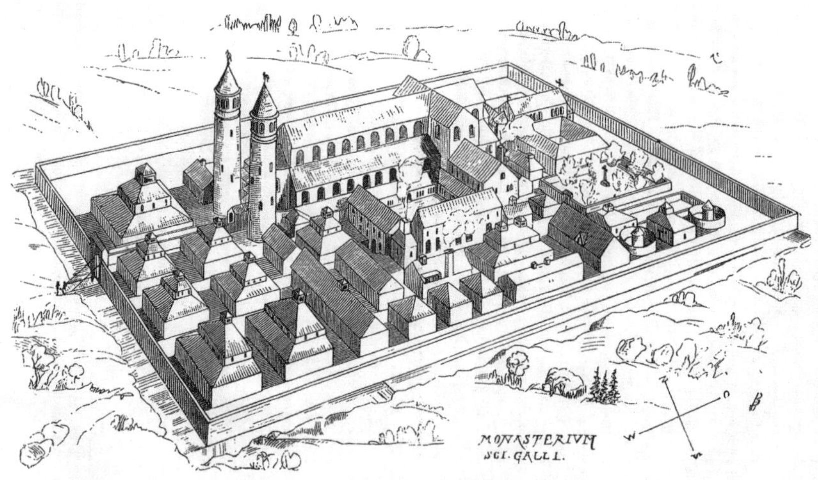

5 & 6. The Plan of St Gall and a reconstruction drawing by Johann Rudolf Rahn[15]

rest of the world, setting up their monasteries in remote valleys and making themselves as self-sufficient as they could, in order not to have to rely on charity. To accomplish all this they worked with lay brothers, who were not monks but still belonged to the community. Unlike the Cistercian monks, who regularly cut their hair (the tonsure) and shaved, lay brothers wore beards. They had their own on-site living quarters and were tasked with managing the monastery's economy. Providing for their community was the sole responsibility of the monasteries, and they contained flour mills, bakeries, breweries and wine presses, and processed what they grew on their estates themselves. They produced food and drink, and manufactured clothes and shoes from the wool of their own sheep and the skin of their own cattle. Tanners turned the skins into leather and cordwainers produced footwear for the monks, and everyone who lived in the monastery was equipped with new pairs of shoes once a year – one pair of leather shoes for work during the day and, for the monks, an additional felt pair for night-time, to keep their feet warm during nightly prayers.

As you can easily imagine, this resulted in overproduction; furthermore, the products were of such high quality that people outside the monasteries also wanted to get their hands on them, and the Cistercians were able to sell not only shoes but textiles, tools, agricultural instruments and roof tiles.

Partnering with nature: hydraulic power

The Cistercians harnessed water for their on-site farming activities and became renowned hydraulic engineers. No monastery was without its own watercourse, which supplied drinking water, disposed of sewage, irrigated the gardens, filled the monastery's fish ponds and powered the mills, including flour mills and bark mills for the tanners.

A panegyric to water penned by Bernard of Clairvaux's biographer in the early thirteenth century beautifully illustrates the way that the Cistercians treated water practically as a 'cooperative partner': the author rhapsodises about how an arm of the Aube, on whose banks the monastery had been built, ran between the abbey's numerous workshops to support the monks in their tasks. He describes the river almost as an over-eager colleague: having entered the monastery, the river first impetuously throws itself into the mill, where it makes itself busy and moves about to help grind the wheat between the millstones and drive the fine sieve that separates the flour from the bran. Thence it travels to the neighbouring brewery, where it fills the kettles, and then into the fulling mill, where they produce cloth, and where it by turns raises and drops the heavy hammers, thus sparing the fullers much exertion. The waterway then moves on to drive the wheels of the bark mill. Foaming, it emerges from the millwheels then calms itself down, grows gentler and separates into several smaller arms, visiting the monastery's various places of work as it runs along, constantly keeping an eye out for anyone who needs a hand, whether to cook, sieve, crush, irrigate, wash or mill. It never hesitates to get stuck in. Before it leaves the monastery, it collects the rubbish and makes sure that the place is clean and tidy.[16]

Thus, nature is brought on board as a partner. The Cistercians were also known for their enthusiasm for construction and played an important role in land development, including clearing forests, draining swamps and building dams and dykes.

Sharing communities and market participation

Despite – or perhaps because of – their diverse economic activities, the ideal of self-sufficiency ultimately eluded monastic sharing communities. They depended on marketplaces for things such as salt, or the iron from which they fashioned their tools. This alone would have forced them to participate in the market; but they also needed somewhere to sell their products.

Cistercian monasteries became extremely successful production and consumption communities and turned themselves into a cash-rich big business.[17] The monastery of Salem near Lake Constance, for example, had 310 members in 1311, of which 130 were monks and 180 lay brothers; Bebenhausen monastery had 60 monks and 130 lay brothers in 1262–81, and the considerably smaller monastery of Schöntal had 45 monks and 35 lay brothers in 1330. Add to that the many people who belonged to a monastery's wider *familia* – the 'familiars', whom we would now describe as 'associate members', prebendaries who had purchased the right to live there, visitors, hired hands and servants.

The economic success story of medieval monastic sharing communities is overshadowed by accusations that they betrayed the ideals of their own communities. Where did their magnificent economic successes leave their voluntary vow of poverty? Their peers, in particular members of other orders, never tired of talking down the competition. Where, they asked, have the ideals on which they were founded disappeared to? Can a monk call himself a monk when he has a belly as big as *that*?

Ultimately, the criticism only highlighted the dilemma of a sharing economy: it works, and evidently not only in terms of breaking even, but in terms of making a profit. Again and again, the very success of these economic communities of monks and nuns would prove their undoing.

Commons, and the Art of Internalising the External

Are sharing communities good for the environment? Do co-operatives manage their economy in a more sustainable way? Do user communities exploit the planet less than the private sector? These are pressing questions – as we realised in 1987, when the World Commission on Environment and Development (WCED) published its report, entitled *Our Common Future* (also known as the Brundtland Report, after the WCED's chair, former Norwegian prime minister Gro Harlem Brundtland). Our 'discovery' of sustainability dates to this report, which concluded that the globe's critical environmental problems were the result of great poverty in the southern hemisphere, coupled with unsustainable consumption and production patterns in the northern hemisphere, and called for a strategy that jointly tackled development and environmental issues. It also coined a term we are all familiar with today: 'sustainable development', which it defines as 'development that meets the needs of the present without compromising the ability of future generations to meet their own needs.

In the first instance, these questions are about the future of the 'global commons', i.e. the resources whose long-term use is crucial to humanity's survival: water, the Earth's atmosphere, soil and breathable air. Our increasingly complex environment and economics have exposed the limits of traditional forms of national sovereignty: political borders can't stop the pollution of our water, air and soil; we are all affected, and only have a future if we work together.[18] From this perspective, the whole world is a single, global sharing community.

The action points recommended by the WCED were duly noted, but since then we have either refused to accept the need to protect our global commons or simply ignored it.

How the forests taught us about sustainability

The idea of sustainability as an economic principle necessary to human survival had already been formulated long before the WCED. More than 250 years earlier, a man called Hans Carl von Carlowitz (1645–1714) published a book entitled *Sylvicultura oeconomica* (lit. 'economical forest management'), which has been described as the moment the concept of sustainability was born.[19] Carlowitz was the head of the Saxon Mining Office in Freiberg, which was famous for its silver mines. Even back then, the Saxon forest was already being extensively exploited, principally for mining iron, coal and silver: fire was an indispensable resource, and the demand for wood rose as Saxony's mining industry expanded. In his book Carlowitz proposes that timber shortages could be offset by methodical reforestation. He suggests that we should maintain a healthy balance between our wood consumption and our forests' regenerative powers; we ought to use forests 'gently' and give young trees time to grow, in order that future generations may benefit from them in perpetuity. We have to treat forests with great care, he writes, and organise the conservation and cultivation of trees so as to ensure a 'continuous, steady and sustained yield'. This was the first time that the phrase 'sustainable use' appeared in writing.[20]

Anna Amalia von Braunschweig-Wolfenbüttel, Duchess of Sachsen-Weimar (1739–1807), later implemented Carlowitz's ideas: as her son's regent, she pioneered new forest management methods, culminating in the enactment of the 1775 Weimar forest ordinance, which regulated the 'conservation' of forests and the 'management of timber shortages'. The aim was to 'assume due responsibility for future generations'; timber would no longer be 'extracted' at the current generation's 'discretion or [to meet its] needs', and instead the claims of 'posterity' would be taken into consideration. A new mode of thinking had entered the Saxon forests, which anticipated the twenty-first-century notion of sustainability: its economic yardstick was not 'demand' or 'the market', let alone rich people's need for luxuries, but the 'true power of the forests', i.e. the resilience of the ecosystem.

As Heinrich Cotta – who founded the Royal Saxon Forestry Academy in Tharandt in 1790 – said, we have to 'obey Nature, who is subject to no external law, but allows us to inquire into her and discover her own laws'.[21] At the close of the eighteenth century, a finance professor at Marburg University called Heinrich Jung-Stilling included the term 'sustainability' in an early precursor to Maslow's hierarchy of needs. Starting with basic

7. Deforestation *c.* 1700, as illustrated by Carlowitz in his *Sylvicultura oeconomica*

needs such as housing, clothes and furniture, followed by anything that makes us 'merry and bright' (e.g. music and other arts), he arrives at the top of the pyramid, which consists of 'opulent' and false needs that merely benefit us, without consideration for the wider community or future generations. In fact, he includes providing for others among the fundamental human needs.

In the case of forests, this means specifically 'cutting down no more and no less in a year than can grow [in a year], so that we may secure the wherewithal to meet the timber needs of our descendants'.[22] With their various demands and policies concerning sustainable forest management, Carlowitz, Braunschweig-Wolfenbüttel and Jung-Stilling were responding to the shortcomings of their day, as described in both word and image in Carlowitz's *Sylvicultura oeconomica*.

Illustrations such as the one above suggest that people were cutting down trees indiscriminately, but it's unclear who was actually at work there. In whose employ were the loggers, and when did the deforestation start? The illustration doesn't mention that the deforestation was itself a consequence of a rise in demand for timber from the Erzgebirge mining industry, which was imposed and run mainly by the state, i.e. the Duchy of Saxony-Weimar.[23]

The pretty tale of how sustainability was discovered in early eighteenth-century Saxon forests is apt to convey the impression that exploitation and deforestation used to be rife, that forestry was wholly unregulated, and that there were no laws, environmental standards or certification requiring reforestation. Was this really the case? No. Regulated, sustainable forest management clearly existed long before Carlowitz wrote down his thoughts on the matter.

How we managed forests sustainably before we invented 'sustainability'

An excellent illustration of sustainable forest management in the Middle Ages are the forestry cooperatives located in what is today Alsace and southern Palatia. The *Haingeraiden*, a name that refers to both the forest as a resource and its community of users, were village associations that followed certain rules and regulations on the sustainable use of the forests that surrounded them.[24] The name is nowadays applied to woodland associations in Alsace, Rheingau, Wettereau and Palatia. The Palatian *Haingeraide* was a continuous, in the main densely forested area of about 180 km^2 stretching from the River Speyerbach in the north (near the city of Speyer) to the River Queich in the south (near Landau). The *Haingeraide* association, comprising thirty Palatian parishes, had exclusive rights of use. The forests did not belong to individual parishes but to the association as a whole, with the area further divided into five sub-*Haingeraide*. A given village never enjoyed usage rights over a continuous area, only over 'frontwoods' and 'backwoods', sometimes located hours apart. The villages themselves were also almost always located outside the forests.

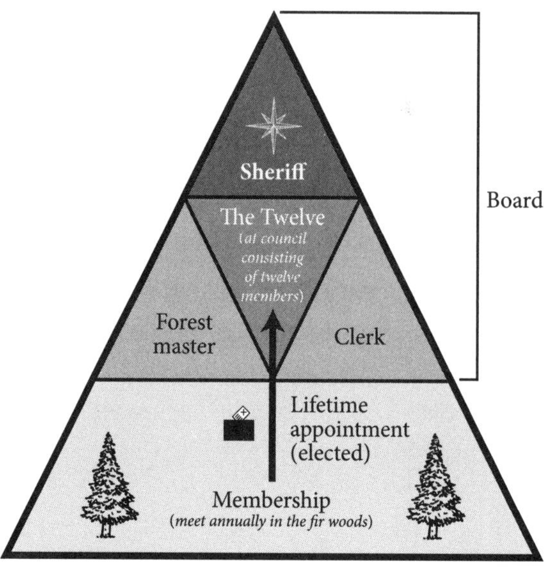

8. Organisation of the *Haingeraiden*, medieval forestry cooperatives in Alsace and Palatia

The forests supplied nearly everything the villagers needed to live – firewood, construction timber, pasture and more. In addition, the villages periodically used them as temporary farmland: they chose a defined area, felled the trees (obtaining valuable timber), burnt off the remains, used the ash as fertiliser and planted crops on the vacated tract. After a few years, they would turn the land over to cattle for twelve months, before restoring it to the forest for new trees to grow. The foliage was useful too, chiefly as bedding for both man and beast; nuts, berries, mushrooms and fruit were a key component of the diet; villagers collected resin from conifers and used tree bark to wrap cheese; oak bark was invaluable for tanners; and charcoal burners supplied an important raw material to the village blacksmiths, who forged nails, knives and horseshoes.

A forestry cooperative was a sophisticated organisation: it was headed by a *Geraideschultheiß* (a *Schultheiß* being a sort of sheriff), and he, his twelve deputies from the associated villages, a forest master and the *Geraideschreiber* (a clerk) formed the *Haingeraide*'s board. The sheriff and 'the Twelve' were elected, and convened at least once a year for a sort of AGM 'in the fir woods'. Since time immemorial, this had been the place where community matters were discussed, conflicts resolved and rule violations sanctioned. There was also a *Geraidekiste*, a kind of archive (*Kiste* = chest) in which the association's certificates, files and current records were stored. To ensure that no one made any changes to the official list of rights and obligations without prior agreement, the *Geraideschultheiß* was the only one with a key to the archive. The *Zehntmeister* ('tithe master') also played an important role supervising the cooperative's operations; he made sure that the usage rights were properly observed, regularly inspected the forests, reported any damage and put out open fires. One of his chief tasks was also to mark the trees that could be felled.[25]

Trouble in the Siebelding Valley

In early 1736, the town council of Landau unilaterally decided to fell trees in the Siebelding Valley's communal forest and float the logs down the Queich to Landau.[26] Landau was a member of the *Haingeraide*, but the rules stipulated that all such decisions – especially as pertained to log-floating – could only be taken by the association as a whole. Unsurprisingly, then, the other members wouldn't stand for it. They first took their complaint to the *Geraideschultheiß*, who reprimanded Landau. But Landau didn't react. Instead, its council commissioned French entrepreneurs who sent their lumberjacks into the Siebelding Valley. This was too much for the cooperative. Its members got together, entered the woods at night and hid the loggers' axes and saws. When the loggers returned the next morning and couldn't find their tools an almighty row broke out, leading to fisticuffs.

Things did not end there. The local landowners – the king of France (Landau had been his territory since 1680) on the one hand and the Palatine Elector on the other – got involved and initiated legal proceedings. The court closely examined the parties' claims: did the *Geraideschultheiß* really have jurisdiction over the members of the cooperative? Did Landau really have to submit to majority decision, without the ability to issue any logging orders whatsoever of its own accord? Should Landau be given its own key to the *Geraidekiste* and appoint its own forest masters? Finally, and most importantly: now that Landau was in France, were French entrepreneurs entitled to fell trees and quarry rocks in the communal forests, for use in the construction of fortifications and royal palaces? In the course of the October 1736 negotiations, almost every single one of these matters was decided in favour of the *Haingeraide*. The court reasserted that Landau had acted unlawfully. It also transpired that what Landau needed most of all was firewood for the French garrison, which had been created at Vauban in 1688 and massively expanded since then. It was thus not the members of the *Haingeraide* who benefited from the logging, let alone the forest itself – merely the royal seigneur.

Although the court vindicated the *Haingeraide*, the 'excesses' of the Siebelding Valley prompted a revision of the cooperative's usage rights. In 1740, the French state issued new set of statutes under the pretty-sounding title of '*La Geraide*'. They started off by declaring that the main problem all along had been the fact that the Palatine Elector owned the association's villages located on his territory, but had no authority over their communal forests. To solve the issue, the French proposed to check the files in the cooperative's archive, a process that ended with the French king being given the power to veto all future decisions. Furthermore, the *Geraideschultheiß* would henceforth have no jurisdiction, and every village now had the right to extract as much firewood as it liked from the forests.

The cooperative was also ordered to copy the entire contents of the archive and cut extra keys to it, and to hand these over to the sub-*Geraiden*. By way of justification, they invoked the principle of equality before the law. Lastly, French entrepreneurs would be allowed to take as much wood from the forests as any one of the Twelve allowed them to have or, as the case may be, sold to them. The authority of the cooperative was thus perfectly hollowed out, in the name of rationalisation and increased efficiency.

Communal forests – good for sustainability, bad for progress

This example illustrates the pressures experienced by these regulated forest associations. The communities' understanding of how to manage their forests in a sustainable way was discredited as inefficient. Floating logs, for instance, was certainly an easy and relatively cheap way to get logs to where you needed them, but under the old regulations you were only permitted to do it in exceptional cases, because of the damage it caused to riverbanks and adjacent fields. In 1740, however, lawyers determined that floating logs caused no such damage at all. The traditional rules governing the use of the communal forests were what we would call 'sustainable': based on collective experience, they were described as inefficient and in part severely restricted the rights of individuals, yet they were rooted in the desire to ensure that the forest could continue to be used as a resource in the long term. In the course of the eighteenth century, this knowledge base was systematically eroded, and communal property was declared the enemy of progress. When the *Haingeraiden* were razed to the ground in 1819, the *Rheinische Intelligenzblatt* commented that 'we have long known that there is only one way to prevent the devastation of these invaluable forests and ensure that they are better managed, and that is to remove them from communal ownership'.[27]

The *Haingeraiden* are just one of many examples of how commons were successfully managed in the past. History offers up an astonishingly broad spectrum of such arrangements, bringing together individuals, households and legal entities – such as the right to graze your herd on common pastureland and the right to collect wood in wooded commons, as well as collectively managed inventories of real estate, machinery, stables and storerooms. Not only these, but flour mills, hammer mills, wash houses, bath houses, bakeries, kilns, oilseed presses, cheese cellars, barns and grain stores, workshops, potteries and brickworks were often managed collectively; and in many places, people collectively organised and financed the draining of swamps, the laying and maintenance of sewage pipes, and the construction of bridges, roads and irrigation systems.[28] When did we actually forget all this? Why do we nowadays think of commons as predominantly 'tragic'?

The obsolete notion of 'the tragedy of the commons'

As we look to the future, the collective use of resources is a major concern. The Earth's forests, waters and atmosphere are goods that are used by all of us, collectively, and we therefore have to manage them collectively too.

In his sensational 1968 article 'The Tragedy of the Commons', biologist Garrett Hardin argues that it can only end in tears. To illustrate his point, he asks us to imagine a mountain pasture that is open to everyone. Any intelligent, rational farmer in the village will want to graze as many cows on this pasture as possible, because it costs him nothing; he also directly profits from it, because he can sell the milk he gets from his cows without having to pay for the feed. In addition, he only suffers a fraction of the 'negative utility' resulting from any damage incurred from overgrazing, because the effects are borne by the community as a whole. Furthermore, any negative effects are delayed until such time as the pasture is completely ruined. Consequently, a farmer who does not try to graze as many cows as he can on the common pasture is a foolish farmer, because he isn't maximising his personal gain. Every farmer is 'locked' into this system, and 'ruin is the destination toward which all men rush, each pursuing his interest in a society that believes in the freedom of the commons. Freedom in a commons brings ruin to all.'[29]

We find ourselves instinctively nodding in agreement. The scenario coincides with our everyday experience: think of all those rows about the office kitchenette, where dishes and rubbish pile up and no one can be bothered to fix the tap. Whatever is used by all is neglected by all (as Aristotle says in *Politics*, 'Property that is common to the greatest number of owners receives the least attention').[30]

The resounding success of Hardin's article thus comes as no surprise. It is one of the most cited academic texts of the twentieth century, in almost any discipline, and still forms the basis of much research done on commons.[31] So, what does Hardin propose we do? He puts little store in technological innovation. In his view, the only solution is for a state – a strong state – to regulate the individual's right to participate in the common resources by limiting the freedom to breed; for 'freedom to breed will bring ruin to all'.[32] Statements like this have led some to accuse Hardin of racism and xenophobia.

The laws of sustainability, or 'Elinor's Laws'

The most famous opponent of Hardin's 'tragic' theory was the economist Elinor Ostrom, winner of the 2009 Nobel Prize in Economic Sciences. She believed that the collective use of common resources (i.e. commons) is actually feasible,[33] and brought a third power into play, alongside the market and the state: people's ability to organise themselves and to cooperate. She believed that members of user communities, who are simultaneously producers and consumers, have a substantial interest in maintaining the terms and conditions of their economic and social existence. They know the specific conditions, and therefore often work considerably more efficiently – out of self-interest as well as keeping an eye on sustainability – than an external 'authority' or market mechanisms ever could. Yet the realisation of a user community's full potential depends on a variety of factors.

Under what conditions, then, can the common use of common resources work? Ostrom and her team came up with eight 'design principles' for a sustained regime of common-pool resource systems – Silke Helfrich, Germany's leading commons scholar, calls them 'Elinor's Laws':[34]

1. 'User Boundaries': commons are not a no man's land, and generally have defined user groups. The first law concerns the need to establish 'clear and locally understood' boundaries that separate legitimate users from non-users, and specific common-pool resources from the wider socioecological system.
2. 'Congruence with Local Conditions': the rules for the use and regeneration of the commons must be appropriate to local conditions. They must not put too much strain on people, and must harmonise with each other; 'the distribution of costs [should be] proportional to the distribution of benefits', i.e. profits and losses must both be shared.
3. 'Collective-choice Arrangements': anyone affected by a 'resource regime' must be allowed to participate in the decision-making processes concerning regulations and, just as importantly, any changes to regulations.
4. 'Monitoring': both user and resource need to be monitored for their protection. The monitoring will be done by the users themselves, or by individuals accountable to them.

5. 'Graduated Sanctions': rule violations should be controlled, and any sanctions are to be graduated, i.e. starting low and becoming more severe if a user repeatedly violates a rule. The sanctions must be convincing and practical.
6. 'Conflict-resolution Mechanisms': the rules of the user community must include 'rapid, low-cost, local' resolution mechanisms for conflicts within the community or between the community and local authorities. This includes clarity around the local spaces where such conflicts may be resolved.
7. 'Minimal Recognition of Rights': functioning commons need a minimum of state recognition of their rights as users, and the right to set their own rules.
8. 'Nested Enterprises': in most cases, commons are closely interwoven with a larger resource system. Ostrom believes that we need local centres of responsibility ('polycentric governance structures'), which are connected to each other on various levels. Governance won't be centralised and hierarchical, but local.

Forgoing short-term wins

History can certainly show us examples of successful commons; yet their organisation never ran along laissez-faire lines. There were always clearly defined membership rules, and adherence was closely monitored and any violations were sanctioned. Many rules concerned deliberately forgoing gains, something that sounded 'unviable' to the ears of modernity's 'maximisers of efficiency', who therefore systematically pushed to abolish local user communities.

Because commons were always orientated towards local idiosyncrasies, they were an obstacle to the idea of central state control as imposed in the nineteenth century; by then, the idea that arable land would lie fallow at regular intervals, or that timber-rafting – which was, after all, so efficient – was strictly prohibited no longer suited state policy, because such rules meant that huge profits were being forfeited. Yet they continued to adhere to certain practices, such as fallowing, giving up potential profits. These days, we would say that the environmental costs were priced in – i.e. people paid for them, so to speak, by not damaging the environment in the first place. Such far-sighted planning benefited everyone in the long run. Even their descendants.[35]

Were he alive today, Hans Carl von Carlowitz would probably want to work with Ostrom, or indeed with the historian Tine de Moor, both of whom have revisited old commons regulations. Since Carlowitz wrote his *Sylvicultura oeconomica* we have rediscovered the fact that people are very much willing and able to cooperate and act sustainably, even if it means limiting their own personal gain.[36]

Water: fishing on Lake Constance, 1350–1900

Another example is fishery. How were the fishermen of Lake Constance able to use the lake as a collective resource for centuries, without depleting it? The historian Michael Zeheter has found clear parallels between their regime and the way we think about these issues today. Lake Constance's fishermen knew that preserving the fishing grounds was in their interest. They weren't motivated by ecological considerations or the desire to protect the environment; for them, sustainability was nothing short of a survival strategy.

In what follows, therefore, we won't be looking for evidence that modern ideas around sustainability already existed in the past – quite the opposite: the real question is when it was that we lost our capacity for long-term thinking and acting for the benefit of future generations in the first place.[37]

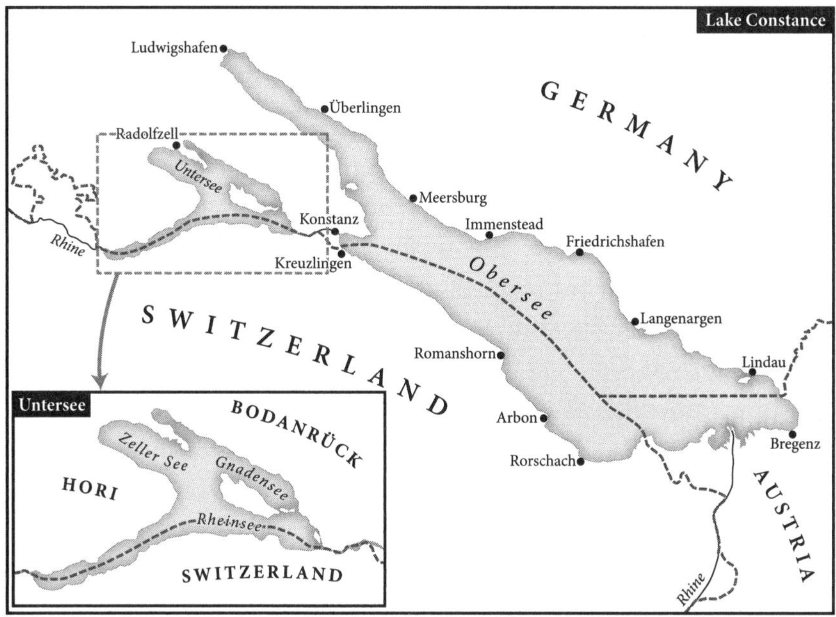

9. Lake Constance and its neighbouring states

When you're on Lake Constance, you are in international waters. The governments of the three countries that border it – Switzerland, Germany and Austria – have never been able to agree how exactly to divide it up between them, and the Upper Lake is under joint jurisdiction to this day. There are historical reasons for this: for centuries, the monasteries of St Gall and Reichenau island, the prince-bishop of Constance, the Cistercian abbey of Salem, the dukes of Nellenburg and Tettnang and, finally, the four free imperial cities of Buchhorn (now Friedrichshafen), Lindau, Überlingen and Constance (until it was conquered by the Habsburgs in 1548) all shared the lake and its shores. They all owned territory bordering the lake, which they gave to fishermen in fealty. Yet aside from these privately held legal titles, the shores were free for everyone to use. This applied equally to the Lower and Upper Lake.[38]

However, in practice only expert fishermen were able to make use of the commons, because the lake's deep waters required special know-how. Working out on the open water was difficult and dangerous. The fishermen used dragnets, gill nets, creels and rods to catch all kinds of fish. Among them were the famous *Bodenseefelchen*, a whitefish especially easy to catch during spawning season in November–December and a source of protein that, dried and smoked, could be stored for long periods; perch, which locals called *Egli* or *Kretzer*, caught mainly with rods or gill nets; pike, a highly desirable reed-dwelling predatory fish; and plenty of carp, roach, rudd, tench and bream, although these were exclusively bought and eaten by people who couldn't afford any other.

Fish was a staple diet, and locals didn't have to rely on preserved saltwater fish such as pickled herring or dried cod commonly eaten in other parts of Central Europe, which were in any case much too expensive, thanks to high transport costs and customs fees. Lake Constance's fisheries did not constitute a subsistence economy but were integral to a stable economic cycle. The fish were perishable goods that had to be sold quickly at regional markets, chief among them being Constance and Lindau, frequented not only by townsfolk but also by the inhabitants of the surrounding countryside and the monasteries. These customers guaranteed a constant demand for fish, which incentivised the local fishermen to increase their profits. Not only that, but they felt a pressure to intensify their fishing, because a simple way to grow those profits was to ramp up their exploitation of the lake's waters. Given that Lake Constance was a commons, there was no governing authority which could have prohibited overfishing.

If we are to believe Hardin, therefore, it was a classic candidate for a commons tragedy: a renewable but limited resource, whose users could benefit personally from its exploitation. There was no shortage of incentives to increase fishing on the lake: more nets, or more efficient, close-meshed ones, or more fishermen, would have made individual users more competitive. What was missing was a higher authority which could, for example, set quotas. Instead, the users decided things for themselves. The lake was neither privately owned nor centrally regulated by the state, but collectively fished by locals who all had equally free access to it.

Still, Lake Constance obviously avoided the fate of a commons tragedy. Why? Zeheter's studies have led him to conclude that the critical success factor was the direct participation of the fishermen themselves. They and the relevant local authorities were equal stakeholders with equal responsibility, and decided how much you could catch and the methods you could use. To that end, the fishery guilds in Constance and Lindau formed a cooperative which, from the late fourteenth century onwards, took over policymaking powers from the patrician families.

The regulations instituted by the guilds show that they knew all about the latest methods, right down to the last detail. Not only that, but they evidently went on the offensive when it came to dealing with specific abuses, establishing rules with regard to the materials your nets, traps and rods could be made of, determining closed seasons and setting catch limits to help with the conservation of certain fish species, and defining punishments for violations, which ranged from fines and forfeits to imprisonment.

The level of detail contained in the regulatory documents clearly shows that they were created from the bottom up, not imposed from above – something also evidenced by the constant tweaks and revisions made to the rules during regularly scheduled fishery conferences, where they discussed everything that needed discussing. The negotiations were led by a guildmaster, an older, experienced fisherman who also acted as liaison with the town council.

Understanding resource fragility

Even the earliest known regulations show an awareness of how fragile the renewable resource called 'fish' is. The cooperatives agreed that to guarantee long-term supply they needed to protect stocks by imposing closed seasons and catch quotas. To do that, they continuously negotiated new, practical measures to prevent overfishing. A 1531 letter from the Constance guildmaster to his colleague in Überlingen shows that they were acutely sensitive to the potentially negative consequences of overexploitation: if all fishermen stuck to the rules, wrote the Constance guildmaster, and didn't catch young fish, the lake would be able to replenish its stocks – even though there currently appeared to be hardly any fish in it.[39] Today we would describe this as a 'sustainability initiative'.

Yet their key motive was nothing to do with ecology or environmental protection for its own sake, but a comparatively selfish desire to protect their livelihood. You could even say that the Lake Constance fishermen were a significant step ahead of us: instead of arguing about whether or not protecting the environment was important, they looked at the matter realistically, had a clear understanding of the consequences of their actions, and regulated the behaviour of everyone involved with the aim of securing their long-term survival. Various sources mention how ignoring the laws they had collectively passed would create chaos on the lake, which would have a negative impact on long-term yields. Sustainability was clearly defined in economic terms: if they did not stick to the agreed rules, their yield would decline in the long run.

There was also an important social component in play: if they did not stick to their rules, they would be unable to meet their fellow citizens' demand for fish. They also always explicitly considered the interests of their less well-off customers; and their efforts were complemented by the introduction of market regulation concerning catch sales, with price caps set for some species to frustrate racketeers and shield poorer buyers.

The cooperative also agreed minimum standards of quality and freshness, and required day-old fish to be marked as such by cutting off the tail fin.

Thanks to the combined regulation of the fishing industry and its market, Constance and Lindau's guilds ended up controlling a significant chunk of the lake's business. They thus set the standard, and fishery laws subsequently became the preferred method for regulating activity on Lake Constance. Other sovereigns – such as the imperial abbey of St Gall – subsequently passed their own versions.

Sustainable fishing strategies

The regulations obviously worked, or they would not have remained in use for centuries. They were regularly debated and renegotiated at fishery conferences, and adjusted to suit prevailing climatic and economic conditions. Zeheter has analysed thirty-four fishery regulations and contracts issued between 1350 and 1774, and established that the parameters sometimes shifted considerably during that time – never arbitrarily, but always in response to changing conditions. Whenever a law proved useful, it remained in place for centuries. For example, a 1455 regulation stipulated that a gill net's mesh size should be thirty-seven *Band*; the use of old gill nets would be allowed for another year, but after that only nets with this bigger mesh would be permitted.[40] The rule was evidently considered a sensible one until 1774. Meanwhile, the specifications for dragnets changed all the time. At one point, wider meshes were introduced to allow some bigger fish to escape, but the next iteration of the relevant rule added a special exemption for roach-fishing, where close-mesh nets would be permitted; the roach population of early 1600s Lake Constance must have been sufficiently healthy that there was no risk of overfishing.

The cooperative was clearly flexible, and willing to adjust regulations as and when necessary to suit the needs of both the fishermen and the conditions in the lake. The same goes for the 1700s: both centuries saw a sharp rise in the local (human) population, and the region's agricultural capacity was pushed to the limit. Fish was a food source whose supply you could easily increase by intensifying production, so to speak, and the discussions held at fishery conferences suggest that the number of fishermen was continuously growing. During this period, we generally notice a growing tension as short-term interests vied with long-term strategies, and a compromise had to be found between expanding the fishing industry to meet rising demand and ensuring that fish would remain in sufficient supply for future generations.

So they needed to change tack. Instead of interpreting the constant tweaks to regulations as proof that they didn't work, we now see that therein lay their advantage. The evolution of Lake Constance's fishing industry from the late Middle Ages to the 1900s was a success story: the fishermen used the lake's resource – the fish – efficiently for centuries, without causing a permanent decline in stocks or experiencing any serious problems in providing the local population with sufficient fish. They avoided the tragedy of the commons – but how?

According to Zeheter, two things played a key role: firstly, the fishermen regulated themselves, which meant that they created rules that they knew from experience were reasonable; their voices were heard at conferences, their knowledge was valued by the authorities in charge, and the fishermen themselves thus instigated every single modification made to the regulations. Secondly, non-locals who were not subject to these rules could be excluded from using the resource. Or, to put it the other way round: the regime required that any fisherman who wanted access to the key markets had to submit to the rules of the commons. Anyone who fished there, regardless of where and regardless of who employed him, was bound by the rules of the lake. The fact that fish are perishable goods of course helped convince outsiders to cooperate, since it was practically impossible to sell enough at faraway markets to make circumventing local regulations a realistic proposition.[41]

The mountains: Alpine commons

Since time immemorial, Alpine pastures have been shared by the inhabitants of the valleys. How exactly this happened is something we largely have to assess indirectly, relying on archaeological sources such as ruined huts in former summer pastures high up in the mountains, historical livestock trails, changes in vegetation due to seasonal manure, and other traces imprinted on the landscape over the centuries by the mountain pasture economy.

The first useful written sources date from the late Middle Ages, the oldest among them being the Swiss *Alpbriefe*, or 'mountain pasture certificates', which were increasingly common in the late fourteenth century. One particularly illuminating example stems from 1416 and concerns the pastures at Mühlebach and Ueblis in central Switzerland.[42] In a nutshell, it includes provisions concerning the maximum head of cattle allowed, specifics regarding which mountains form part of the user community in question, and droving and pasture maintenance schedules; it stipulates that jobs such as cleaning and clearing the pastures are shared by the community and carried out as and when necessary, and that on specific dates all pasture users – together with as many farmhands as are required, based on their share of the pasture – must help tidy up; anyone who fails to show up on the day has to pay a fine or make up for it later.

It also states that if someone does not use their right to drove they will be credited a third of their interest balance; and that no one may dispose of their usage rights. Finally, it names five *Leider* (bailiffs) who are in charge of monitoring adherence to the rules and issuing fines when they are violated. We can conclude from this that the communal use of mountain pastures, too, required regulation – even the oldest extant ordinances contain clear guidelines and access restrictions, and regularly include an addendum to the effect that changes will be made if a majority considers them necessary.

These examples from the Swiss Alps are often interpreted as evidence that cooperative economies of that kind are best suited to local, settled, stable, long-term communities of a manageable size and little social or geographical mobility. In other words: only somewhat 'backward' societies can afford to engage in communal husbandry, which renders the model unfit for a modern, connected, global and highly mobile world.

Those who argue along these lines are labouring under two misapprehensions: on the one hand, they overestimate how isolated village communities are; on the other, they underestimate their mobility. It is a common mistake to think that in the old days, people – particularly rural populations – spent their whole lives in one and the same village. It may be true of many, but it is also not true of many. Sources relating to villages in central Switzerland, for instance, show that they were far more mobile than you might expect: there is much evidence of temporary migrants, both female and male, and of young shepherds and dairymen who worked abroad.

Even their supposed social stability doesn't always tally with modern expectations: in many collectives a village woman (*Talwip*) played a key role, making important decisions on matters affecting the collective, while the men, or 'milkmen', took care of the manual labour.[43]

Transhumance in the Pyrenees

In this section we will take a look at transhumance economies and their collective use of mountain pastures, using the example of the Pyrenees of southern France and northern Spain. Whereas Alpine pastures are used only in the summer, Pyrenean herds are out and about all year round. Each season they are driven to a different pasture, often hundreds of kilometres away, and the journey can take several weeks. This form of commons can be traced back to antiquity, and it wasn't until the latter half of the nineteenth century that it dropped off sharply, following the large-scale privatisation of land.

The technical term 'transhumance' comes from the southern French dialect word *transhumer*, which suggests 'ground' or 'soil' as well as 'region' and 'land', and translates roughly as 'cross-country pastoralism'. It partly overlaps with both pastoralism and nomadism, and is characterised by the constant swapping between winter pasture in the lowlands and summer pasture in the highlands. It has been practised chiefly in the Mediterranean, particularly in regions with high mountain ranges which are cool and damp in the summer and cold and usually snow-capped in winter – from Portugal via Italy all the way to Turkey and Armenia, and from southern France via Catalonia to Andalusia.[44]

The wandering shepherd of Montaillou

'Well shod for his long journeys in a pair of good shoes of Spanish leather – the only luxury he allowed himself – detached from the goods of this world, careless of the almost inevitable certainty of being arrested at some time by the Inquisition, leading a life that was both passionate and passionately interesting, Pierre Maury was a happy shepherd.'[45] This is how the historian Emmanuel Le Roy Ladurie summed up Maury's state of mind. Maury was a nomadic shepherd who practised transhumance. He came from Montaillou, a village about 100 kilometres west of Perpignan, halfway between Toulouse in the north and Barcelona in the south, and part of a wide network of villages that predominantly made their living from sheep and grazed their flocks on distant pastureland all year round.[46] The nomadic shepherds of this region (involuntarily) left behind quite extraordinary evidence of their existence: written declarations of their ideas and world views, everyday lives, relatives and friends this and that side of the Pyrenees, which have proved a veritable treasure trove. In them, the microcosm of a mountain region is made visible as if by a magnifying glass. Let me briefly explain how this came about.

Montaillou is a very famous, perhaps the most famous, village in France. Famous, however, not for its wandering shepherds but for its heretics, the Cathars. The entire village once faced the inquisitor, and Le Roy Ladurie wrote an account of it in 1975 which became one of the most famous history books of the twentieth century. It focuses entirely on the villagers' depositions to the Inquisition between 1318 and 1324, which the court clerks translated from Occitan into Latin, copied on to parchment and bound into folio ledgers. Thanks to them we can hear the voices of people whose words would not normally have been recorded, and they provide us with a wealth of information and astonishingly detailed insights into everyday nomadic shepherd life in the late Middle Ages.[47]

The counts of Foix were Montaillou's seigneurs. The House of Foix's official representative was the castellan or châtelaine, who lived in the château overlooking the village. In Maury's time the chatelaine was Béatrice de Planissoles. From the fortress, terraces of houses and gardens descended all the way down to the church. The villagers, workmen and farmers were smallholders, and archaeological digs have shown that they cultivated the land intensively, planting oats, wheat, barley and especially turnips.[48] Altogether, there were fifty-five houses in the village, and people often lived with their livestock under one roof. Household structures were fluid, and sometimes temporarily included employees – there were no serfs in Montaillou:

all servants were contracted – and people always had guests. Many of the women were migrant workers. Multi-generational households were rare, and the villagers' statements suggest that solidarity was determined less by lineage than by a wide-ranging relationship network that included both kin and neighbours.[49]

Pierre Maury was born in about 1282, into a family of weavers. Like almost all families in Montaillou, the Maurys were also crop and livestock farmers; and, like almost everyone in the village, they were adherents of the Cathar Church. One of Pierre's brothers was a woodcutter, two of his sisters were married off at a young age and three other brothers were also shepherds. Thanks to Pierre's detailed statement, we know a surprising amount about his life as a wandering shepherd. In around 1300, when he was eighteen or so, he worked on the commons of Montaillou; that autumn, he moved out of his parents' house and went looking for work in the lowlands, in what is today the department of Aude, where the weather was warmer. He was hired as a shepherd by his cousin Raymond Maulen in Arques, and had a brief relationship with a certain Bernadette, which ended, however, when others convinced him that he should seek the daughter of a 'good Christian', i.e. a Cathar, for a wife.

A wealthy Cathar living in Arques called Raymond Pierre subsequently offered him the chance to become his son-in-law, but because the daughter was not yet old enough to marry Maury was asked to wait a little longer. Meanwhile, his future father-in-law contracted him as a shepherd. Maury's trial testimony reveals that the households in these villages saw a constant coming and going. The Inquisition was, of course, more than anything else interested in dubious intentions, and the presiding bishop's questions were very specific: we thus learn that Pierre worked as a shepherd in the highlands and would descend into the valley once a week to fetch bread, on which occasions he regularly encountered guests at his employer's house. Among those present were fellow sheep breeders, shepherds and itinerant Cathar preachers, to whose sermons Maury enjoyed listening as they sat together over dinner. At some point, he was converted. Famous preachers such as Pierre Authié, Prades Tavernier and Guillaume Belibaste fascinated him.

It appears to have been common for guests to spend the night, and Pierre repeatedly mentions having eggs and bacon for breakfast. His descriptions almost always end with the pithy comment, 'I went back to my sheep.'[50] By this time, he must have been around twenty years old. He spent the majority of the summer in the mountains, in a place called Rabassole, where he and seven other shepherds – whose names were, like everything else, meticulously documented – occupied a *cabane*. The term *cabane* was used to describe both the hut and the temporary team of shepherds inhabiting it: 'I was the hut leader or *cabanier*,' Maury told the Inquisition. 'I was in charge of the cheese-making ... I gave cooked meat, cheese, milk, and bread to passing believers in heresy.' The fact that his comrades on the mountain pasture considered him their leader is no surprise: the records show that everyone thought of him as a good worker, and his employer said that he always wanted Maury to be head shepherd, to 'rule over the other shepherds'.[51]

We also know that in 1305, towards the end of the summer, he left his employer in Arques and started working for a man called Barthélemy Borrel, whose sheep were at that time grazing in the Pyrenees, near Tortosa in Catalonia. Maury and two helpers went south, crossing the Pyrenees into Catalonia with other wandering shepherds and itinerant labourers looking for work, or on the run from the Inquisition. In summer they used the pastures on the northern slopes of Foix, in winter the warmer pastures on the southern slopes of the Pyrenees.

Maury describes each of his work contracts in minute detail; he regularly changed employer, often working for women, and the flocks' owners – for instance Ramond Boursier from Puigcerda, for whom he worked in the southern Pyrenean highlands in 1310 and 1311 – often moved with them. Maury later worked for a Catalan called Barthélmy Companho, whose flock was looked after by eight shepherds, two of whom also came from the Montaillou area. Now and again, he lived with his aunt Guillemette, who had emigrated and settled near Tortosa, where she ran a highly successful business.

What is interesting is that Maury rented out his own flock while he grazed other people's sheep in the mountains, with profits and losses shared equally by both parties. And so nomadic life continued: six weeks in Cerdagne in the north, on the border between Catalonia and Roussillon, then, in the summer, he drove sheep belonging to a certain lady called Brunissende up to the mountain pastures in the Ariège highlands, always accompanied by helpers who were young relatives or other shepherds with their own flocks. In autumn, Maury returned to southern Catalonia and took the flock of his elderly employer, Arnaud Faurés, to the winter pastures of the Plana de Cenia near Tarragona. One summer, he wandered north to graze his sheep alongside those of some fellow Montaillou shepherds close to the Puymauren Pass near l'Hospitalet.

And so it went, on and on, in a continuous migration from summer to winter pastures in Catalonia, Cerdagne, Aragon and Ariège. Unlike the mountain pasture economies of central Switzerland, the wandering shepherds of the Pyrenees moved from place to place all year round. This way of utilising collective resources was essentially a form of private enterprise. Various sources describe the *boria* as the cornerstone of mobile transhumance – a *boria* being the barn with its stables and pens, as well as a shepherd's business, which consisted of wide-ranging relationship networks on both sides of the Pyrenees. For example, Maury's aunt Guillemette was one of his chief business partners.

A wandering shepherd's business relationships were based exclusively on contracts with ever-changing employers, usually wage contracts with set terms which may or may not include a share of the profits, depending on the risks involved.[52] The lines between wage labour and leasehold were fluid; the shepherds also had their own animals, which they sometimes leased to others or used as a form of payment. Thus Maury once pledged thirty of his sheep as part payment for 100 sheep he bought from a breeder called Raymonde Barry.[53]

Conflicts over usage rights are also mentioned in the depositions, with cases of villages or landowners asserting their legal rights over pastures that were either traversed or grazed on by the wandering shepherds' flocks. In the course of one interrogation, Maury told the story of how he was grazing his sheep among the peaks above Flix, near Tarragona, when the bishop of Lerida sent twelve armed men from Bisbal de Falset up to the mountains to charge him and the other shepherds there with breach of the peace and confiscate their herds. According to Maury, the shepherds did not even dispute the bishop's rights. Instead they settled the case out of court, so to speak: Maury served the armed men – who were exhausted from the arduous climb to the lofty pastures – an opulent feast, to which he also invited other shepherds from Cerdagne, Catalonia and Ariège. They all ate and drank together, and the bishop's henchmen were appeased.[54]

The fact that the pastures belonged to individual communities was no reason not to use them. One record mentions that, for two summers, Maury grazed his sheep at the Pal Pass in the territory of the municipality of Baga near Barcelona, and for one summer at the Cadi Pass, on Josa land, near Gerona. References in witness statements to territorial boundaries like these suggest that municipalities might have charged shepherds a levy for using their land. Shepherds would also graze their sheep near villages, on private or parish land that often nominally belonged to the local landowner, without being penalised for it.

On what principle the shepherds divided pastures up between them is unclear. Sometimes they allocated them with the drawing of lots, as the Montaillou shepherds did whenever they drove their animals to the Arques pastures. On the Catalan side of the Pyrenees, the conditions were stricter. If you wanted to use land that belonged to a village, you either had to apply for citizenship or marry a local girl. This is what happened to young Jean Maury, a nephew of Pierre's. When he wanted to graze his sheep in Casteldans, a village near Lérida, the local council demanded that he should marry immediately, or move on with his flock before his sheep stripped the village's pastures altogether. He could not find a woman who would agree to marry him in such haste and was initially forced to leave. He moved to the neighbouring village of Juncosa, where he met a woman called Mathena who was willing to become his wife.

The wedding ceremony usually marked the first step towards 'settling' in a village. Most shepherds ended their nomadic life when they married and had children. Maury, too, got married, albeit only briefly, to the lover of a Cathar priest called Guillaume Belibaste. The priest's lover was pregnant, and it seems that Maury married her to provide his friend with an alibi. Three days was all it took, after which their marriage was dissolved by Belibaste himself. As far as Maury's relationships with women are concerned, it was seemingly common then for shepherds to bring a girlfriend or lover with them into the mountains, one summer at a time – a seasonal relationship, so to speak, which would end as quickly as it began.[55]

Le Roy Ladurie's descriptions of transhumance in the Pyrenees are practically rhapsodic. The wandering herdsmen had no place to call home; and even when they did manage to accumulate a certain amount of wealth from their shepherding and other work, they were unlikely to have their heart set on owning a property. Mobile as they were, they hardly had use for four walls and a roof. Maury, too, was interested more in a wealth of human connections: from those transient, cheerful love affairs which provided companionship on the pasture and in the tavern to his relationships with siblings, cousins, aunts, uncles and friends. He felt comfortable in this network. He embraced his fate, and loved his work and way of life. To him, his sheep meant a freedom he wouldn't have dreamt of swapping for the supposed charms of settling down – which some of his friends and employers tried to persuade him to do by offering him marriage, adoption, a house and suchlike. He preferred to be a rolling stone, without a home and yet at home everywhere. With his lifestyle, property would merely have been a burden. He was also relaxed in how he handled his wealth: whenever he lost money or sheep he didn't mind too much, really, for he knew that, sooner or later, his two hands would provide.

In the fourteenth century, the shared use of Pyrenean pastures for grazing sheep was largely operated as a private enterprise and regulated by contracts. In those days there were no large-scale municipal or district flocks of sheep (*ramados*) – these only started appearing in this part of the world in the nineteenth century. In the late Middle Ages, i.e. in Maury's day, the flocks still belonged to individual owners or small associations of private citizens.

It is therefore wrong to think of 'community spirit' as a prehistoric mindset inherent in remote and 'backward' mountain regions. On the contrary: cooperatives only started replacing commercial enterprise some time later.[56] We also must not overestimate the importance of the village community in a shepherd's life. His real social unit was the aforementioned *cabane*, the mountain huts where those small groups of self-employed men lived together for the season. Here they produced cheese, sheared the sheep and hosted passing travellers, making them something like supra-regional communication centres and places of cultural exchange. Archaeological digs in Montaillou have revealed the remains of spinach stuck to cooking utensils, which suggests that the wandering shepherds brought spinach into Central Europe from Al-Andalus.[57]

Although Pyrenean transhumance was a form of contract-based commercial commons, there's no evidence that there were written rules and regulations of the kind recorded in the Swiss *Alpbriefe*. Nonetheless, there were guidelines – for example regarding what routes to take, how to deal with local conditions, and how long you could graze your flock in a given pasture if you wanted it to be fit for use the following year. This know-how was passed on from one generation to the next when experienced herdsmen took budding shepherds with them on their journeys as apprentices and companions. When we recall the feast Maury put on for the bishop's henchmen, we get the sense that any conflicts that transpired were solved rather idiosyncratically and creatively. Le Roy Ladurie believes that the primary reason why this culture was able to survive into the nineteenth century was that its economy was based on self-preservation rather than growth.[58]

'What is important is not to make the world a better place, but to protect it.' Odo Marquard

Scholars unanimously agree that, from a historical perspective, Hardin's thesis is untenable. However, Hardin was interested less in the commons of a bygone era than in the ruthless exploitation of the global commons, and in that context he is surely right to warn us not to assume that people have an ecological conscience and will behave responsibly.

Yet Hardin is somewhat misleading in portraying pasture commons as always freely accessible to everyone, and thereby precludes (no doubt unintentionally) the very possibility that commons can be used successfully. His second mistake is to assume that in any given situation a rationally thinking person will by definition focus on what they can personally get out of it.

Both premises are flawed. 'Unlimited right of common' is an adynaton – which is to say as rare as a purple cow. It has never existed. Furthermore, describing commons as a system where profits are privatised and losses shared is plainly wrong; as is the idea that 'rational thinking' implies the pursuit of self-interest. Are foresight and long-term planning not the human brain's most remarkable qualities? An intelligent farmer would surely be unlikely to willingly destroy mountain pastures, and thereby their children's future livelihood. What do they stand to gain by selling gallons of milk now, knowing that their descendants will be left impoverished when the commons ceases to exist?

In addition, the assumption that people are unlikely to cooperate at the very least requires further explanation, now that recent studies in behavioural sociology, behavioural economics and experimental psychology have shown that the opposite is true. Michael Tomasello, for one, would disagree with the notion. People are very much capable of cooperating constructively. The problem is not the collective use of resources; what will drive us to ruin is if we start acting in the way that economists describe in their textbooks.[59]

The principles governing historical commons

Without exception, the approach taken by the examples raised here – and they represent just a small sample from a broad historical spectrum – follows a clear economic logic, one that has, through the centuries, proved a way to use our resources in a sustainable manner. Daniel Schläppi, an expert on commons, has summarised the principles that drive cooperative economies like these as follows: thrift is as central to how they are structured as the desire to preserve the given resource. The idea that the common good is secured by constant economic growth is nowhere to be found.

The people involved were mainly concerned with sustaining the source of their livelihood and continuously practised long-term economics. They internalised externalities such as long-lasting environmental damage by factoring short-term losses into their plans, and were continuously aware of the ecological context. They were experts in sustainability before they ever knew the word – at the same time that, unlike us today, they were interested not in protecting the environment but in preserving their livelihood.[60]

Beguinages: Female Communities, Urban Gardens

Sharing, then, brings with it riches and facilitates sustainability; and sharing also gets things done. Examples of this can be found not only among monks and nuns, mountain farmers in the Alps, migrant shepherds in the Pyrenees and the inhabitants of Palatine forests: many of our cultural masterpieces owe their very existence and long-term survival to community action. Among them are some of the monumental Gothic buildings in European cities that are so popular with tourists – Notre Dame in Paris, for example, and the town hall in Brussels. They were conceived as communal projects, and completed only thanks to the collective effort of various citizen groups.[61] Such large-scale initiatives are evidence that the towns and cities considered themselves sharing communities. This by no means undermined their business acumen or economic creativity; on the contrary: the pursuit of economic well-being, it seems, did much to foster a community spirit, which in turn contributed to people's economic well-being.

This becomes especially clear when we look at thirteenth-century European society. The climate was mild. People had it good. Business was booming. Trade and cities flourished. And precisely in those places where these developments were most acutely felt – the Flemish trading towns and port cities of Bruges, Antwerp, Ghent, Leuven and others – a new form of urban community was emerging: groups of women who had left their families to live in beguinages. Beguinages were equally supported by the towns' rulers, charitable foundations, the Church and wealthy citizens. Those that still exist today famously contain Europe's oldest urban green spaces. They were founded by individual charitable benefactors but maintained thanks to the continuous, collective commitment of their residents, as well as all sorts of urban interest groups. They were diverse places, ranging from more or less loose associations of neighbours who lived alone to multi-occupant households and communities with hundreds of occupants. The women lived together, sometimes prayed and worked together, but only rarely shared their property. These unusual urban associations allowed their members an unexpected degree of freedom, and are the kind of supportive and empowering community that we might well be inspired to emulate.

Avant-garde sharing communities

What are beguinages? In terms of urban planning, they are a topography found chiefly in Belgian and Dutch cities. They consist of several houses, squares, streets, gardens, a church or chapel, a hospital, commercial premises such as breweries, mills, bakeries and barns, as well as spaces used for agriculture, providing a locally managed food source on the outskirts of town. They are almost always enclosed either by a protective wall with one or two gates, or by canals. Some beguinages even have their own moorings, or perhaps a small port. Urban architects distinguish two types of layout: the 'street beguinage' (*stratenbegijnhof*), where the homes and businesses were erected along streets and alleyways; and the 'court beguinage' (*pleinbegijnhof*), where the living quarters were arranged around one or two largish squares containing a church or hospital. The ones that are still around are mainly blended types, which are the product of several centuries' worth of building works, although they often follow older layouts – Leuven's Groot Begijnhof being one such example.[62]

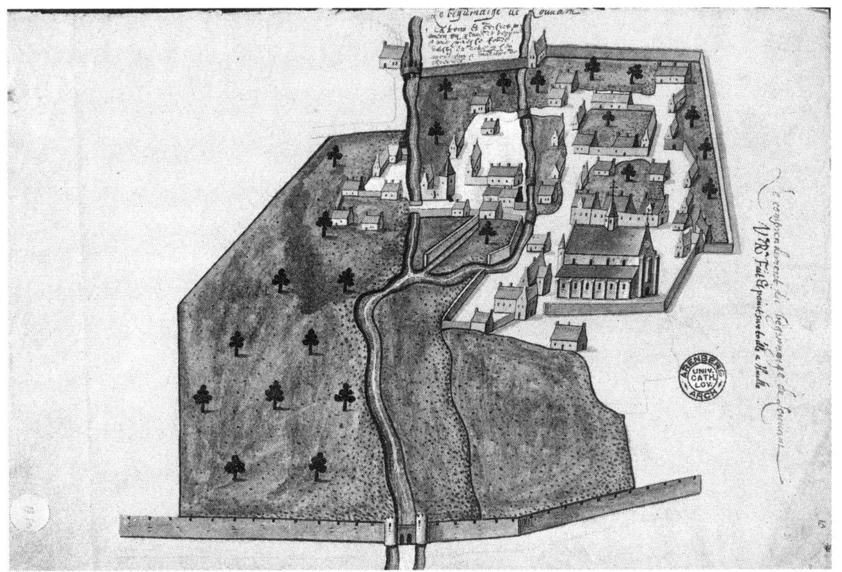

10. The Groot Begijnhof in Leuven: a blend of court and street beguinage (colourised drawing by Pierre de Bersaques, *c.* 1598–9)[63]

World Heritage Sites

Beguines and beghards (their male counterparts) lived all over Europe, but beguinages were confined to Dutch and Belgian cities. We know of seventy-seven such architectural groupings, twenty-six of which have been preserved; in 1998, UNESCO added thirteen of them to its list of World Heritage Sites for their architectural value, the way they have integrated green spaces, and as examples of Flemish tradition. The extant buildings date back to the seventeenth and eighteenth centuries and boast populations of ancient trees, comfortable terraced houses, picturesque squares, clean air, gardens and generous parks – and all that right in the city centre. Let's take a short stroll through a few of them.[64]

The beguinage in the town of Hoogstraten, situated close to the Dutch border in the far north of Belgium, was founded in the fourteenth century as a court beguinage located right next to the town hall. In the seventeenth century, it was significantly altered and expanded to house 160 beguines in sixty-two houses. These whitewashed one- and two-storey buildings occupy a generous open area east of the church. The ensemble also includes an old cemetery. The entire site was extensively renovated in the late twentieth century, and rededicated with a big festival. The beguinage of Lier, meanwhile, is a typical 'street beguinage'. It consists of 156 houses, and a hospital that was destroyed in a fire and rebuilt by the city in 1970. The highly desirable, centrally located apartments have since then been rented out as affordable homes for less well-off citizens. The Groot Begijnhof in Mechelen – which housed an astonishing 1,500–1,900 women at the end of the sixteenth century – has recently been turned into an attractive residential area. Sint-Alexius in Dendermonde (Termonde) is the very epitome of a court beguinage, with sixty-one houses arranged around a triangular space. The site was created in 1288 and originally surrounded on all sides by the waters of the Dendre. The buildings we see there today date from the seventeenth century, but the layout is very much medieval.

The Bruges beguinage of St Elisabeth Ten Wijngaarde was founded in the thirteenth century. Its name – literally 'of the vineyard' – suggests its original location on the edge of the city's vineyards, probably outside the city walls. Yet as Bruges expanded during the thirteenth century, the beguinage became part of the city and grew into an autonomous neighbourhood enclosed by a wall and a canal. Bruges's sixteenth-century street plan (see illustration, p. 80) clearly shows the many different building types contained within: there are small, single-family houses, as well as larger communal buildings; the prominence of the church (no. 42), which was constructed in the centre of the large square, is typical for many beguinages; close to the west gate, beyond the three trees, you can see the hospital,

11. The Dendermonde beguinage is typical of a court beguinage

which has its own little chapel; and its external walls can be discerned to the east and south, but are obscured in the north and north-west by rows of houses edging the beguinage. The beguines' homes are arranged around the two squares and along the street. The settlement's main entrance lies east of the church (centre left in the image), and could be accessed from Wijngaardstraat via a bridge across the canal; a further entrance can be seen at bottom right.

The bridge across the canal leading to the 'vineyard square' and the seventeenth-century gate is still there. What is particularly impressive about the beguinage is the generous green space at its heart, in the midst of whitewashed, mostly two-storey houses. The church with the little Gothic spire, which also survives, is on the edge of the site, somewhat hidden. Some sources also show evidence of agricultural structures including stables and barns.

12. The St Elisabeth Ten Wijngaarde beguinage in Bruges, 1562

Ghent has no fewer than three beguinages, one of which was home to 410 beguines and 65 children.[65] The beguinage of Sint-Truiden is particularly remarkable for its extensive agricultural spaces, a herb garden and the only well-preserved example of a 'beguinage farm' (*ferme béguinale*).

Cities of ladies

These extraordinary urban landscapes were created by women. It was also almost exclusively women who lived and worked in them over the centuries. Even contemporary accounts mention 'beguine towns' (*civitas beghinarum*), which prompted the

13. Bruges: beguinage with access bridge and Gothic church

14. Bruges: the central green space surrounded by the beguines' houses

historian Walter Simons to give them the rather apt epithet of 'cities of ladies'.[66]

What were they all about? A beguinage was a community of women who lived either alone or with one or several other women, with or without private staff, in a private home or in purpose-built communal housing. They all pursued their own line of work, and came from every social stratum. There was no such thing as communal property. Some had been married and had children, others were young 'pious virgins'. They rarely took vows. When they moved in they merely agreed to abide by house rules and obey the 'mistress', and could leave the community as casually as they entered it, for example to get married. Some deliberately decided to live in poverty, others kept their property and assets. They lived a life of intensified piety, but remained lay members – even if outsiders often perceived them as nuns.

Beguinages were not something like supra-regional associations of like-minded women, but they did evolve in similar ways across many regions. We don't yet know why. Nearly all were founded in the thirteenth century, and the necessary capital and land were obtained via charitable donations from local benefactors, 45 per cent of whom were female. Leading figures among them included Joan of Constantinople and her daughter Margaret, who, as countesses of Flanders and Hainaut, ruled the area for seventy-four years (1206–80). The queen of France, too, founded beguinages, as did aristocratic ladies such as Jutta, the widow of Waleran de Montjoie (Sittard), or wealthy nuns or canonesses such as Isabelle de Houpelines (Mons) and the abbess Guda von Rennenberg (Thorn). However, the majority of benefactors were worldly ladies, often widows, who turned the land and buildings they owned into urban beguinages, or decreed that they should be turned into them after their death.[67]

The beguinages that survive may give the impression that all beguinages were more or less the same – not so.[68] There was no overarching master plan; the donors merely provided an open urban space that could be turned into plots for buildings and accommodation. Just like any other neighbourhood, the sites evolved gradually, and they were repeatedly expanded and converted. The main reason for their expansion was the arrival of new residents: it was the beguines themselves who took the initiative to erect their houses, which they paid for either out of their own pockets or with donations. In many cities, large-scale building or conversion projects were supported by the Church and the community: Hamburg's beguines thus financed their conversion project at the turn of the sixteenth century with the help of money raised by the bishop from selling off indulgences, and with donations from Hamburg's Blue Nuns and some local families.[69]

Urban capital was thus purposefully channelled into beguinages. At times, non-members would try to buy their way into them, for instance by acquiring real estate on the site; and contemporary statutes and court actions show that the mistresses of some beguinages tried to secure the right of first refusal for members of the community – but it appears that they only succeeded in a few individual cases. It wasn't until the modern era that the houses became the communal property of the beguinages and were leased back to individual women for the duration of their lives. Throughout the Middle Ages, however, the houses remained the property of the women, who either sold them or left them to other beguines in their will or to relatives, who then sometimes sold them on to other beguines.

Origins

Historians use the term 'semi-religious' to describe the beguines' way of life; they were intensely pious, but not actual nuns.[70] The term 'beguine' (Latin *beg[u]inae*, *begutae*) first appears in the early thirteenth century. Its precise meaning is unclear: its origins have variously been attributed to the Belgian saint Begga, to Lambert le Bégue of Liège, and to the term *bigin*, short for *albigeois*, a term sometimes used synonymously with heretics and apostates.[71] Sources dating back to the twelfth century and later also use the more neutral term *mulieres religiosae* for women who led a life of piety away from their families, in a community of like-minded women. Some people objected to this, others – such as an anonymous thirteenth-century chronicler from Colmar – delighted in the multitude and diversity of female communities founded during this time.[72] Their way of life seemed alien to nineteenth- and twentieth-century minds too, with some arguing that they constituted an 'excess' of women, or that the Church was confining these women to (lay) convents.[73]

The notion of women leading independent communal lives doesn't quite fit our idea of the Middle Ages. We instinctively think that we know what was normal 'back then', and what was normal was surely a settled, traditional family. However, this turns out to be one of modernity's most consequential inventions. There used to be much greater diversity – from academic colleges and overseas merchants' communities, to religious (monastic), military (e.g. mercenaries) and nomadic communities (e.g. migrant shepherds). And this diversity included beguinages, and when we examine the available data we see that – depending on the specific case – their share of the total local population constituted between 1 and 8 per cent; while at the start of this century, just 5.9 per cent of Germans were living in shared accommodation.[74]

How to organise an urban sharing community

Why did the bishop of Liège, Robert de Thourette, take the beguines who lived in his bishopric under his wing? For they must be the 'ladies' he had in mind when he forbade anyone from attacking or insulting 'the pious ladies'. The women wore

Small beguinages (35–100 beguines)

Beguinage	Year/Period	No. of residents
Breda	1535	32
Zoutleeuw	1526	36
Hesdin	1324	38
Tienen	1526	39
Valenciennes	1485	49
Kortrijk	1526	52
Turnhout	1480	60
Bergen op Zoom	1526	65
Lier	1480	69
Cantimpret (Mons)	1365	84

Medium-sized beguinages (100–400)

Beguinage	Year/Period	No. of residents
Champfleury (Douai)	1272	100
St Catherine, Antwerp	1526	101
Groot Begijnhof, Leuven	1526	125
St Catherine, Diest	1558	144
Ten Wijngaerde, Bruges	1455	153
Groot Begijnhof, 's-Hertogenbosch	1526	183
St Catherine, Tongeren	1322	230
Herentals	1480	266
Klein Begijnhof, Ghent	1500	269
Dendermonde	1480	275
Wijngaard, Brussels	1526	326

Large beguinages (1,000–1,900)

Beguinage	Year/Period	No. of residents
Groot Begijnhof St Elisabeth, Ghent	Late thirteenth century	610–730
St Christophe, Liège	Mid-thirteenth century	1,000
Groot Begijnhof St Catherine, Mechelen	Late fifteenth century	1,500–1,900

15. Population figures for twenty-four beguinages

a special attire which shielded them from such assaults because it signalled – like a police officer's uniform or judge's robe – that they were backed by a strong community and enjoyed the protection of both Church and city. One of the main problems of this new communal urban lifestyle was its very openness: the beguines were testing life in a community away from the safety of their families as well as outside the walls of a convent, and it is therefore easy to see why their house rules focused particularly on interactions at the intersection of town and beguinage, and why we regularly find statements to the effect that residents may not leave the complex without permission.

Let us examine this interaction between beguinage and town more closely by looking at the house rules of St Stephen's in Aachen: these state that permission to leave could be granted either by the mistress or – and this addition seems to me crucial if we want to properly understand this policy – by a fellow resident. Translated into today's language, the policy basically says: 'For your own protection, you must inform someone before you leave the site, and let them know when you plan to return.' Rules regarding overnight absences, likewise, are formulated in diplomatic terms: overnight stays outside the beguinage are not forbidden, but a beguine must first obtain the consent of the beguinage's mistress or priest.

It was a form of supervision that suggests concern rather than surveillance, and we discern a similar approach to participation in extramural festivities: it might sound strict to us that beguines were not allowed to accept invitations to weddings, childbirth celebrations or dinners, but the rule's concluding clause – '… if there is any cause for concern' – says it all. Again, the regulations surrounding overnight guests initially seem drastic: beguines were not permitted to bring someone into the beguinage, or put them up for more than eight nights, without prior permission from the mistress or priest; and the fact that they were forbidden from speaking to men during night-time,

or from opening a door or window in order to speak to them, might evoke a smile – but the addendum 'without good reason, or unless strictly necessary' speaks volumes.

The 1333 revised version of St Stephen's house rules bans the beguines from bathing with men, and declares that they ought to avoid the company of men who secretly enter the beguinage late at night, when the beguines are on their way to church for evening prayer – which tells us that this must have been common practice; and the express demand that beguines should attend church every Sunday hints at the fact that they did not usually do so.[75]

It seems, then, that everyday life was far more 'ordinary' and worldly than the nineteenth-century image of pious women wearing white veils would suggest. This is not to say that they were not motivated by piety, but that they were far more than 'pious ladies', and none of the sources suggest that their life-style was the same everywhere. These days we would probably call it a 'localised grass-roots movement'. The only quality that characterises all beguines, at all times and in all places, is their facility for adapting to local social and economic conditions. In historian Letha Böhringer's words, 'these women were brilliant at reinventing themselves'.[76]

'You talk, we act'

Many of the women living in these supportive and empowering communities have left behind records of their thoughts. Some wrote controversial works in which they criticised their times – such as *The Mirror of Simple Souls* by Marguerite Porete, who was burnt at the stake. Others left behind their traces in comparatively unspectacular writings; in the late thirteenth century, a Dominican friar in northern France published a collection of stories designed for inclusion in sermons, and among them is a riveting exchange between a professor at the University of Paris

and a beguine. In this dialogue, the beguine explains the difference between scholars who are perpetually engaged in research and women who actually *do* something:[77]

You talk, we act
You learn, we do
You analyse, we choose
You chew, we swallow
You negotiate, we buy
You warm up, we catch fire
You suppose, we know
You ask, we take
You work, we pause
You lose weight, we put it on
You ring, we sing
You sing, we dance
You flower, we bear fruit
You taste a little here and there, we eat.

We can scarcely imagine that the anonymous Dominican ever used these words for a sermon; but he did write them down. Perhaps he was fascinated by her thoughts, and by the way she opposes two types of knowledge – university scholarship and the intuitive knowledge of women who act – in carefully constructed pairs. She uses the paradox, a popular stylistic tool in mystic discourse, to express her superiority over contemporary academia.

Beguines generally saw themselves as the ones who took action, who got things done, while men wielded words, analysed, negotiated and now and again tentatively initiated a project or two. They were women with something to say, who had learnt that actions speak louder than words. Greta Thunberg would no doubt have found like-minded supporters in these communities.

The beguine of Douai and her watercress nursery

Today, we know beguinages as urban gardens and oases; and we have very little idea as to how their gardens and agricultural spaces were once managed. However, we can glean some information about this in a roundabout way, for instance by looking at their architecture, which displays some similarity to that of large farms on the edge of medieval towns: just like these estates, beguinages were enclosed by a wall and usually set up just outside city walls. Their layout in general also often suggests a farm.[78]

At the close of the 1200s, as cities rapidly expanded and walls shifted outwards, many beguinages found themselves in, or on the edge of, the city centre (as we saw with St Elisabeth in Bruges); and the open spaces contained within the complex perhaps fulfilled a function not unlike that of gardens in monasteries and large farming estates. Beguines were allowed to build churches and create cemeteries, just like monks and nuns, and their cemeteries were usually arranged as green spaces; you might even say that the dead helped create these urban oases.

There is much evidence to suggest that beguinages were partly self-sufficient. For example, 'house' breweries supplied beer to the residents; it is unlikely that they ever sold it to outsiders (although there is a beer in Tongeren called Dagelyckx which is advertised as 'beguine beer'), but we know from surviving invoices that they did sell the pomace as animal fodder and fertiliser.[79] Some beguines traded in fruit and vegetables planted by others. One example is Maroie le Cresoniere from Douai – whose name ('le Cresoniere') suggests that she ran a watercress nursery of sorts, renting out 'wet plots' for planting cress and probably dealing in both plants and seedlings.[80]

The 1262 house rules of the beguinage in Valenciennes stipulate that members must earn their living among other things from mowing and harvesting (*miessoner*); they don't explicitly mention that they worked the fields in other ways, but the

16. Beguine farm in Sint-Truiden, Belgium

community did own a farm – called De la Basse-cour – which it rented out, and who's to say that the beguines did not take on at least some of the farm work? Farms and agricultural spaces both inside and outside beguinage walls are also frequently referred to in connection with the beguinage hospitals, for example in Bruges and Valenciennes;[81] and in Valenciennes, Tongeren, Dendermonde and Sint-Truiden some beguines 'did farm work in nearby fields, herded animals, raised poultry, or grew vegetables for the urban market'.[82] Sint-Truiden is where you will find the only surviving beguine farm, which is still intact and dates back to the eighteenth century.

'Successful businesses, like happy people, leave no trace behind.'[83]

Unlike, for instance, credit transactions (of which more later), farming was one of those activities that rarely needed written records. Perhaps dealing with nature – looking after animals, cultivating gardens, sowing and harvesting – was simply so much part of everyday life that it required no special effort or mention. This is the familiar historian's dilemma: we can only know what has been recorded in writing; everything else is mere speculation. This has far-reaching consequences, because we usually only put pen to paper when there is some kind of conflict. Amicable business is settled with a handshake, not a court case.

Our view of the past is therefore blurred by bias, and we regard much of it through the lens of strife. That's when people start writing things down, to record who owes how much to whom, what belongs to them, who is right and who is wrong, who has won and who has lost; they hire solicitors, notaries and jurists to produce certificates, create laws, establish chronologies and provide proof. All the many relatively harmonious dealings, relationships, negotiations and processes in human history have simply disappeared: they happened, went well, worked out. That's it. And no one remembers them, because no one wrote anything down. They didn't need to. Everything worked out fine, and was instantly swallowed up by the bottomless well that is the past, never to be seen or heard of again.

Perhaps the beguinages' farming activities are an instance of those successful ordinary businesses that only rarely find their way into the written record. By this I don't mean to claim that the world of farming knows only happy people and happy outcomes – but their disputes with unpredictable nature, not least the unpredictable weather, were possibly ones in which certificates and contracts were of little use.

Prototypes for modern urban gardens?

Something else we know exceedingly little about is how the beguinages' gardens were originally laid out and cultivated. Beguinages were not static entities. Like the towns and cities in which they were located, they changed constantly. Their fields were not the only victim of urban expansion; the sites themselves changed too.

Seventeenth- and eighteenth-century construction layouts survive in today's cityscapes; but what we know of medieval gardens largely stems from medieval art and literature (recently augmented by experimental archaeological research projects, such as the reconstruction of Lorsch Abbey).[84] Fortunately, we have access to a sort of template for medieval gardens: the Plan of St Gall. On it are marked, among other things, four different types of garden together with instructions for planting – a square garden, a vegetable garden, an orchard and a physic garden. As monastic culture spread across Europe, so did these garden types; and it is not unreasonable to assume that they may have supplied the blueprint for beguinage gardens too. Furthermore, we can speculate that the women cultivated and used their gardens, fields and farms according to the relevant local customs.

That some beguinages proved robust enough to survive to this day is certainly a stroke of urban-architectural luck, and the beguines' wonderful ability to adapt and change makes their history very much worth studying, as an example of how sharing communities of the past were able to live sustainably. However, we must reckon with a few disappointments: beguines were not guerrilla gardeners; and beguinages were neither intercultural, interactive gardens, nor citizen initiatives aimed at transforming urban spaces into green oases by planting aromatic herbs and some edible fruit in plastic buckets.[85] They were not designed for romantic reasons, as bucolic relics or parallel rural universes, but as a necessary component of a town's economy. A few decades ago, historians believed that the combination of communal life and peri-urban farming was evidence of a naive-utilitarian relationship with nature. A lot has changed since then, and we are rediscovering the possibilities of 'urban farming' – not as a relic, but as an integral component of the urban economy.[86]

Sharing communities as empowering communities

Were beguinages sharing communities? Their members shared urban living spaces. They shared their everyday lives. In the Middle Ages, they only shared their property in exceptional cases,[87] but despite this – or perhaps because of it – beguinages offered amazing opportunities to share and utilise resources to shape communal life.

Beguines had a right to private property. They also had an independent income, whether from work, renting out property, an inheritance, or 'widow's thirds'. City regulations declared them legally competent to conduct business. They could also construct their own homes, and depending on their means made them large or small, and more or less luxurious. Depending on the size of her house, a beguine would live alone, with other beguines, or with friends or relatives. Staff – i.e. maids – are frequently mentioned. Evidently, it was not obligatory to take a vow of poverty.

A beguine did not have to live in voluntary poverty but she could do so, as long as she was able to feed herself, be it by working or from what she had brought with her when she entered the beguinage. Being a beguine was thus not a social leveller: 'Rich women became rich beguines, and poor women were (and remained) poor beguines.'[88] Those who were poor or destitute were helped by beguinage-run charities, which helped them find a place in the settlements' convents. There they found shelter and were given enough money to pay for lighting, heating and building maintenance. Above and beyond that, though, they were expected to provide for themselves.

Again and again, the beguines' financial independence is underlined. In economic terms, they were autonomous agents. Their accounts were sometimes audited by the town or bishop; for instance, Hamburg's beguines had to submit theirs to the city council's auditor at the end of each financial year. But the auditor did not interfere with how they ran their affairs. Instead he consistently signed everything off, even accounts that had obviously been falsified.[89]

The beguines of Hamburg

Hamburg already had a beguinage in 1255, but that year an endowment from the count of Holstein facilitated a new building in Hamburg's Steinstraße in the parish of St Jacobi. Further buildings were added, and by the time they were torn down in 1850 the site consisted of two houses perpendicular to the street, used as accommodation; various operational buildings; the mistress's garden; two squares, one lawned and one cobbled; and wells and outdoor toilets.[90]

The beguinage's account ledgers for 1481–1546 give us a fascinating glimpse into the everyday lives of its twenty to twenty-seven beguines. Anyone who wanted to move into the convent had to pay a one-off entry fee of thirty-two marks or bring with them a life annuity of two marks a year. In addition, there was an annual fee for board and lodging ranging from one mark to six marks. Every member was registered by name, and children paid between five and ten marks. At any given time, there were between seven and eighteen children in the beguinage; these were usually the young daughters of Hamburg families who lived there as pupils. Fourteen books that can be traced to the beguinage have survived, suggesting that there was a library and that at least some of the women could read and write. Other beguinages elsewhere, too, ran similar schools. Among the girls taught by the Blue Nuns in Hamburg in 1482 was a certain 'Elsebe, who was with Alleken Bruns', i.e. a girl who 'belonged' to a beguine called Alleken Bruns and thus paid only two marks and twelve shillings (instead of ten marks). She was probably a ward or relative of Alleken's. When a beguine died, her property passed to the beguinage (not her family); whereupon the *Mesterinne*, that is, the mistress of the convent – who was also in charge of bookkeeping – arranged an estate sale. The proceeds, and any capital the deceased had possessed, were added to the community's coffers. Occasional entries concerning such sales in the beguinage's earnings statements show that its inhabitants came from all walks of life: while some left little more than their bed sheets and a couple of skirts, others also left furniture, china and other household objects.[91]

How did they make money?

The beguines did not live on handouts. How exactly they financed themselves and managed their affairs varied from community to community; and their family circumstances and social background, choice of work, religious orientation and how their property was structured also played an important role.[92] Some beguines had their own income and led almost self-sufficient lives in their beguinage house, others were members of large groups who took care of everything as a community. Provisions and income were not shared everywhere as in Hamburg, and not everywhere – as evidently in Ghent – did they lead a communal working life to the rhythm of songs and prayers.[93]

There is much evidence to suggest that the inhabitants of the great Flemish beguinages were mostly employed in local textile production and manufacturing. For instance, numerous municipal ordinances concerning beguinages have survived, a noticeable number of which deal with questions concerning the textile trade. Flemish beguines chiefly worked with cloth: according to Walter Simons, they 'hackled, combed and spun wool, napped or otherwise finished the woven woollen cloth, prepared it for dyeing, or cut and prepared flax for the production of linens'; and court beguinages, 'with their spacious meadows and gardens close to the waterways, were convenient locations for washing and bleaching woollens and linens'. They also made clothes, and may have been embroiderers too.[94]

Beguines and the financial markets: Marseilles

You will often read that beguines took care of the sick in Europe's cities, but the latest studies suggest that this was not generally the case; at least not in the Middle Ages, although they may have done so more often in later times.[95] Many earned an income from their property, made charitable donations[96] or turned up in the financial markets in Hamburg, Hanover and elsewhere.[97] Notaries' files from Marseilles give us an unusually detailed insight into the economic activities of the beguines of Roubaud, who regularly appear as moneylenders.[98] They lent start-up capital to young newly-weds so that they could open a bakery or cordwainer's, invested in grain and real estate, and even dealt with Lombards, i.e. money changers – what we would today call professional bankers.

They also engaged in long-distance trade, albeit very cautiously, given the considerable risks involved: a beguine called Nicolave once lent money to an entrepreneur called Chabert Aydini on the condition that he did not invest the sum in overseas dealings, arguing that the *risigo maris* was too great. (Incidentally, the word *risigo*, or *risques*, comes from Arabic and originally denoted the danger of trading on the high seas, whence it entered every European language.[99]) Some registers also show that the beguinage in Roubaud had almost regular appointments with notaries. Documents such as these illustrate the extent of the beguines' sphere of activity, and demonstrate that the women were engaged in a form of economic sovereignty made possible only by their status as members of a beguinage. They undoubtedly acted in their own interests too, and invested money to make a profit, thereby directing the flow of capital in the town where they lived. They were able to do this because they were beguines, and therefore stakeholders in their community's social capital. Beguine communities were thus distinctly empowering.

In conclusion

These female sharing communities enriched the towns and cities to which they belonged. The beguines' way of life was instructive, and has frequently acted as a prototype for other communal projects, such as Augsburg's famous Fuggerei housing development and charitable foundation. Their example is energising. They weren't merely pious church mice and nurses, as historians used to believe – indeed, they played a crucial role in the world around them. They were trusted figures: their schools educated the towns' children, and they were asked to manage local charities and hospitals; they understood the culture around dying, were experts in intergenerational thinking, ran urban farms, gardens and associated businesses, and injected capital into the urban economy by acting as creditors.

They would never have achieved all this as individuals, living outside a beguinage. It was only with the backing of a sharing community, modelled on contemporary monasteries, that they were able to become legally 'competent', and thus attain a degree of independence that gave members of these collectives unprecedented scope for action. Beguinages may indeed be one of the best examples the past has to offer us of how a shared life can mean greater freedom than living and working on your own – and they demonstrate that the best kind of sharing community is an empowering one that makes the otherwise impossible possible.

3

RECYCLING

In the context of human history, throwaway societies are uncommon and short-lived phenomena. Of course, over the past 300,000 years we have never *not* produced rubbish, but for a long time one of our strengths was that we knew how to make pretty much full use of the resources at our disposal. Discarding something meant forgoing something valuable; it meant forgoing the benefits of energy we had already invested. Our ancestors were far too smart not to put every last ounce of the world's resources to good use. Why leave behind the mammoth's bones, its ivory? Why throw away the warm fur? Nearly everything was valuable. There was no such thing as waste. Bones could be used to build homes, fur turned into clothes and bedding, and ivory carved into flutes and other musical instruments. Even mammoth dung could be utilised: dried, it made for a splendid fire. The only time our ancestors left something behind was when they had to run away. The only time they produced waste was when there was a surplus. Yet times of plenty were usually brief, largely because whenever we discovered or created a paradise, we also managed to quickly and thoroughly ruin it.

Our refusal to waste anything has therefore played a crucial role in our long-term survival: given that there was little profit to be made in a linear economy, recycling gave us a selective advantage. For millennia, what we now call a 'circular' economy was in fact the gold standard of economic management. When something broke, we patched or fixed it; second-hand markets flourished (product recycling); we took defective products apart and reused their components (material recycling); and reusing or repurposing 'rubbish' was an integral part of the economy. So those 30,000-year-old mammoth-bone flutes are really a perfect example of what we would now call 'by-product recycling'.[1] Even as late as 1906, Charlottenburg (when it was still an independent town rather than a district of Berlin) introduced police by-laws requiring residents to separate their rubbish into three containers: (1) ash and sweepings, (2) food waste and (3) commercial/industrial waste (paper and rags). A waste disposal business then processed the ash and sweepings into fertiliser and the food waste into animal feed, and delivered the rags and scrap paper to paper manufacturers for reprocessing.[2]

Until the end of the Second World War, raw materials were the most valuable resource in any production process. Then, during the second half of the twentieth century, people in Western industrialised nations forgot everything they had learnt about recycling and repurposing.[3]

'1950s Syndrome': Turning the World into Waste

Christian Pfister, Professor of Economic, Social and Environmental History at Bern University, coined the term '1950s syndrome' to describe the sharp rise in energy consumption and waste production we witnessed in the mid-twentieth century. The spike began when cheap oil suddenly flooded the global market,[4] creating a glut that made exploiting other raw materials cheaper too. The price of raw materials consequently dropped, and when raw materials are as good as free, the products manufactured from them have practically no value either. They become disposable. As Reinhold Reith puts it, we saw 'more and more essentially still useable materials exiting the economic cycle'.[5] During the latter half of the 1900s, human consumption and behaviour patterns that made the most of our resources became ever less important: when there is a period of overabundance, cultural techniques involving the sparing use of resources become obsolete. However, today they are once again much needed – more than ever, in fact. The art of recycling may even become *Homo sapiens'* key survival strategy.

Menders and Second-hand Traders

Case study: the Frankfurt job market

Our cities were once full of people who mended things. In the early 1900s, the macroeconomist Karl Bücher spent years combing through Frankfurt's city archive on a quest to discover how people earned their living in the Middle Ages.[6] His chief sources were the city's asset tax rosters, eighty annual volumes spanning the period 1320–1510, supplemented with information found in the 'mayor's books', which contained notes on town council decisions and other business; court records, whose trial summaries provide an invaluable insight into working life in Frankfurt; municipal account ledgers, particularly the city's detailed records of sums paid to messengers and builders for services rendered; and a 1438 property register, and citizens' registers for 1387 and 1440.

More than 1,500 different job types ...

Bücher's investigation brought three surprising facts to light. Firstly, people were engaged in no fewer than about 1,500 different occupations.[7] The sources list an abundance of job types, ranging from millwright, lumper, confectioner and wool broker to scissors merchant, solemaker and napper. Some came with a multitude of subdivisions, and there were forty-five types of smith alone, from plain smith to 'locksmith, blacksmith, bladesmith, combsmith, boltsmith, scissorsmith, whitesmith, crossbow-smith and bow-smith, as well as goldsmith, silversmith and bucklesmith'.[8]

... of which a surprising number were done by women

The second surprise is that women are present everywhere in the tax rosters. Bücher marvelled at how many of them worked for a living, and at the time was only able to explain it by hypothesising that there was a 'surplus' of women in Frankfurt.[9] Recent studies, however, prove him wrong; the historian Sabine von Heusinger, for instance, has discovered that women regularly turned up in guild membership registers in the Middle Ages, both in Frankfurt and elsewhere, and that the only difference between them and their male colleagues was that they were exempt from military duty. The oldest extant lists date from around 1355, and women appear as full members in every one of them. The shipping guild, for example, explicitly mentions women, the coopers' guild gave them exactly the same rights as men, and the butchers' guild permitted widows to take over their late husbands' work – its records even show that they not only sold meat, but slaughtered the animals themselves. Tawers had both male and female apprentices, smiths granted women full rights too, and the milliners' guild demanded that all prospective members – 'male or female' – meet certain requirements. Finally, the fishery guild conferred equal status and privileges on guild members' daughters and sons, and permitted the daughters to marry outside the guild. Moreover, the fishing council's ordinances of 1388 state that no seller of fish, 'male or female', may display more than two troughs of fish on the market. Less surprisingly, perhaps, female textile workers – dressmakers, wool weavers, silk knitters and cloth shearers – were also granted full status alongside men. Gender-equal wording, which is slowly coming into use again, was clearly the norm back then, with guild statutes regularly using the 'male or female' formula.[10]

Ruzsen, Lepper and Plecker: Frankfurt's fixers

The third surprising discovery is that there was a prevalence of jobs related to mending and refurbishing things. People who did these were generally called *Ruzsen*, *Lepper* or *Plecker*, preceded by the product they specialised in (e.g. a *Schuhruzse* was someone who repaired shoes). It seems that they were frequently mobile, that is, had stalls at fairs or markets and did their mending – whether of shoes, knives, pots or clothes – locally. We know that theirs was a profitable trade because they started appearing in Frankfurt's tax records right from the start, and regularly so from 1320 onwards. For instance, an average of between ten and sixteen cobblers paid asset tax to the city in the 1300s, peaking in 1372 with twenty-six.

Menders: bothersome competitors

Unlike cordwainers, who specialised in producing new shoes and boots, cobblers patched or revamped old ones. It appears that competition between makers and menders everywhere was stiff; their patrons evidently had trouble distinguishing between the two, and would occasionally buy a new pair of shoes from a mender.

Again and again, we come across council ordinances that try to prevent or resolve clashes, and some guilds – including those that regulated the 'repair professions' – added suitable clauses to their constitutions. Thanks to these, we can reconstruct some of those conflicts. In 1386, for example, when Charles IV gave Frankfurt the power to reorganise its guilds, the city council adjusted its regulations, which among other things now decreed that members of the cobblers' guild were henceforth entitled to sell new shoes. The addendum that they could do so only on specific market days suggests that the cordwainers were unhappy about the menders encroaching on their territory. These sorts of issues occur throughout the history of Frankfurt's repair

17. Portrait of the shoe mender Ott Norlinger, from the 1549 'household books' of Nuremberg's Twelve Brothers charity. He is sitting at his bench mending a shoe with 'wire' (tarred yarn). In front of him are a pair of shoes, some ready-cut soles, a cobbler's knife, an awl and a circular cutter. On the wall hang two lasts, with two more on the floor, together with a tub. On his right are some shelves with finished shoes.

industry, all the way into the early modern age: one council ordinance from 1500 declared that 'cobblers are to repair shoes, boots, soles and other such things, as of old, and in times when they are not busy are permitted to produce slippers and soles; but they must not sell them in Frankfurt in between trade fairs.

18. A chair mender, a scissor sharpener and a knife sharpener in Milan (late eighteenth century)

They must also not employ an assistant without first obtaining the proper permission.'[11]

The repairs business was astonishingly specialised. There were professional menders not only of shoes, but of all other useful objects, from bags to knives, jugs and pots.[12] Buildings, too, needed regular upkeep. This was the realm of the *Humpeler*, who would repair the masonry and other things; the carpenters' guild 1498 constitution orders its members – who were in the business of constructing new attics, as well as working on new houses – to let the *Humpeler* do their work in peace and stop hiding their tools. Like the cordwainers and cobblers, the building trades clearly got in each other's way, and the carpenters were striking back at their presumably less well-trained and cheaper rivals. The same statutes also attempt to draw a clear line between them by declaring that a *Humpeler* must only repair a building, never build a new one.[13]

The problem back then was the same as now: repairs were not in a producer's interest. Unsurprisingly, a cordwainer who makes his living from selling people shoes isn't going to be particularly happy about having his profits reduced by a cobbler who insists on making them last longer.

Second-hand markets

The same goes for people who sold old clothes, who were called *Altgewender* (equivalent to the medieval English 'botcher'). They turn up in the tax rosters with as much regularity as cobblers, which indicates that they too were an integral part of the professional landscape. The 1361–2 roster lists six of these, most of whom were women, and all of whom paid their taxes as per the city's laws.[14] However, Frankfurt's tailors were worried about the competition these second-hand sellers posed, so the city revised its trading regulations in 1440: in addition to a section on how to deal with competition from 'foreign' (i.e. non-Frankfurt) tailors, there was now a clause stipulating that clothes menders could only sell what they could fit into their shops, and must not employ more than one person (except family members).[15] There was also the *Kleiderhocke* or *Cleyderhockin* (second-hand clothes seller), who was almost inevitably female: the tax roster of 1428, for instance, lists a certain *Gele eyn cleyderhockin*.

The (female) *Unterkeuferen*, meanwhile, seem to have acted as second-hand brokers and agents for all sorts of things, including properties, tools, furnishings and clothes. Anyone who bought furniture with a view to reselling it had to be on good terms with the city's craftsmen, of course – after all, you needed them to restore the items before you could sell them on. An ordinance from 1485 expressly declares that an *Unterkeufere* could only act as a broker, and must never buy or sell 'old things, be it harnesses, bedding or household goods' herself. *Unterkeuferen* were paid when buyer and seller completed their transaction. In addition, they could act as valuers in inheritance matters, for auction houses or pawnbrokers, although no more than two *Hockin* may be engaged in any one case, and their day rate was fixed at three shillings plus expenses for board and lodging.[16]

Studies of Nuremberg's historical occupations show that the situation there was similar: in the fifteenth century, there were second-hand traders who sold goods on behalf of out-of-town merchants, and municipal documents, regulations and court records frequently mention professional *Fürkeuflin* who appear to have been both traders and brokers – selling hand-me-downs on their own account, while also being employed by the city as experts in used goods. *Underkeufeln*, meanwhile, exclusively brokered deals related to grain, clothing, spices or land, and were forbidden from dealing on their own account.

At the end of the fifteenth century, *Fürkeuflin* was an exclusively female occupation; to become one, all you had to do was show that you had the wherewithal to run your business.[17]

History's blind spot

The cultural techniques of mending and repurposing have been studied only little so far, with most research driven by museums.[18] As with women and the repair professions, historians have tended to ignore second-hand markets too – undeterred by the fact that the circulation of used goods once formed a major part of the medieval marketplace. Textile and furniture markets, for instance, were dominated by used goods until well into the nineteenth century. One reason why they have been overlooked all this time is that historians have tended to focus on production, commerce and crafts; another, according to the historian Laurence Fontaine, was the invention of political economy in the late eighteenth century, when the definition of what constituted a 'market' narrowed considerably, and any business not involving a currency transaction was consigned to the dustbin of outdated, pre-modern economics.[19]

Thanks to Fontaine, there has now been an increase in research into second-hand markets. In her 2008 book *Alternative Exchanges* she cites the novelist Louis-Sébastien Mercier's wonderful description of the flourishing second-hand markets among the columns of Les Halles, the magnificent market halls in the centre of Paris, in his 'Tableaux de Paris' (1781–89). There, you could buy every last thing you needed to furnish your house from basement to attic, from beds and cupboards to chairs and tables. Even if 50,000 people descended on Paris in a single day, they would still have found everything they needed, and there was plenty to go round.

The weekly St-Esprit market on the Place de Grève, a little further out of town, sounds even more spectacular: it was used for executions on most weekdays, but on Mondays – the executioners' day off – it was turned into a market for women's and children's clothes. This is where the second-hand traders' wives, sisters, cousins, daughters and aunts met. Mercier describes petites bourgeoises, brothel owners and stern, frugal housewives rubbing shoulders as they bought whatever they needed: caps, dresses, shirts, shoes, even bed sheets. Policemen in civilian clothes also regularly attended the market, because it was popular with thieves looking for somewhere to offload their loot.

Mercier calls it the official second-hand wardrobe (*défroque*) of the entire province, where a dress belonging to a president's dead wife might be bought by a respectable hausfrau, and a poor worker's daughter might acquire a cap once worn by a marchioness's maid. It was better not to know where the clothes came from: after all, an innocent girl might well find herself wearing lingerie in which an opera singer had danced only yesterday. In the evening, the charming business came to an end. The goods disappeared as if by magic. Not a single little cloak was left behind, and all those boundless riches would not be seen again until the following Monday.[20]

Mending – the cultural technique of the future

Menders and second-hand markets played a key role in pre-modern urban economies, and the trade in used goods was not the domain of the poor. So when, exactly, did we stop fixing stuff?

Why can we think of hardly any repair professionals nowadays, other than perhaps cobblers or the people who fix our mobile phones? There are several reasons:

1. Repairs aren't worth it. Jumpers are so cheap that it would cost more to have an old one mended than to buy a new one.
2. Planned obsolescence – i.e. the unusability built into a product from the start, for example by including parts that won't last. In 1932, the real estate broker Bernard London wrote a paper entitled 'Ending the Depression Through Planned Obsolescence', in which he suggested that goods such as tools, household devices and shoes should be produced using materials with a limited lifespan. Once those materials failed, the entire product would become unusable. Doing this would help kick-start the economy again. In London's view, we can only afford products with a long lifespan when all is well with the economy. During recessions we need to keep demand constant, and if in doubt incorporate 'breaking points' in a machine's mechanism or textiles.[21]
3. 'Anti-repair' design is making it increasingly impossible to fix devices – not only mobile phones, but things like kitchen appliances, TVs, printers, computers and cars.

Times are changing, however, and both consumers and producers increasingly value self-sufficiency and independence. Higher-education institutions now offer design courses that prioritise repairability and reusability. Movements like iFixit advertise with the slogan 'Repair is good for manufacturers, good for the economy, and good for the rest of us.' Its founder, Kyle Wiens, argues that we should all have the 'right to repair', and that we should take charge and fight for our independence as customers.[22] More fixable mobile phones are coming on to the market, and mending in general is enjoying a comeback. Many of us are willing to pay more to have devices maintained and repaired – but the problem is that there are not enough people around who know how to do it, and producers are far more interested in selling new things.

This is why we find ourselves flailing about in endless repair loops. We take the car to the garage for its MOT, the broken toaster back to the electronics store, the mobile phone with the iffy connection somewhere else … it shouldn't have to be like this. Things were different once – and they can be different again. For the customer, at least, it's the dream. Just imagine: wouldn't it be lovely if, instead of your broken toaster, phone, floor lamp, hairdryer or whatever collecting dust in the back of a cupboard, there was a mobile repair service that came by regularly to check if you have anything that needs fixing? Repair and recycling services are an entire job sector waiting to conquer the market. New job sectors are born every day, and it is high time we reinvented the repair professions we once knew.

Paper: A Global Market Disruptor

For 2,000 years, paper was a 100 per cent recycled product. Until the introduction of wood pulp in the nineteenth century we made it entirely from scraps – old clothes, rags, worn-out ship's ropes and tailors' clippings. It was a classic example of waste recycling. Then, with the dawn of modernity 200 years ago, wood-based paper conquered the market, starting a new and – for our planet's trees – fateful period in its history.

It is now time for us to bring that chapter to a close. Unprecedented technological advances mean that we can once again turn to alternative raw materials. If the will is there, we can make the switch. Despite increasing digitisation, the paper industry is still flourishing. In fact, global demand has risen over the past

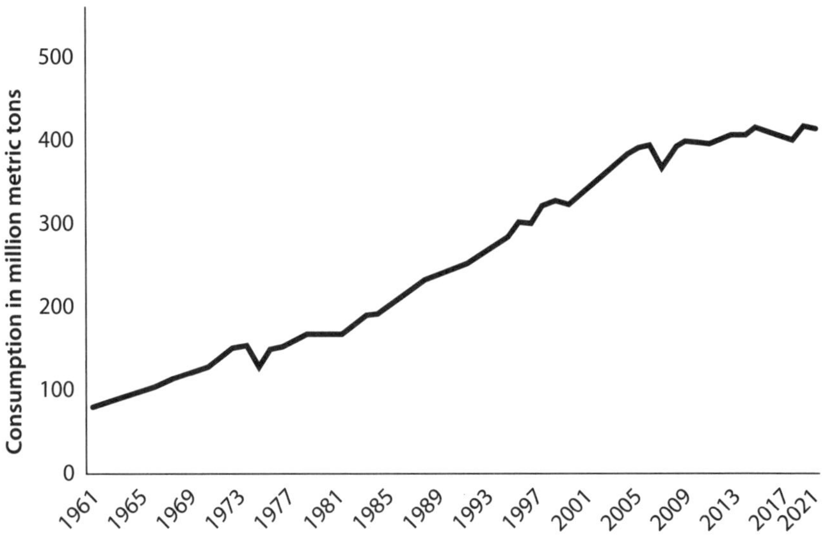

19. Rise in global paper consumption between 1961 and 2022: despite digitalisation the demand for paper continues to increase

four decades, from 170 million tons in 1980 to 423 million tons in 2017. We currently estimate that the number will double again in another forty years.[23] The reason for this is an unexpected side effect of digitisation: the boom in online shopping has resulted in a spike in demand for packing materials. However, all over the world forests are being decimated by increasing aridity, wildfires and drastic deforestation, which means that our supply of wood is running low.

Is there a way for us to meet our demand for paper without destroying the world's trees? If so, how? By using less paper? By refining the technology? By making more and more paper from less and less wood?

The history of paper suggests that there may be other solutions.

20. A 1637 illustration of a Chinese papermaker

A short history of paper

In technical terms, paper is a flat, primarily plant-derived material produced by suspending cellulose fibres in water and then draining the water through a fine sieve; the resulting fibrous substance is then pressed and dried.[24] The process was first developed in north-western China in the second century BC, in what is now the autonomous Uyghur province of Xinjiang. There, archaeologists have discovered paper that was produced using methods previously employed in bast fibre processing and felt production, whereby plant fibres were pounded and softened, and the resulting pulp spread over a flat sieve and then drained and dried.[25]

According to the traditional Chinese narrative, papermaking was invented in the late first century AD by Cai Lun, who lived in Leiyang, which was then the seat of the Eastern Han dynasty. Cai Lun was an imperial engineer, and – like many high-ranking officials at the time – a eunuch, in charge of the emperor's armaments and instruments.

The fact that he invented paper is, as far as we know, first mentioned 400 years after his death, in the fifth-century *Hou Hanshu* or *Book of the Later Han*. The text describes how, in the old days, books and documents were usually made out of strips of bamboo tied together, which held bundles of precious silk sheets. The sheets were extremely expensive, and the bamboo strips heavy and unwieldy; and so Cai Lun came up with the idea of making paper out of tree bark, bits of hemp, rags and remnants of fishing nets. His process worked, the emperor was delighted, the new product was officially adopted by the empire, and Cai Lun was elevated to the nobility.[26]

Paper – a recycling revolution

Cai Lun's innovation resulted in one of the most spectacular revolutions the world has ever witnessed. Like most things, it didn't come out of nowhere. Also like most inventions, it can't actually be credited to just one person; at best, it was the result of one or more people making connections between bits of information gleaned in various fields of knowledge. What Cai Lun did was take a familiar production process and apply it to a new material, i.e. textile waste. Instead of 'silk' – most likely paper created from mulberry fibres – he exclusively used recycled fibres, expanding the raw material pool at a single stroke, meaning an exponential increase in output. This groundbreaking new material was then distributed far and wide, first across China and then, in the course of the third and fourth centuries, to Korea, Japan, Central Asia, Southeast Asia, Nepal and India. By the eighth century it had firmly established itself in Middle Eastern paper production centres, with major manufacturing firms in Syria (Damascus), Iraq (Baghdad), Egypt (Cairo) and the Byzantine Empire. Istanbul still commemorates the Byzantine papermakers in the district of Kâğıthane (originally called Vorvisis), whose name literally means 'papermakers' place'.[27]

The belated arrival of European paper

The oldest evidence of European paper production dates to Moorish Spain (Al-Andalus), where archaeologists have unearthed evidence of it in tenth- and eleventh-century Jativa / Xátiva (near Valencia), Córdoba, Toledo and the Balearics. In addition, Arab, Genoese and Amalfian merchants imported paper from Cairo via Kairouan (Tunisia) and Valencia. But it wasn't until the thirteenth century that the history of European paper proper began.[28]

The main reason why paper took so long to enter the European market was simple: we did not think we needed it. After all, we had parchment (animal skin that has been stripped of its hair, stretched and dried),[29] a writing surface widely used in Europe since the eighth century, when it overtook papyrus in popularity. Parchment is more durable than papyrus and easier to get hold of, being a sort of by-product of livestock farming.

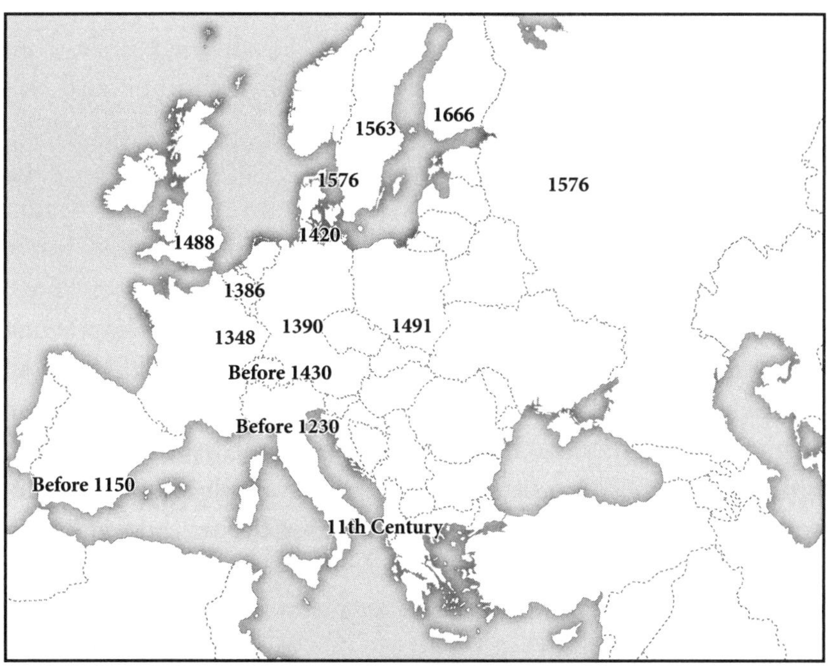

21. How the art of papermaking spread across Europe

It did take a fair amount of time and effort – cleaning, scraping, liming, stretching, drying, smoothing, more scraping – before you could actually write on the skin of a sheep, cow or goat, but the advantage was that people did not have to depend on Egyptian imports.

The conservatively minded occupants of Europe's notaries' offices, lawyers' chambers, courts and monasteries therefore didn't think innovation was necessary. As everyone knows, all change requires an initial investment, and the powers that be didn't want to give up on tried and tested technologies and processes without good reason. Yet they could not hold out for long against the paper revolution: at some point Europeans, too, wanted documents made out of something other than mere parchment. The 'age of white magic' had arrived.[30]

How did this new paper get to Europe?

Perhaps a resourceful merchant from Amalfi or Genoa convinced a Cairo papermaker to leave his workshop behind and join forces with him in Italy instead; or maybe an enterprising Egyptian businessman sold the secret of papermaking to the Italians; then again, perhaps (as one legend has it) a crusader imprisoned in Syria or Egypt learnt the art there, and introduced it to Europe on his return. We simply don't know. All we do know is that at some point in the thirteenth century the art of papermaking became established in Italy.

Genoa, Fabriano in Ancona and Amalfi near Naples still argue about which of them can lay claim to having invented European paper. According to one narrative, Amalfians had been producing and exporting it since long before the thirteenth century. Unfortunately, the city archives were destroyed in a fire, but it certainly seems plausible, given that the Kingdom of Sicily, to which it then belonged, was deeply influenced by Byzantine and Arab culture. Moreover, it is the only scenario that explains why Italian archives contain so many paper documents dating back to the eleventh and twelfth centuries. There's much to support Amalfi's claim, then; unfortunately, there is no real evidence that it is true. In fact, the oldest piece of real evidence comes from thirteenth-century Genoa, in the shape of a 1235 contract between a papermaker and the city council.[31]

Contemporary Italians, however, considered Fabriano the birthplace of the new technology, and there are official documents dating from 1283 concerning the production of paper in the town. What we know for certain is that, from the late 1200s onwards, papermaking flourished in northern and central Italy. There were entire paper mill districts centred on Fabriano, which soon became a serious paper exporter, both overland and via the port of Fano on the Adriatic coast. Today, you can see the oldest extant products of European papermaking in Fabriano's Museo della Carta e della Filigrana. From Italy it spread across the rest of Europe, and paper mills sprouted everywhere like mushrooms, with Ulman Stromer's mill on the banks of the Pegnitz in Nuremberg, which opened in 1390, perhaps the most famous of all. In the 1400s, when Johannes Gutenberg invented the printing press, paper manufacturing across Europe soared – and as demand for paper increased, so did the demand for rags.

Innovations: rag recycling

Paper produced from recycled textiles dominated the market primarily because manufacturers were constantly optimising their processes and improving the product. Let us now take a brief look at their innovations. The seventeenth-century pedagogue Comenius's school textbook *Orbis sensualium pictus*[32] provides us with some wonderful illustrations and descriptions, as you can see in image 22.

Everything in this illustration that has a number is described in the accompanying text: 'In the old days, they used tablets made

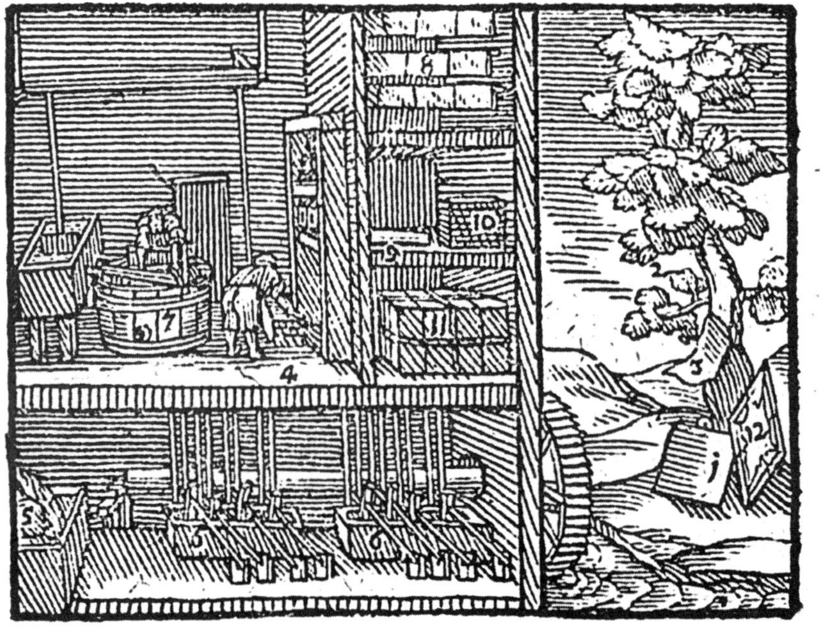

22. Illustration of a paper mill in Comenius's *Orbis sensualium pictus* (Nuremberg, 1658)

of spruce wood (1), leaves (2), bark (3) or [...] papyrus to write on. Today we use paper. Paper is produced by the papermaker in the paper mill (4) out of old rags (5), which are pounded and turned into a pulp (6), and then poured into a mould (7). The sheets (8) are hung up to dry (9). Of these sheets, twenty-five make a quire (9), twenty quires make a ream (10) and ten reams make a bale (11). Things that are meant to last for a long time are written on parchment (12).'

New technologies and processes

Three technological innovations in particular meant that recycled paper was regarded as superior to old-school parchment and became a resounding success.

Firstly, the process for milling rags was made more efficient by the introduction of hammer mills, whose mechanics were based on the fulling mills already in use in textile manufacturing. You can see the workings of a seventeenth-century mill in the bottom left-hand section of image 22. Engineers had designed several strong hammers for these mills, which pounded against a grooved metal base plate. There were four to six vats set up in a row, where the rags were shredded by an array of increasingly slender hammers. The whole thing was driven by a large water wheel, also visible in the picture, which enabled the staff to keep the mill running constantly and dictated the rhythm of their work.

The second major change was substituting a rigid mould mesh made of metal wires for the traditional cloth-covered frames or flexible bamboo or stalk mats. To do this they employed the latest methods from the world of wire-drawing: ever thinner wires were stretched across the moulds, allowing for the paper to be more and more finely structured, and enabling the papermaker to control the density of the sheet. Pre-shaped figures made from copper wire could also be sewn or soldered on to the rigid metal moulds, becoming the watermarks in the finished sheet which attested to the paper's origin and quality. Instead of leaving the freshly pressed fi bre mat on the mesh to dry it was transferred to a felt ('couched'), so that the vatman could immediately reuse the mesh for the next sheet, while the coucher drained the freshly moulded one, hung it up to dry and prepared it for its final pressing.

A third innovation was the invention of 'sizing' – the process of coating paper in order for it to absorb less ink. Arab workshops had been using starch to do this, but in the late fourteenth century European manufacturers increasingly turned to animal glue, which made the paper more stable and durable.

In addition, papermakers made some organisational changes: European rag recyclers expanded into manufacturing, employing large numbers of specialists whose working life was rigidly scheduled, with production increasingly concentrated into designated papermaking districts.[33] Moreover, their part in the process depended on all sorts of other trades and suppliers, too, from ragmen to animal glue manufacturers.

There were also constant attempts to improve the quality of the paper, for instance by treating the sheet surface with chemicals that made it more user-friendly for scribes and printers. Even the processing of rags was continuously fettled; for instance, fermenting and treating them with milk of lime before milling turned out to produce a finer grade of paper. The highest degree of sophistication was achieved by European print shops during the fifteenth century, as they tried to imitate the appearance of parchment.

New kinds of raw material

Unlike coins, for example, or iron chains and millstones, you only rarely see medieval shirts, petticoats or other clothing in museums. This is because textiles don't have a very long half-life. They quickly start yellowing and crumbling, and their survival chances are therefore much lower than those of, for instance, weapons. This means that our image of the past is considerably skewed, and perhaps overly martialised. Why is it that, when we think of the Middle Ages, we almost inevitably think of battles? The reason is that weapons, then as now, are made from durable substances, and a comparatively large number have thus survived into the present day, while everyday objects, from shopping baskets to hammocks, were made from perishable stuff, and would decay on the rubbish heaps of the past without leaving a trace.

Another reason why only a few clothes have made it all the way here from the Middle Ages is that from the thirteenth to the late nineteenth century, textiles were an integral part of the recycling industry. Any worn-out clothing, from underwear to cloaks, as well as bed sheets, tablecloths and tapestries, were resold rather than thrown away. Cloth of any kind was valuable. You could make a lot of money from it, because every last scrap, no matter how small, was highly sought after as material for the production of new textiles – and paper. Indeed, the rag trade was dominated by paper manufacturers and traders, who would engage small subcontractors to acquire rags on their behalf. These were the famous rag-and-bone-men or ragpickers, who went door to door and bought up any old clothes or scraps people might have lying about. Most worked for a single client, usually a paper miller or printer, and in some places it was such a competitive market that you needed a permit.[34]

As the demand for paper grew, old clothes became ever more valuable as a raw material. The most expensive were white ones, made of linen or fustian – a linen-and-cotton blend produced first in Italy, and from the late fourteenth century onwards also in southern Germany, including Ravensburg, Ulm, Biberach, Regensburg and Augsburg. Dark textiles were less valuable, as were woollen textiles (animal-based yarns are much shorter than plant-based ones, and therefore yielded lower-quality paper).

Collection permits and bans on rag exports

Whether linen or fustian, rags were a highly desirable raw material. Having said that, they also rather limited the amount of paper that could be produced. Things came to a head in the eighteenth century, but even in the late Middle Ages we find businesses complaining that there are not enough rags to go around. Paper mills and ragpickers fought hard over the stuff, and contemporary ordinances show that whenever a new paper mill was granted a licence to operate, it was assigned one specific district from where it could obtain its rags.[35]

Again and again, too, we come across edicts prohibiting this or that region from exporting rags. The purpose of these measures was to ensure a constant supply of raw materials. The oldest rag permit we know of was issued in Switzerland in 1467, to a paper mill owner in Berne.[36] In 1490, Nuremberg banned rag exports altogether. Paper millers also worked closely with paper merchants, who wanted more regulation too. Then, starting with the second half of the fifteenth century, printers entered the paper market in a big way; book-printing presses needed a reliable supply of high-quality paper, which they either bought wholesale at fairs in Frankfurt am Main and Leipzig or obtained by contracting, buying shares in or leasing paper mills. In the early seventeenth century, printers who worked for city authorities, universities or regional governments also encouraged their municipal government or local sovereign to protect paper stocks by prohibiting the export of rags, and limiting the ragpicking trade with permits.[37]

Rag-smuggling in Leipzig

As the following anecdote from Leipzig – the unofficial capital of books – shows, things got tense in the 1700s[38] when, with monotonous regularity, the city issued edict after edict prohibiting the export of rags. In May 1785, one among many such orders threatened anyone caught in the process with severe punishment: their entire cargo, including 'horses, carts and harnesses' would be confiscated. Anyone who collected rags without an official permit faced the same consequences. These laws evidently did not go far enough, for accusations of illegal ragpicking and rag-smuggling across the Saxon border did not fade after that.

You can tell how grave the situation was from the fact that Leipzig's printers and papermakers – who were, after all, business competitors – joined forces. They were fighting for their very existence. Until then, Saxony had been the market leader in the manufacturing of paper and printing, and the whole of Prussia, Brandenburg, Bohemia, Moravia and even Austria printed their publications on Saxon paper; and if they didn't bring the smugglers under control, the regional paper sector would suffer serious losses. When the Leipzigers discovered that, on top of all this, there was a threat of a hostile takeover from 'abroad' – a Berlin paper merchant named Ebert was buying up the entire stock held by Saxony's mills before they had even started producing it – they took action and convinced the city council to give one of them the exclusive right to collect rags in the area.

The man in question was the paper merchant Gottlob Leberecht Lehn. (His first names mean 'praise God live right'. The surnames of his two colleagues below mean 'hard man' and 'fat head'. And they say Germans have no sense of humour.) In January 1790 he appeared before the council to make their case: foreign carriers and other persons were buying up all the rags in Leipzig, he said, and the resulting shortage of raw materials had seen a spike in the price of paper. He proposed an interesting solution: if the city authorities gave him alone the 'freedom to collect rags in the city of Leipzig and environs', he would either pay them an annual fee or give them a specified volume of paper gratis. In this he was backed by his colleagues, including Johann Christian Hartmann and the Leipzig printer Breitkopf. It must be said that Lehn was not exactly pure as the driven snow, having himself been involved in rag-smuggling in connection with mills in Brandenburg – but a ragpicking monopoly was the only chance they had of controlling the market. The plan worked: three months later, on 31 March 1790, Lehn was granted the monopoly he had asked for, and his 'licence to collect' stipulated that all sales would be limited to Leipzig.

However, Leipzig's papermakers and printers were not done yet. They also asked the authorities to (a) charge a 40 per cent export tax on Saxon paper, and (b) make it easier to import high-grade paper from France, Holland and Switzerland. The authorities agreed to this too, if somewhat belatedly (on 29 January 1793), and declared 'that paper imported into Saxony must not be subject to any tax whatsoever, and that ragpicking is to be properly controlled'.

Documentary evidence of this kind gives us a fascinating insight into some of the common issues encountered by the sector; it also shows how hard it was to regulate the market, and that problems surrounding the supply of raw materials constituted a major threat to printers and publishers, as well as paper producers.

'Don't these scoundrels keep any in stock?'

The Enlightenment was no doubt the main reason for the huge increase in demand for paper during the eighteenth century. It was the age of books, pamphlets and newspapers, and eminent philosophers were as affected by the rag shortage as was their growing readership. Imagine if printers had been unable to print the *Critique of Pure Reason* (whose first edition comprised almost 800 pages), or – worse, perhaps – if no one could have performed Mozart's *Requiem* because paper had to be rationed.

That the possibility was at all conceivable is attested to by a letter from Mozart's father Leopold to his publisher Jakob Lotter in Augsburg, dated 7 July 1755:

> Monsieur mons tres cher amy!
>
> [...] I should be sorry if paper were to ruin our fun. I always was and still am of the opinion that one should not be overly cautious when it comes to recording the results of great endeavour on handsome paper. Can you not have the paper sent on condition that it is up to standard? There cannot be only one papermaker in the whole world. Don't these scoundrels keep any in stock? Do they have to make

> it first? Enough! You had better wait for the good stuff; I would otherwise be sorry for your effort, because I very much want it to catch the eye, such that one might never again hear people say what I have heard them say, namely that only Hamburg and Leipzig make beautiful books [...]
>
> Your obedient servant,
>
> Dr Leopold Mozart[39]

What if they hadn't found a solution? It does not bear thinking about. What would have happened to all the artistic and intellectual creations of the age? Without rags, Mozart's *Magic Flute* would never have existed – never been printed, never performed. Bach, Handel, Haydn and all the other great composers of the eighteenth century, the writings of the Enlightenment thinkers, Voltaire's letters to Frederick II of Prussia, Rousseau's *Émile* and Adam Smith's *The Wealth of Nations* ... the whole Enlightenment project would have had to be aborted – and all because of a shortage of rags.

Raw material shortages and the urgent need for innovation

Thankfully, it did not come to that. The papermakers, scientists and engineers of the age were no less creative than the great artists and thinkers, and conducted impressive experiments to find additives that could be used in papermaking. Today, these experiment-happy entrepreneurs would probably all be given awards for innovation.[40] They succeeded because they drew on the experience of previous generations, rather than trying to reinvent the wheel. In fact, manufacturers had been experimenting with additives for a long time: the Lunckwitz Mill near Zwickau was producing paper that consisted 'in large part' of materials 'other than rags' as far back as 1672; in 1695, Georg

Balthasar Illy was producing paper made from a combination of recycled paper and manufacturing waste in his paper mill in Schleusingen; and in 1712, a certain Engelbert Kaempfer recommended the use of Japanese papermaking techniques, which did not use rags at all but tree fibres.

'Try telling a papermaker that you can make paper from wood, plants, etc. Few will believe you.'

In the eighteenth century, Jacob Christian Schäffer began an extraordinarily fruitful investigation into possible alternatives to rags for use in paper manufacturing. He was a man of many talents. Born in Saxony-Anhalt in 1718, he and his five siblings grew up in relative poverty after their father died. However, he obtained a good education, went to university and was ordained a priest in 1741, at the unusually young age of twenty-three.

Until his death in 1790, he worked tirelessly not only as a priest, but as a natural scientist, medic, entomologist and inventor. He gave lectures at international conferences, was granted an honorary professorship by the Danish king, and was celebrated by posterity as the 'Leonardo da Vinci of Querfurt'. His writings are proof of his many gifts, both academic and practical. Alongside prayers for the dead and New Year sermons, he published works including a text on medicinal herbs (1759), a guide to insects (1766) and treatises on liver fluke in sheep (1762) and 'implanted worms in teeth, and some possible remedies' (1756). To describe his countless inventions is to enter an early modern laboratory: among other things, he invented a low-energy oven to help with the current shortage of wood while also protecting the forests,[41] and his crowning achievement in 1766 was a 'convenient and highly advantageous washing machine', a prototype of the modern device (now on display in the Miele Museum in Gütersloh).

To counteract the paper shortage, Schäffer conducted – as summarised in the title of a two-volume work he published in

1765, which was translated into Dutch five years later – 'experiments and models for producing paper without the use of rags, or containing only a very small amount thereof'.[42] In his book he argued that the world needed to find alternative raw materials from which to create paper, if only for economic reasons. He started experimenting with catkins from black poplar trees and with cotton grass, working with a local papermaker called Mackenhäuser. When the latter demanded twenty-five pounds of poplar catkins before he would even consider starting work, the venture threatened to end in failure, because catkins are so light that it would be impossible to obtain enough for such a weight.

They consequently started off using very small amounts – with disappointing results. The cotton-grass paper was 'of a terrible quality', falling apart whenever you bent or folded it. It looked as if all Schäffer's efforts and financial investment had come to nothing.[43] The paper made from the catkins was slightly better, almost like 'proper' rag paper, but it was not white enough and the sheets were anything but uniform. In the end, it turned out that Mackenhäuser had not only left the raw materials in the milk-of-lime bath for different lengths of time, but surreptitiously mixed rags in with them. So Schäffer decided to buy his own paper press, and hired a junior papermaker to work under his direction.

Learning from nature: eighteenth-century bionics

The humble wasp, something of a born papermaker, suggested an even more promising solution to Schäffer. It wasn't the nests that interested him, but the widely known fact that wasps use wood pulp to create the paper-like walls and honeycomb structures of those nests. So he examined them to see if it would be possible to copy the process, i.e. to develop a technique to extract the same substance from trees that wasps use to produce 'wasp paper'.

23. Black-poplar catkins with seeds in Schäffer's *Versuche und Muster ohne alle Lumpen oder doch mit einem geringen Zusatz derselben, Papier zu machen* (1765), Plate 1

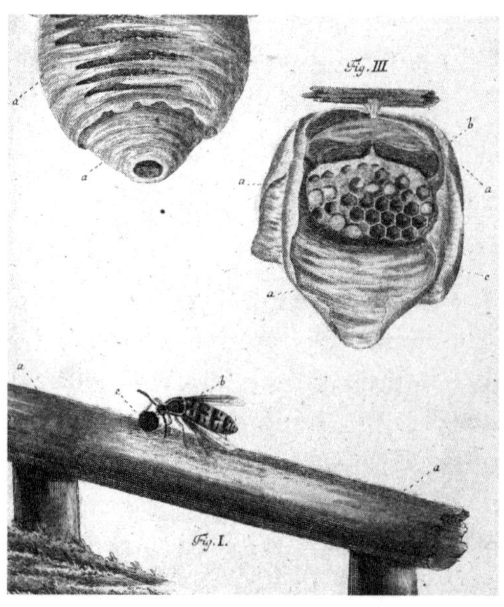

24. Wasps' nests provided the inspiration for wood-based paper. From Schäffer, ibid., Plate 2

Some experts dislike innovation

The reaction to Schäffer's experiments was twofold. Paper production experts were sceptical; they were focused on making conventional methods more efficient, and simply couldn't imagine using alternative materials; as Schäffer put it, 'Try telling a papermaker that you can make paper from wood, plants, etc. Few will believe you.'[44]

One such man was Georg Christoph Keferstein, a Saxon paper miller who appears to have been incensed by Schäffer's suggestions: in 1766, he wrote a booklet in praise of the sophisticated art of papermaking addressed to his fifteen sons, warning them against using the Regensburg dilettante's new-fangled inventions.[45] He listed six reasons why Schäffer and others like him were wrong:

1. 'It doesn't work!' Just as you can't make wheat from oats or gold from iron, you can't make paper from hemp (though, as an experienced papermaker, he ought to have known that linen comes from hemp).
2. 'To what end?' What use is it to know that dry leaves can be ground down and turned into a sort of useless wastepaper? None at all.
3. 'We don't need alternatives!' We will always have rags. 'Therefore, we will continue as we have been, and only make paper from rags; because for as long as there are people on German soil, they will need clothes; and every person wears out about two shirts a year, which end up in the paper mill without my needing to make an anxious effort.'
4. The market will sort out any issues; there is no need for new techniques, and supply and demand determine production: 'I orientate my actions on my merchants and my incoming stocks.'
5. 'Mere scaremongering!' The paper shortage has been

wildly exaggerated. Economic crises are nothing new. The current one is a consequence of the Seven Years' War, and the demand for paper will no doubt slow down soon.

6. Let the idiots deliver first: 'silly minds' with silly ideas are nothing new, but until they produce something useful on which you can write and print, 'I will continue to mistrust this invention'.

Yet Schäffer's experiments also drew some support. His work received an exceedingly positive review in the *Allgemeine Deutsche Bibliothek* praising his tireless experiments, which had produced evidence that paper could be made from things other than rags. It concluded with the proposal that manufacturers should take his work on board and develop commercial production processes: 'The author's efforts deserve the praise and support of papermakers, who may be able to achieve on a large scale what he has been unable to complete on a small scale.'[46]

Papermaking materials experimented with in the eighteenth century included the following.

Wasps' nests: Before Schäffer, in 1719, the French scholar René Réaumur delivered a lecture at the Académie des sciences in Paris on the paper-like nests of wasps. People subsequently experimented with all kinds of wood, but it took until the second half of the nineteenth century before they successfully used it in paper production.

Recycled paper: This was another promising candidate. Manufacturers had long been mixing small amounts of old paper into their rags, but recycling will only work properly if you can de-ink and de-colour the old paper in an efficient way. In 1774, Justus Claproth from Göttingen solved the problem by rinsing the paper in fuller's earth. The long-term consequences were remarkable: in the mid-twentieth century, the US was a leading force in the field of paper recycling;[47] today, used paper makes up more than 80 per cent of all new paper stock.

Plant-based paper – and a brilliant marketing idea: Two famous French entrepreneurs, Anisson-Duperron (director of the Imprimerie Royale) and Léorier Delisle (director of the paper mills of L'Anglée near Montargis, south of Paris), experimented with all sorts of materials, including nettles, moss and comfrey, as well as with innovative marketing strategies. Nowadays, we would say that they were trying to market paper as a 'lifestyle product'. What Delisle did was print two books in small print runs on two or three different types of paper each: Pelée de Varennes's *Les loisirs des bords du Loing* in 1784, and the Marquis de Villette's *Oeuvres* in 1786. The project was less successful than he had hoped it would be, and only few orders were placed – but these stunning, extravagant print runs are considered great treasures from the history of printing.[48]

Straw: Among the paper types produced in Delisle's Montargis mills were ones made of different kinds of straw. At the turn of the eighteenth century, a papermaker called Matthias Koops (who may or may not have been from Hamburg) promoted the use of straw paper all over Britain, and in 1800 published the first book ever printed on it, entitled *Historical Account of the Substances, Which Have Been Used to Describe Events and to Convey Ideas from the Earliest Date to the Invention of Paper*.[49] Koops patented a process involving straw, and founded the Neckinger Mills paper factory in Bermondsey (London). He too tried to market the new paper by producing hybrid editions, and printed each book on two types: the first half on previously printed old paper, the second half on straw paper. Research conducted in the 1950s shows that this really was made largely of straw, with only a small percentage of rags mixed into it.

Constructing the mill had been expensive: the cornerstone alone, which was imported from Scotland, cost £150, nearly £16,000 in today's money – a mind-boggling sum. Yet just two years after it became operational it went bankrupt, having accumulated debts of £10,500. The problem was not that the paper didn't sell, but that Koops had designed the factory on a scale that vastly exceeded his needs.[50] However, even though the project failed, you could argue that it marked the birth of the modern paper industry. We seem to have forgotten all about straw paper, but it proved popular across the world in the nineteenth century, with factories springing up everywhere in Europe and the US. In the 1950s, when the predatory exploitation of forests was recognised as a major problem, straw paper became fashionable once again. However, the subsequent economic boom put an end to these concerns.[51] There is no alternative to wood, the argument ran, because wood is cheapest. And so it is – as long as you disregard the environmental damage done by deforestation, and by the large quantities of sulphuric acid used to separate the lignin and resins from the cellulose.

Science vs reluctant experts

If the history of paper has taught us anything, it is that experimentation pays off – even, and especially, wherever the mantra 'there's no other way' holds sway.

There will always be people like paper miller Keferstein, who don't see the need to take action. As so often, though, history has made the decision for them. In 1766, Keferstein could not imagine that paper would ever be made from anything other than rags; similarly, when the first mainframe computer was developed in 1943, Thomas Watson, chair of IBM, miscalculated gravely when he declared that 'I think there's a world market for maybe five computers.' How did Keferstein and Watson get it so wrong? Certainly not because they didn't know enough, or weren't experts in their field. No: the reason they got it so wrong is that too much self-confidence and sticking stubbornly to tried-and-tested methods can make you blind to new developments, and the needs of both current and future generations. 'These people are stuck in a rut, and don't want to know about anything new that they haven't come up with themselves',[52] is how a friend and supporter of Schäffer's described the resistance to his experiments. If Keferstein, instead of wasting his time writing edifying pamphlets for his sons, had taken Schäffer's experiments seriously and applied his discoveries, he might have become known as the co-inventor of wood-based paper. Yet, like most paper manufacturers, he chose otherwise.

'It takes twenty years to make an overnight success.' Eddie Cantor

Let us hope that this scenario won't repeat itself. Our search for alternatives to wood-based paper is running full steam ahead: straw paper is being successfully produced and marketed again, the Meldorf paper factory in Schleswig-Holstein is producing paper and cardboard made from grass, and grass is also increasingly used in packaging.[53] Anna Jones's recent cookbook, *A Modern Way to Eat*, was even printed on apple paper.[54] Anyone who is investing their time, money and energy in developing the recycled products of the future should take heart: your efforts will pay off in the long run.

Bricolage and Assemblage: Antiquity Repurposed for the Middle Ages

Our third example from the recycling industries of the past concerns the charm of the old, and the value added by the passage of time. The trade in 'vintage' products involves things that have become rare by virtue of their age and the process of selection, and which are therefore valuable. The patina of old age thus turns mass-produced objects into 'one of a kind' pieces, which acquire a whole new intrinsic value through the mixing of styles and creative historicism.[55] This goes for everyday clothing, fashion items and furniture as much as for creative concepts, business ideas and, yes, politics.

Charlemagne's penny or *denier* is a prime example. Not long after he was crowned emperor of the Romans in 800, Charlemagne ordered the recently introduced silver pennies to be re-minted, and when it came to reproducing his likeness on the coins he unabashedly exploited the tools of the past, recycling the profiles of Roman emperors – appearing on the coin with a laurel wreath on his head and a Roman toga about his shoulders – and replacing the old inscription CARLUS REX FRANCORUM (Charles King of the Franks) with KAROLUS IMP[ERATOR] AUG[USTUS] (Charles Emperor Augustus). As we can see, recycling not only makes things more beautiful but adds to their significance.

Historians rarely describe such activities as a form of recycling, and terms like *renovatio imperii*, Carolingian Renaissance and 'the legitimisation of power' at first glance seem to have little to do with us today – but they all concern the practice of reusing the past to improve the present. Only in art history has upcycling produced its very own field of research, called spolia scholarship, which deals with recycled antique building materials.

Unfortunately, the traditional designation of these materials as *spolia* ('the spoils') inevitably brings to mind looted art. In some cases, of course, it is entirely warranted, such as with the Horses of St Mark's in Venice, stolen by the Venetians during the sack of Constantinople in 1204 and triumphantly installed above the basilica's portal. And when we witness the tragedy of a column which, felled and quartered, has turned into a worn-out flight of basement steps, we often talk about how ancient Rome was ruthlessly stripped and ruined by medieval builders.

But such associations are otherwise largely mistaken, for most *spolia* are evidence less of looted art than of how brilliantly the late-classical and medieval construction trade mastered the art of recycling. Archaeologists are still discovering medieval stores of antique building and decorative materials, which suggests that in the Middle Ages existing resources – in this case, building materials taken from Rome's ruins – were handled both deliberately and judiciously. More recently, scholars have convincingly argued that we should stop using the term *spolia*, with its negative connotations, and replace it with 'recycling'.[56]

The recycling of building materials since late antiquity

In the course of the fourth century, after Constantine the Great moved the imperial seat to Constantinople, Rome's villas fell into disrepair. When the Goths, led by Alaric, sacked Rome in 410 without encountering much opposition, the Eternal City's heyday was clearly over, and depopulation, abandonment and ruin inevitably followed. Who was there to keep up the multitude of secular buildings, the private residences, municipal offices, palaces of state, theatres and great stadiums? Many stood idle and fell apart, and as Christianity spread throughout the empire, more and more temples also stood abandoned. So if a Roman wanted to erect a new building – despite the city's infrastructure issues – why not make things easier for themselves and recycle materials from derelict neighbourhoods? After all, it costs considerably less to reuse old stones than to quarry new ones.[57]

The process was very gradual, however, and it is worth emphasising that Rome did not exactly descend into anarchy. We know that there were numerous legally enforceable building regulations, which shows that the municipal government wanted to stop the arbitrary stripping of vacant buildings – and the very existence of these laws naturally suggests that the activities they proscribe were common practice at the time.

In addition, Roman civil servants were explicitly and strictly forbidden from trading in building materials, with contraventions resulting in draconian penalties. Historians have concluded from this that officials working for the municipal authorities had knowledge of, and access to, lucrative ruins, and were therefore particularly active traders in *spolia*. Ornamental features could only be removed from clearly derelict buildings marked for demolition; and demolition was only permitted in the first place if any marble and columns were made at least officially available for use in a new public building. Exporting antique materials into other cities or provinces was also forbidden, unless the owner of the demolished building and the owner of the proposed new one were the same person.[58]

The constituent parts of ancient temples could be reused in many different ways. Stone steps, for instance, were perfect for wholesale integration into walls, and the bases of columns were often carved into fountain basins, with the columns themselves simply inserted elsewhere, or cut down and converted into a throne or suchlike. They could also be hollowed out and used as coffins, and shorter stumps made good lawn rollers. The often elaborate capitals came with an especially wide range of options: you could easily hollow them out for a baptismal font or a well, or just as easily reduce them to a base for a new column. The historian Arnold Esch has found examples of antique columns turned into heraldic shields, sundials and mortars for grinding fodder. Finally, marble slabs could be stood on end and inserted into walls as pilasters, or hollowed out and turned into sarcophagi. Renaissance sculptors, too, were greedy recyclers of antique building materials: the *Palestrina Pietà* (*c.* 1555), created by an artist of the Michelangelo school, was carved from a massive piece of marble whose antiquity is evidenced by the acanthus motif near the Virgin Mary's left foot.[59]

In the wall of the church of Sessa Aurunca in Italy, you can see a slab with an ancient game of nine men's morris carved into it – and since you can't play on a vertical board, it must have been a flagstone once.[60] Materials appropriated from both temples and secular buildings were nonchalantly deployed in great numbers for use in late-classical and medieval church walls. The oddly patchwork architecture of Pisa's cathedral, for example, strikes even an untrained eye, and as you stroll around the building you'll count more than twenty obvious *spolia*: three ceiling arches, five plates with fragments of inscriptions, five reliefs and seven slabs of ancient roof beams.

Spolia were such an integral part of the look of medieval churches that masons would even copy them; so if you wanted some faux antiquity for your new building, you could have a first-class piece created from scratch. In the crypt of San Michele in Foro in Lucca, for instance, there are window frames that look like ancient ornamental arches but were in fact created by a medieval artist based on classical models.[61]

Recycling Roman building materials in the fourteenth century

How did recycling in the medieval building sector work in practical terms? One particularly fascinating example comes to us from the Italian city of Orvieto.[62] In around 1300, building began on its Gothic cathedral, and except for the Gothic western façade the edifice looks fairly symmetrical, almost plain. You would never suspect that its walls are made from recycled materials. Yet as the ledgers of the construction company in charge (the cathedral works department) show, *spolia* were imported from Rome en masse for this huge church.

There is an invoice from 1321 issued by a team of workers for marble obtained from Roman stonemasons, and several payments were made to proprietors of Roman masonry yards for deliveries of marble slabs. Agents were also sent to the city under orders to find suitable *spolia*, and they evidently enlisted the support of men with local knowledge: one mason (*marmorario*), for example, was paid to accompany an agent for four days and assist him in the location of suitable pieces, and another invoice lists payment due explicitly for 'the detection of *spolia*' (*ad spiorandom pro marmo*). Alternatively, you could work directly with the masons and businessmen who disassembled Roman buildings on-site and offered individual pieces for sale. An entry in the cathedral works department's books of 10 September 1354 mentions an amount of forty-five Florentine guilders – a considerable sum – paid to a certain Alexius for a marble block from the Temple of Jupiter (or a building thought to be the Temple of Jupiter – probably the Porticus Octaviae), which was cut into smaller pieces on-site by a Roman marble mason. Alexius must have been one of the businessmen who had secured permission to exploit the temple, and opened his masonry yard there.

Such and similar entries in the works department's accounts are proof that Roman *spolia* merchants did a lively trade with Orvietan importers. Statues of pagan gods were popular too: with a few chisel cuts, you could convert them into Christian saints.[63]

Other entries concern transportation: two men from Viterbo were paid to carry four marble blocks more than ten miles by ox and cart; and there is a bill for loading several blocks of marble in Ostia, whence the journey proceeded upriver. Before you could do that, though, you needed a *spolia* export licence from the Capitoline Hill, which also cost money. On top of that came customs fees, payable in Ponte Molle, Gallese and Otricoli. In the little town of Orte, on the border with Latium, the Tiber becomes very shallow, and the *spolia* were transferred to carts and taken the rest of the way by land. Technology was very much part of the process, with cranes and other machines being used to help with the dismantling, transportation and reintegration of *spolia*, particularly columns. A sketch by Francesco di Giorgio from the late fifteenth century shows one such – by the look of it, barely functional – construction.[64]

The case of Orvieto shows that recycled building materials can be the pragmatic choice: removing *spolia*, and especially

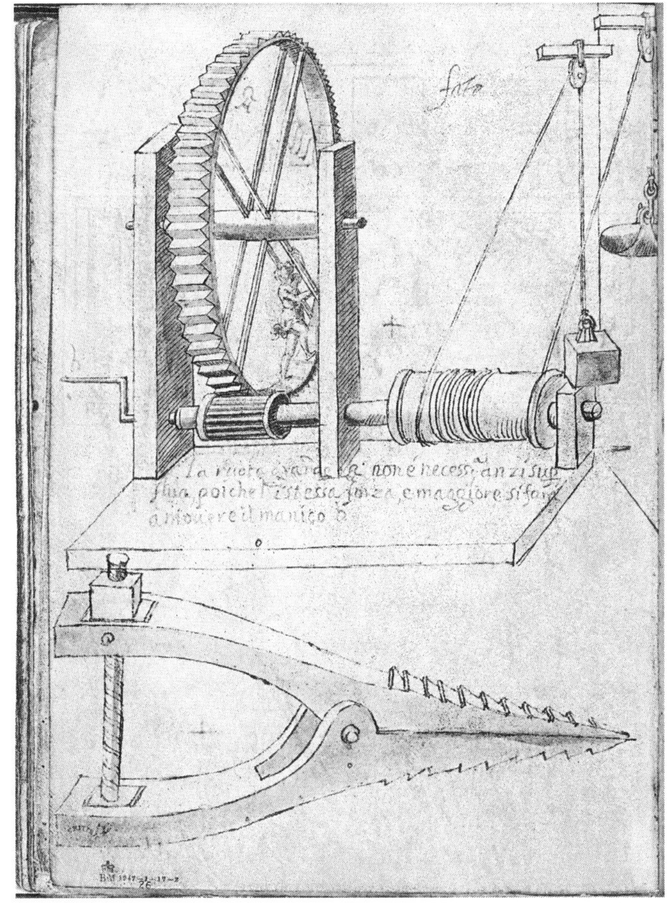

25. Device for transporting antique columns, late fifteenth century

transporting them, was certainly expensive – but still cheaper than producing brand-new ones. Having said that, the cost-benefit ratio could shift considerably, as transportation expenses increased in line with a destination's distance from Rome.

Which brings us to our final example: eighth-century Aachen.

Why Charlemagne had antique columns patched into his cathedral

> 'At Aachen, I saw the well-proportioned columns [...] which Carolus had fetched from Rome and patched into the building.'[65]

When Albrecht Dürer visited Aachen's cathedral in 1520, he was immediately struck by its porphyry and granite columns. When he described them as having been 'patched into' the building, he did not mean to belittle them. In his view, it was only common sense that the architects had reused old building materials – all the more so because they fulfilled the ancient ideals formulated by Vitruvius in the first century BC: they were beautiful, they were old, and they were highly desirable. The columns' eventful history shows just how desirable. After spending a thousand years in Aachen's cathedral, they were taken to Paris by Napoleon in 1795; five of the thirty-eight columns broke during the journey, eight were inserted into the Louvre palace, and the remaining twenty-five were returned to Aachen in 1815, once Napoleon had been retired to St Helena.[66] Why take all that trouble, why all that toing and froing? To answer this question we need to know a bit about the cathedral's history.

The magnificent edifice began life as a plain palace chapel, built between 770 and 794. Charlemagne – then still king of the Franks – had ordered the erection of fortified compounds (or 'palaces', from the Latin *palatium*), in Aachen as well as Ingelheim, Nimwegen and Frankfurt. In 800, when he was crowned emperor by Pope Leo III at St Peter's in Rome, he chose Aachen as his imperial palace and the chapel was – as became traditional for Roman emperors – expanded and turned into an imperial cathedral. To this day, the united Frankish Empire of the early Middle Ages is associated with the term *renovato imperii* (the re-establishment of empire): its model was the Roman Empire, or, more precisely, the Western Roman Empire, which fell in

26. Aachen's cathedral, by Albrecht Dürer (1520)

476 and was now to be reborn in the shape of the Frankish Empire.

Charlemagne took his project very seriously. After the coronation, he decreed that all imperial certificates must use the Roman dating system of 'consular' years, and that all imperial seals must depict the city of Rome. As we know, he also had all coins re-minted to emulate Roman currency. Aachen was to become a kind of second Rome, and on the way back from his coronation in 801 Charlemagne ordered building materials to be imported from Jerusalem, among other places. Ravenna sent a larger-than-life late-classical equestrian statue, and a bronze statue of a she-wolf from the second century AD was imported from the Eternal City to provide a direct visual link to the Roman foundation myth. Although he was only about fifty years old, Charlemagne even made plans for his 'imperial' death, and obtained a late-classical Roman marble coffin.

With all that activity, mistakes were inevitable. The equestrian statue, which was meant to celebrate the resurrection of Rome's magnificence in Aachen, turned out to represent not a Roman emperor but Theoderic, king of the Ostrogoths, who was in effect partly to blame for the fall of the Roman Empire. Somewhat embarrassing, that, and probably why the statue was quickly destroyed by Louis, Charlemagne's successor. As far as the bronze she-wolf was concerned, it turned out to be a she-bear; but no one really minded that one. The marble coffin, meanwhile, had a stunning relief on it – but what it depicted was perhaps not the most fitting subject for a Christian emperor. It told the story of Proserpina, Jupiter's daughter, who was abducted by Pluto and forced to become goddess of the Underworld.[67]

But all these were trivial matters, and did nothing to damage the project as a whole. Charlemagne's *renovatio imperii* is and will remain the prime example of a ruler exploiting the past to assert their right to power, and reshaping the present to suit their vision. Napoleon did exactly the same a thousand years later, when he decided that he simply had to have those columns for his new imperial seat of Paris.

Recycling creates unforgettable buildings

In this account of how recycled building materials were used in Aachen, I have ignored a small but significant detail: chronology. By 800, construction of the palace of Aachen had already been under way for thirty years. When it started, Charles was still merely king of the Franks – a very successful one, yes, but his future was as yet uncertain – and he was eager to import old building materials from northern Italy.

We know this because he discussed his plans with other powerful politicians. From letters he wrote in the year 787, for example, we learn that Pope Hadrian I gave him permission to export building materials, mosaics, marble and art works from the floor and walls of the former imperial palace in Ravenna. He also obtained marble columns and mosaics from Rome, from the ancient imperial residence in Trier, and apparently also from the Romanesque church of St Gereon in Cologne.[68]

We also know that he loved bathing, and had Roman baths built in Aachen, a move that was also a form of architectural recycling. The baths of the ancients turned Aachen into a city of leisure, providing a ruler whose empire stretched from northern Spain to the North Sea with respite from a tiring life on the road.[69]

The throne of Charlemagne: bathroom or gambling hall?

For a long time, historians argued over whether or not the venerable throne of Charlemagne was actually built during Charlemagne's reign, but recent tests have confirmed that its origins are in fact Carolingian. We can safely assume, therefore, that the throne provided future rulers with somewhere to sit during all of the thirty-two coronations that subsequently took place in Aachen cathedral.

The throne is made of marble slabs, but where we might expect finely worked material of the highest quality, we instead find graffiti: pre-Carolingian scribbles adorn the sides and back of the throne, and there are crosses, pilgrims' badges and even an inscription in Old Georgian. The riddle of what the marble was originally used for remains unsolved. Its numerous Maltese crosses, similar to those on the columns of the Church of the Holy Sepulchre in Jerusalem, suggest that the plates arrived from Jerusalem or its environs.

The one concrete piece of evidence we have is the nine men's morris grid scratched into the right-hand slab, which suggests that it may once have been the sort of game board commonly found in Roman baths. If it was, it would mean that

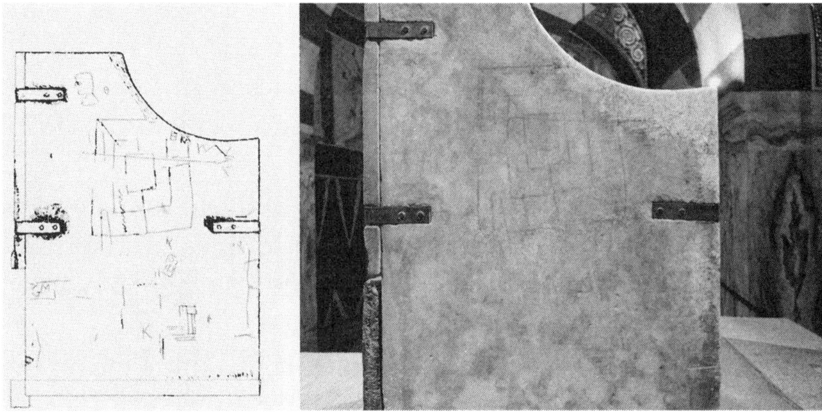

27. Armrest of the throne of Charlemagne, Aachen cathedral

the venerable old throne of Charlemagne was constructed from marble taken from the floor of a Roman bathroom. Others argue that the throne's sides – which are about two centimetres thick – are too thin to have been used as flooring, and that they were more likely used as tabletops. The board game would thus have been a games table, probably resting on a wooden support; in which case the famous throne of Charlemagne in Aachen was recycled from the fittings of an ancient gambling hall. You can't help but smile at the everydayness of it.[70]

Bricolage and assemblage

This last example proves again how common recycling once was. Whether floor slab or gambling table, Charlemagne's throne was at any rate not constructed from the remains of the Temple of Jupiter on the Capitoline Hill. Its makers simply used whatever was to hand. While the 1800s and 1900s disparaged such treatment of antique materials as a bungled attempt to revive a never-to-be-attained past, for us today it evokes something very different: bricolage, assemblage and recycling are key terms for our century, which is to a high degree '*spolia*-orientated' (as Bruno Klein puts it), much more even than the modernist early twentieth century was.[71]

As our awareness of ecological issues grows and these processes once again become fashionable, we are able to draw on a wealth of experience – for in pre-modern everyday architecture, repurposing and reusing recyclable materials was, simply put, the gold standard.

4

MICROFINANCE

In the Middle Ages, fundraising initiatives, endowments and microfinance were considered basic components of socially and economically sustainable behaviour. It was common practice to use donations from wealthy citizens, and successful businesses were keen to exercise what we now label 'corporate social responsibility' to finance not only social or charitable ventures (beguinages, almshouses, colleges, and so on) but large-scale public undertakings too, such as new roads and bridges (including the famous bridge of Avignon).[1] Another source of funding were indulgences, which some historians have compared to emissions trading:[2] like carbon emissions now, 'sin' emissions were deemed unavoidable in the Middle Ages, and all you could do was try to regulate and offset them. Indulgences worked roughly like modern crowdfunding initiatives, with all the attendant opportunities as well as risks. They were used to finance major infrastructure and creative projects, and sustained some of the most important Renaissance artists, from Raphael to Michelangelo. Yet they also show that the crowd's patience can eventually run out, and were a major trigger factor for the Reformation.[3]

Oslo, 10 December 2006. It's the 120th anniversary of Alfred Nobel's death. Nobel, a Swedish armaments manufacturer, made his immense wealth from the invention of dynamite and smokeless gunpowder. By instituting the Nobel Prizes, particularly the one for peace, the man nicknamed 'the merchant of death' even during his lifetime had hoped to somehow make things right. In 2006, the Nobel Peace Prize was awarded to Muhammad Yunus, an economist who had studied in the US and previously been a professor at Chittagong University in Bangladesh, for inventing microfinance. The committee declared that the new financial instrument he had invented would help bring about lasting peace by enabling 'large population groups [to] find ways in which to break out of poverty'. Yunus had shown the world how microfinance can work with his Grameen Bank, which he had founded in 1983 for 'the poorest of the poor', and the Norwegian Nobel committee awarded Yunus and Grameen Bank the prize 'for their efforts to create economic and social development from below'.[4]

Yunus is considered a pioneer of socio-economic sustainability, a subject already known to Aristotle, who believed that market participation was a prerequisite for social cohesion: 'For neither would there [be] association if there were not exchange, nor exchange if there were not equality, nor equality if there were not commensurability,'[5] he writes in his chapter on fair exchange in the *Nicomachean Ethics* (Book V). By 'commensurability' he presumably means something like 'comparability', and Aristotle is thinking here about how equality can be created between very different types of market participants. Money does play an important role, but Aristotle believes that what is more important is what he terms 'need': 'That need holds things together as a single unit is shown by the fact that when men do not need one another, i.e. when neither needs the other or one does not need the other, they do not exchange.'[6] Only exchange creates association. Someone who is so rich that they need nothing is excluded just as much as someone who is so poor that they have nothing to offer.

What is decisive is the fact of exchange as such – or rather, being *involved* in exchange: only someone who has something to offer, regardless of their socio-economic status, can participate in the long term. Market participation thus cannot be reduced simply to the capacity to consume; and it is unclear whether a universal basic income would help create equality, or whether such a transfer payment would merely marginalise the recipient further.[7]

What follows here are three examples of how communities have in the past made efforts towards a financial policy that is socially sustainable.

Microfinance in Italian Cities: The Monti di Pietà

One way was to found microfinance institutions (MFIs). This was the road taken by many Italian cities during the late 1400s and early 1500s. The Renaissance was an age of empowered communities: cities flourished, fought for independence, were proud of their newly won freedom, founded companies and banks, and poured their economic might into strategic partnerships. In 1494, Florence ejected its rulers and became a republic, and, not long after, what must be the most famous statue in the history of art – Michelangelo's *David* – was placed outside the Palazzo della Signoria as a symbol of the self-confident young republic.

It was a time when people in cities started thinking deeply about fairness and the financial markets. Then as now, irregular income and a lack of collateral went hand in hand with expensive credit; poorer households had little or no access to financial services and were forced to pay exorbitant interest rates. People wanted change. In Italy's Renaissance cities, there were comprehensive measures to help the disadvantaged and protect marginalised groups on the financial market. People realised that they needed banks not only for big business, but also for the 'little' people – and that was how the *monti di pietà* came about, communal credit facilities in the shape of 'institutional' pawnbrokers.

These new financial institutions were initially confined to towns and cities, but later extended their credit offering to the local countryside.[8] They were non-profit organisations subject to strict ethical regulations: fees and interest rates were kept very low in order not to burden debtors unduly, but also high enough to keep the operations going and avoid their slipping into the red. Perugia kicked things off in 1462, followed by Orvieto, Gubbio, Spoleto and other towns in Umbria, the Marche and Emilia Romagna. Within three decades there were fifty *monti di pietà* in Italy, rising to 130 in the year 1500, and by the end of the seventeenth century there were 500 of them.

There was hardly a city in Italy without a *monte*. The one in Florence was founded in 1496, about the same time that Michelangelo was commissioned to create his *David*.[9] In some ways, the *monti* functioned like municipal versions of sovereign bonds. They existed in many Italian cities, under different names: alongside Monte Commune in Florence there was, for example, Banco di Sant'Ambrogio in Milan, Casa di S. Giorgio in Genoa and Monte dei Paschi in Siena. The *monti frumentari* were analogous institutions whose capital contributions consisted of grain rather than cash – capital was 'paid in' in the form of natural produce, to prevent grain price inflation in case of shortages.

The *monti delle doti* (*dote* = 'dowry') were another common sight. There, local fathers deposited money to save up for their daughters' dowries, which was repaid with interest when the daughters reached marriageable age. The equally widespread *montes mortuorum* did the same for funeral costs.[10]

What, precisely, is a monte di pietà?

The *monti di pietà* (Latin *montes pietatis*) are literally 'mountains of pity'. Specifically, they are mountains of capital used to fund charity in the shape of loans to the poor. In those days, the term *monte* was applied to all kinds of capital reserves, particularly communal ones; municipal banks, that is, whose stock consisted of compulsory deposits made by affluent citizens. The capital thus 'piled up' was strictly earmarked for community investments. One of the most famous examples is the Florentine Monte Commune, which was founded as far back as the late 1200s to help the community finance an ever-growing number of public projects, and as bridge financing in case of war or food shortages. The whole thing was funded by wealthy residents, whose assets were periodically valued by the city treasury in order to determine the amount they would be compelled to pay into the coffers. These injections of capital usually earned around 5 per cent interest. Investors did not get their deposits back, but they were allowed to sell their earnings; and because they were in effect a reliable long-term annuity, speculators soon started trading them.[11]

The mystery of medieval microcredit[12]

Why is it that we have forgotten all about these late-medieval MFIs? One reason concerns the historical sources available to us: the problem is not that there are too few of them, but too many.

The *monti*, those 'mountains' of charity, have left behind mountains of documentary evidence too: endless statutes, accounting ledgers, registers, lawyers' reports, lists of pledges and any number of other administrative files. Much of it is still waiting to be processed by Italy's archivists, and what makes things still more difficult is that the way those banks were managed was decidedly complex. Most *monti*, with the exception of those in Tuscany, employed the double-entry system, where everything that happened – all the information concerning every single microloan extended to every single person – was recorded in a ledger and then copied into several other ledgers, including the cash flow register (*quaderno di cassa*), the master pawnbroker's ledger (*libro mastro*) and a book listing all accounting operations in chronological order (*libro giornale*).

Administrative processes, staff numbers and job titles also varied from city to city, as did the value and duration of the loans issued, the banks' organisational structure and who managed them. The medieval world was not as keen on norms as the modern world; people generally responded to regional conditions and adjusted regulations to suit local needs.

In short, researchers have their work cut out, and it takes many years of training and enormous patience to get to grips with the structure and internal logic of the extant sources – an effort that understandably scares off many scholars today. Economic historians made some advances in the early 1900s, and local historians have meticulously reconstructed the history of their *monti*, but their discoveries have gone comparatively unnoticed outside Italy. That is one reason why many people have never heard of these medieval MFIs. Another is that they have long been woefully neglected by economic historians, in part, perhaps, because the history of microloans was unlikely to win anyone academic plaudits. Historians therefore preferred to study the big banking dynasties of the past and the financial transactions of princes and kings. The glamour of high finance simply promised greater fame than the more lowly everyday business of microloans.

It was only with the creation of the Centro Studi Monti di Pietà in Bologna in 2001 that these banks – and their significance in terms of sustainable development goals and moral economics – have finally been given the attention they deserve, by historians as well as the general public.[13]

Anyone who becomes rich while creating more and more poverty ought to be ashamed

The motives of the founders of these medieval MFIs can be easily deduced from the economic and social conditions of the era, and the efforts people made to eradicate usury and poverty.[14]

In addition, the northern Italian cities of the late Middle Ages were pivotal centres of the Commercial Revolution, whose most notable markers were the emergence of major trading companies and the spread of commercial accounting, as well as an increased specialisation in all areas of economic life. The monetary economy expanded, and new financial instruments and banks were created. According to Robert S. Lopez, the Commercial Revolution changed the face of European towns and cities to an extent only equalled 400 years later by the Industrial Revolution, and the marketplace supplanted the cathedral as the most important centre of urban life.[15]

With progress came riches – but only for some. Trade flourished, business was booming and many people profited; others, though, threatened to be left behind and slide into poverty. For them, participating in the market's activities became ever more difficult, among other things because it was becoming harder for them to access capital. The local financiers, moneylenders, who were often Jewish but also included Christians, issued credit to lucrative businesses and were thus an essential driver of urban economic growth.

Everyone knew that moneylending – in other words, a functional financial market – was indispensable to economic success; and because a significant proportion of it was transacted via Jewish financial institutions, most cities were keen to ensure that they remained in place and drew up contracts (*condotte*) to regulate the credit business. They set interest rates that satisfied the merchants and large investors, and, since overseas trade was often risky, profit margins were considerable, and more than a few businesses defaulted on their loans, the rates were very high indeed, usually between 10 and 40 per cent. These terms made taking out a small loan impossible, and seamstresses and bakers, for example, soon found themselves unable to obtain the credit they needed to purchase textiles or flour wholesale. The sword of Damocles of financial and social ruin hung precariously over the heads of many formerly self-sufficient urban citizens.

Most of the time, it was the cities themselves who tried to halt the increasing imbalance. Every community worth its salt could and would not put up with it for long – the view being that anyone who becomes rich while creating more and more poverty ought to be ashamed. The chorus demanding better access to credit for the less well-off grew louder, and the interest rates of professional moneylenders were attacked left, right and centre.

In this environment, new forms of microfinance for ordinary citizens could not help but flourish: here it was the town council, there the bishop who took the first steps, creating new forms of affordable microloans and amassing 'mountains' of capital exclusively to guarantee market participation for all. There was nothing at all dishonourable about having to hand over pledges. In a society in which saving was not an easy matter, and where even banks were unable to offer attractive savings terms, functional everyday objects frequently served as a 'store of value'. Buying clothes, household goods, jewellery or furniture was a way to save up for a rainy day – if need be you could trade them, use them instead of cash (to pay bills, dowries or legacies) or even turn them into cash by pawning them. The contents of a household thus had a double identity: on the one hand its objects were used every day, on the other they were stores of value to be utilised in times of need.

The fact that the *monti* accepted many types of collateral made it easier to turn stores of value into cash, and helped keep the capital markets going. Much as Rumpelstiltskin sought to convert straw into gold, the motto here was to convert goods into cash.[16] The process worked extremely well, because once you had enough cash you could turn it back into stores of value – clothing, saucepans and suchlike.

28. Bologna's Palazzo del Monte di Pietà, next to the Cattedrale di S. Pietro

Bologna: a classic success story

In April 1473, Bologna opened its first *monte*. However, since it could not secure sufficient financing and the public offered only modest support, the bank was forced to close again in December 1474.

It took another thirty years before they tried again. They had more success this time, because by December 1504 the political climate had changed. The new ruler of the papal states,

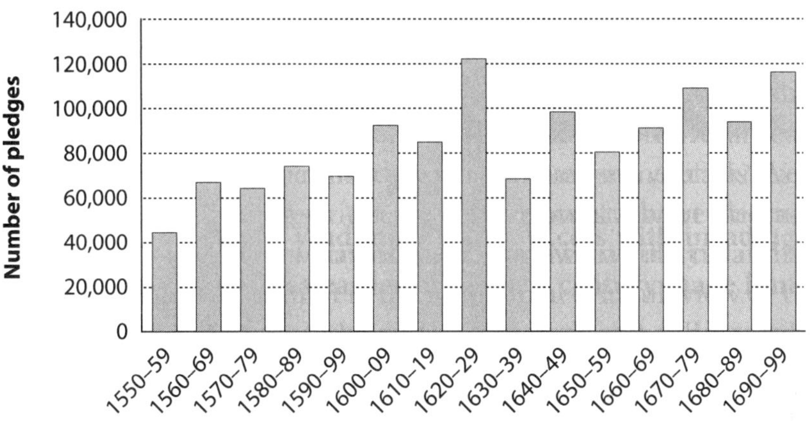

29. Pawns taken to the monte, 1550–1700 (ten-year average)

Pope Julius II, was in favour of a communal bank for the poor and issued a bull in 1507 for the creation of a new *monte*. It became clear that to meet the needs of the poor, all you had to do was control the lower end of the urban credit market. The *monte* was therefore given the status of a municipal bank, and was able to attract private donations by matching them with public money. The bank's capital stores grew, and the city encouraged guilds and fellowships (today's professional associations) to transact their business through the *monte* and deposit their capital there. This second attempt proved extremely successful, and in the course of the 1500s *monte* branches sprang up all over the city.

Their evolution went hand in hand with the elimination of their rivals. The new institutions targeted traditional Jewish pawnbrokers in particular: between 1504 and 1519 the number of pawns, or microloans, rose from 5,000 to 20,000; by the mid-sixteenth century this had doubled to almost 40,000; by the end of the sixteenth century it had risen again to 70,000, and in the early seventeenth century, 100 years after the first Bolognese *monte* was founded, it reached 100,000.

Meanwhile, Bologna had a population of between 60,000 and 70,000, meaning that the number of microloans rose from one for every four residents at the start of the 1600s to around two *per resident* at the start of the 1700s. Bologna's *monti*, like many others, continued to evolve all the way into the twentieth century, during which time these banks remained the first port of call for a broad poor- to middle-class clientele.

The model's sustained financial success was chiefly down to the expansion of the MFIs' offering to include wealthy clients. Bank managers knew how to deftly interweave the various needs of their clients: financial services for affluent households became a line of business that brilliantly supplemented the less lucrative business of small-scale lines of credit and helped keep running costs down – which in turn allowed them to keep the rates of interest they charged to poorer clients low.

Padua: embracing change

The history of Padua's *monte* is somewhat different: after a first – failed – attempt in 1469, there was a second in 1491, in this case driven largely by the missionary Bernardino da Feltre with the support of the local bishop. For two months, he not only continuously advocated for the *monte* in his sermons, but tirelessly collected donations for the new bank. After it opened, too, he continued to champion the project. In 1492 he returned to Padua, this time intending to create a fellowship, a *confraternita del monte*, to govern the bank's activities.

No doubt one key reason for its success was that it regularly tweaked its rules and regulations to suit current needs. The people behind it were not afraid of change – they not only updated the statutes in 1522, but reformed the entire management structure in 1534. Another reason for the *monte*'s success is that the city's aristocracy felt that it was their duty to support the poor, and got involved in the running of the bank. In the decades that followed, the *monte* also took on a charitable role, providing food to those in need, and extended loans to the city at times of crisis.[17]

Franciscan 'influencers'

As mentioned earlier, as a rule it was municipal councils, city rulers or bishops who founded MFIs, or sometimes local societies or individuals such as aristocrats or patricians. However, a *monte* was never an easy proposition. You needed the consent – more than that: the capital – of the local citizens, i.e. their moral and financial support. This is where the eloquent Franciscans came into play. There were many charismatic personalities among their missionaries, who were highly respected not only as preachers but, as Tanja Skambraks puts it, 'well-informed experts in the common good'.[18] Paradoxically, their financial expertise and familiarity with the latest economic theories stemmed from the order's ideal of poverty – for, being minimalists, they lived the plainest of lives and saw it as their mission to preach in the towns and cities.

The Franciscan order specialised in the 'economy of need',[19] and most missionaries engaged in the *monti* were members of a newly founded and particularly activist reformist branch of the order, the Observants, who demanded a return to the original ideals of Christianity. As wandering missionaries, these men regularly came in contact with 'little' people and witnessed first-hand the circumstances in which they lived. They knew the self-employed tailor who didn't have enough money to buy cloth. They knew how difficult it was for him to exit the debt spiral he was caught in due to excessive interest rates. They also knew that the poor did save – but at which bank could they have opened an account? None. So they saved by buying solid, costly everyday objects that would hold their value: a trunk, a winter coat, an expensive dress, pots and pans, tools or jewellery.

The problem, therefore, was less poverty than a lack of opportunities for the capital owned by the poor to circulate – in other words, a lack of affordable financial services. The Franciscan missionaries knew all this and actively campaigned for the institution of banks specifically reserved for the poor, arguing that they should be any city's first priority. In essence, their message was: 'If you want to fight rising poverty, you have to make sure that every single one of your inhabitants has access to capital – not only the rich.'

The missionaries bolstered the municipal governments' efforts by acting as spokesmen, organising fundraisers and mobilising depositors, and thus promoted the creation of the *monti di pietà*. Their activities were invaluable in turning the idea into reality, and it was immensely helpful to the founders when one of these preachers not only spoke up passionately for social justice and railed against the mortal sins of parsimony and avarice, but also called for donations and organised processions.

Today we would call people like that 'influencers'. We know more than 140 of them by name: Michele Carcano from Milano was the driving force behind the creation of the oldest *monti*, beginning in Perugia in 1462. Bernardino da Feltre was also extremely influential, and played a pivotal role in the foundation of *monti* in more than twenty towns and cities. Others included Fortunato Coppoli da Perugia, Marco da Montegallo and Michele da Acqui.

None of these men actually founded the banks themselves, but they acted as consultants and cheerleaders of sorts, propagating the idea in their sermons, promoting the *monti*'s aims and benefits, continually publicising what was then still a novel concept, and explaining the details to the residents of the towns and cities. More practically, too, they were often involved in formulating the articles of association, communicating the rules around pledges and loans to the public, raising funds and mobilising sponsors.[20]

The dark side of the story: the monti di pietà and the expulsion of the Jews

The new institutional pawnbrokers for the poor were nearly everywhere in competition with existing moneylenders and pawnbrokers. In many cities their actual rivals were the Christian Lombards and Cahorsins, but when a *monte* was founded the mood exclusively turned against the local Jewish financial institutions.[21] In many places this culminated in mass violence against Jewish citizens. The Franciscan preachers once again played a key 'influencer' role, this time an ignominious one: in their diatribes against usury they repeatedly inveighed specifically against Jewish moneylenders and blamed them for all evils under the sun. Anyone who reads the sermons today cannot help but wince. How could the fight against poverty and the genuine desire to reform social ills go hand in hand with the inhumane persecution of Jewish citizens? What they did was turn a battle fought on behalf of the poor into a battle fought against their Jewish neighbours.[22]

Perugia: a bank for the poor financed by Jewish bankers[23]

Perugia is a prime example: when the Franciscan friar Michele Carcano returned from his pilgrimage to the Holy Land in spring 1462, he publicly demanded in his sermons that the municipal government immediately cancel all its contracts with Jewish moneylenders and create a *monte*. If they did not, he said, they would be excommunicated. The town council met, and agreed to obey Carcano's demands. It cancelled all contracts with Jewish financial institutions on the spot. Yet things did not go quite as planned, because in the event the town could not amass enough capital to found the new bank. The endeavour only succeeded when Perugia, on the pope's behest, renewed its contracts with the Jewish financiers in March 1463 and invited them back to the city, in exchange for a loan of 1,200 florins to found the *monte*. Shortly before that, the pope had already given permission to Jewish bankers to set up their businesses again in the neighbouring town of Deruta.

It appears that the animosity that ensued originated largely with envious townspeople, who systematically spread fake news by suing their Jewish fellow citizens in the town's court. The court dismissed all charges as spurious and exonerated every single one of the accused, but the accusations were out there in the world, and the plaintiffs, unsurprisingly, resorted to casting doubt on the court's impartiality. At around the same time, the *monte* obtained a fresh loan from Jewish moneylenders, this time in the amount of 2,000 florins. It had to rely on Jewish capital to commence operations, and Jewish citizens appear as clients in various *monti*'s cash books, conducting credit transactions and transferring funds. A mid-1500s report by the Dominican legal expert Sisto de' Medici argues that the common good (*bonum commune*) is safeguarded by laws that are based in common sense; and because the presence of Jews is beneficial to the community of a Christian town, it is only common sense to allow them to stay.

Interactions between Jewish and Christian townspeople were evidently complex and multilayered, and their relationship was marked by ambivalence. They simultaneously cooperated and competed, and almost every *monte* in every town and city was founded with money from Jewish backers.

Assisi: the pope as the Jewish bankers' 'silent partner'[24]

The town of Assisi founded a *monte* in 1468, at the instigation of the Franciscan friars Fortunato Coppoli (from Perugia) and Giacomo della Marca. Here, too, this was accompanied by a massive persecution campaign against the local Jews. Fortunato threatened the town government with excommunication if they did not dissolve their contracts with Jewish financial institutions

– and so they did. But soon after, a reprimand arrived straight from Rome, and they were more or less ordered to reinstate the contracts.

In the matter of the foundation of Assisi's *monte*, too, the Roman Curia clearly supported the Jewish bankers: on 16 July 1469 the town elders received a letter sent on behalf of Pope Paul II, signed by the papal treasurer and the papal court's most senior judge, in which these two high-ranking Curia officials conveyed the pope's displeasure at the fact that Assisi had cancelled its agreements with its Jewish residents, and exhorted the mayor and town council to respect them. The missive also reprimanded the Franciscan missionaries: if they wanted to improve the way Christians behaved, it said, they should feel free to do so – but without causing any harm to the Jews, who, after all, respected the law too. The fact alone that their habits differed from those of Christians was surely no justification for harming them. Remind the preachers, the town was told, that they shall of course condemn sin and, if possible, eradicate it; but ecclesiastical law allows the presence of Jews among Christians, and they must be permitted to live life their way. Assisi's *priores* (female directors) consequently renewed the contracts.

Ten years later the town received a further letter, this time from Cardinal Giuliano della Rovere – the future Pope Julius II – in which he confirmed once again that their contracts with the Jews were authorised by the Church, and emphasised that there was no threat whatsoever of excommunication.

Between competition and cooperation

There are many more such examples, which show that, from as far back as the mid-1200s, the Roman Curia had often acted in partnership with Jewish banks. When it proved impossible to reinstate the contracts that had been dissolved the pope frequently offered his protection in other ways, for example by authorising new settlements nearby, where the Jews could continue their business without too great a disadvantage. Furthermore, we can see that the municipal governments weren't interested in hate speech against Jewish citizens; indeed, they repeatedly ejected extremist missionaries. Finally, one of the most important things we have learnt is that most medieval banks for the poor owed their existence to considerable injections of capital – usually in the form of compulsory loans – from Jewish banks. As financial backers, they played a crucial role in the foundation of most Christian MFIs. Not only that, but the latest analyses of the *monti*'s accounts by economic historians show that, in practice, Christian and Jewish credit institutions worked together very closely for a long time and actually complemented each other; and Jewish residents were among the *monti*'s clients, depositing their money in them, taking out loans and acting as buyers at the periodic auctions. This is something we have realised only recently, because the focus of historians used to be so much on the Franciscans' unbearable antisemitic harangues that it skewed our view of actual practices – which played out somewhere between cooperation and competition.[25]

In times of crisis, scapegoats are easier to find than solutions

Yet these recent findings change little about the massive rise in antisemitism that accompanied the founding of MFIs in northern Italy. Animosity and violence against Jewish residents and businessmen was the price exacted by the launch of these banks for the poor. The Jews were the ones who had to pay.

It is difficult to explain why this should have been the case. Perhaps it was an instance of the kind of outbreak of collective violence against minorities – often foreigners, or other members of society that are somehow 'different' – which the French ethnologist René Girard described as typical phenomena during times of crisis. In his book *The Scapegoat* he explains that, whenever there is a catastrophe, plague or war, or when an economy goes through a period of inflation or recession, people fear for their community's survival. He developed a model showing how these social defence mechanisms (can) work almost like a collective reflex: instead of collective solutions, people prefer to look for a scapegoat, whose existence alone suffices to explain the crisis. You can identify the guilty by the 'marks of the victim', which could be anything from a birthmark to superhuman strength, from a club foot to a virgin birth. All you need is for a charismatic person to point the finger at someone who is 'different from us' for them to be identified as the scapegoat. This person is then hunted, tortured and executed.

In these bloody outbreaks of collective violence, Girard argues, the community finds reassurance and renewed strength. Scholars even speak about the 'unifying polarisation of violence', which, however, is only temporary.[26] Maria Giuseppina Muzzarelli proposes that we see the large-scale aggression against Jewish residents starting in the late 1400s – residents who had until then coexisted relatively peacefully and been an integral part of life in these cities – as just such a form of polarising violent excesses. The age of economic upturn also posed huge challenges which the towns and cities tried to counteract by, among other things, creating the *monti*. The binding spell that was the ban on charging interest had finally been broken.[27]

Where did MFIs get their capital?[28]

We will now look at the working practices of these institutional pawnbrokers, or MFIs, in more detail. How exactly did they issue credit to people? Who was in charge? Where did they store the pledges? What were people allowed to use as collateral, and where did the cash come from?

To answer the last question first, there were basically four main sources: firstly, donations, raised via public appeals, from church collection plates to generous sums handed over by affluent citizens, including legacies; in some places they set up a collection point outside the *monte*, which was emptied once a day.

Secondly, the cities would put some of the income they generated from leasing communal land or selling grain into the *monte*. Many also organised processions designed to spread a sense of community through the city's streets, and collected donations along the way. Rome's *monte*, for instance, was set up by a fellowship (*compagnia*), a sort of company or association with more than 5,000 members, each of whom paid money into the bank to replenish its reserves (couples counted as one person). The annual Whitsun procession organised by the *compagnia* was an excellent opportunity for raising money: the event was announced from the city's pulpits three weeks in advance, and Rome's entire elite was invited: senators, nobles and council members, as well as senior envoys from Florence and Genoa, abbots, academics – in short, everyone within reach who was high-ranking or famous. Anyone who took part and gave generously received an indulgence from the pope.

A third regular source of income were the courts – fees, penalties, reparations and stolen goods seized by the authorities. Lastly, there were the tills of already existing institutions that we have already learnt about, in particular Jewish-run banks, which made up the majority of the capital of the new, regulated pawnbrokers for the poor.

Trumpeters, master pawnbrokers and feline pest controllers[29]

If you wanted the microloan business to work smoothly, you needed the right staff. The man in charge was the *depositarius*, who took personal responsibility for making sure that the bank conducted its business properly. Today, we would call him a bank manager. The second-most important position was that of 'pledge master' (*massaro* or *custos*), the man in charge of the pawns – his was a crucial department, because without the proper recording and storing of the collateral the system simply couldn't function. For that you needed a clean and dry storehouse, and the statutes contain detailed instructions for anything from the size of the shelves to cleaning schedules, from monthly inventories to employing a cat to keep the mice away.

The *massaro* had assistants, who collected the pledges from the clients, presented them to the treasurer (*stimatore*) for valuation, then packed the objects up and took them to the stores. For clients, the most important thing was the value of their pledges, and some statutes prescribed that the treasurer should ideally be a goldsmith. Once he had determined the value of the object, said value was entered into a book along with the client's first and last name, a description of the object including its quality (*qualitade de la cossa impegata*) and the amount of the loan granted. All this information was also noted on a ticket, together with the terms, value and duration of the credit, and once the ticket was signed the loan was issued and the sum paid out by a cashier (*cassiere*) or, in some banks, by the *depositarius*.

There were also clear rules about what could and could not be accepted as collateral: clothes and household goods were fine, religious paraphernalia such as Bibles or crosses were not. The bank could not accept stolen goods either. The value of a loan was ordinarily fixed at no more than two-thirds of the pledge's actual value, to avoid serious losses if the client defaulted on their debt.

Such administrative processes resulted in comprehensive account ledgers; from the *monte* in Reggio Emilia, for example, we have seven sizeable volumes of pledge registers alone, showing that the *monti* met their obligations regarding accuracy and transparency with meticulous bookkeeping. As public banks, they were beholden to the citizens – very much unlike private banks, which often deliberately destroyed or failed to

30. An institutional pawnbroker – the Banca di Faenza – as depicted by Giovanni Battista Bertucci in his sixteenth-century painting *Il pignoramento*

keep proper business records in the first place. Once the loan expired, normally after between six and eighteen months, the client would pay back the borrowed money and hand over the ticket in exchange for the pledge. Any pledges not redeemed were publicly auctioned off by a dedicated official (the *venditore* or 'seller'). A trumpeter would announce said auction throughout the city, and the affected client was also informed, in order to give them the opportunity to get together enough money to redeem their pledge after all. If the collateral sold for more at auction than the loan was worth, the profit went either directly to the client, i.e. the original owner of the pledge, or to a charity.

Bertucci's painting *Il pignoramento* is a colourful depiction of the Monte di Pietà di Faenza's day-to-day business. At the bottom of the picture you can see assistants collecting pledges – jewellery, pots and pans, a spindle – and in the foreground you can make out two somewhat smaller figures, helping out the female clients. These are the servants of the *monte*, young assistants (*garconi, fancelli*) who would work for a pawnbroker for a year in return for minimum wage. Today, it would presumably be the sort of internship you would do during your gap year. The official behind the counter, dressed in black with a white collar and about to accept a sack from a client, is most likely the *massaro* or one of his colleagues. Is the official in black behind the counter on the left the *estimatore*, to whom the pledges are passed for valuation? Although he seems to be busy handing over money. Behind the first counter, two scribes at a long table are copying values and payments into the bank's account ledgers, and filling in tickets. A third official in black might be in the process of taking a freshly issued ticket, which he will then pass to the cashier for payment. On the right you can see the pledges being carefully tied into bundles to avoid damage during storage.

The management and administration of urban microfinance evidently required much manpower. The small sums and short durations of the loans involved meant a high turnover and a lot of work, which is why the banks had such a large staff and complex organisational structure.

What Rome's monte can tell us about how MFIs were managed

Each bank had a managing board made up of some of the city's eminent personalities.[30] At the top of the hierarchy was the 'protector', together with three male directors (*provisores*) as well as – remarkably, given that this was the sixteenth century – three female directors (*priores*), who were members of Rome's urban elite (a.k.a. patricians). In addition, there were four deputies (*deputati*), two syndics (*sindici*) and the Council of Thirteen (representatives from each of Rome's thirteen districts).

The constitution of the board makes it clear that the people who set up the *monti* wanted to involve as wide a range of the city's political and social elites as possible. Unlike the bank's officials, every board member was a volunteer. The *depositarius*, situated as he was at the intersection between bank and board, bore the bulk of the burden: he was in charge of the staff, responsible for making sure that everything ran as it should, paid salaries, administered the funds, controlled the pledge registers and was accountable to the board, to whom he reported once a month. The role was taken on by a different member of the city's ruling class each year, which suggests that engagement with community MFIs was part and parcel of membership of the Roman elite.

Who were the clients?

Only those in need were entitled to credit from the *monte*, and you had to live either in town or in the immediately surrounding area, the *contado*. Sources repeatedly mention *pauperes pinguiores*, 'the strong poor' or – literally – 'the fat poor', i.e. people who could earn a living with their hands and needed cheap credit to sustain their business. They generally had no or only very little property to put up as collateral.

Modern historians often group them together under the label of ordinary people. To call them the 'lower classes' would be misleading, because they technically included over 90 per cent of urban society in the Middle Ages. Medieval contemporaries used different categories. The *pauperes pinguiores* were people

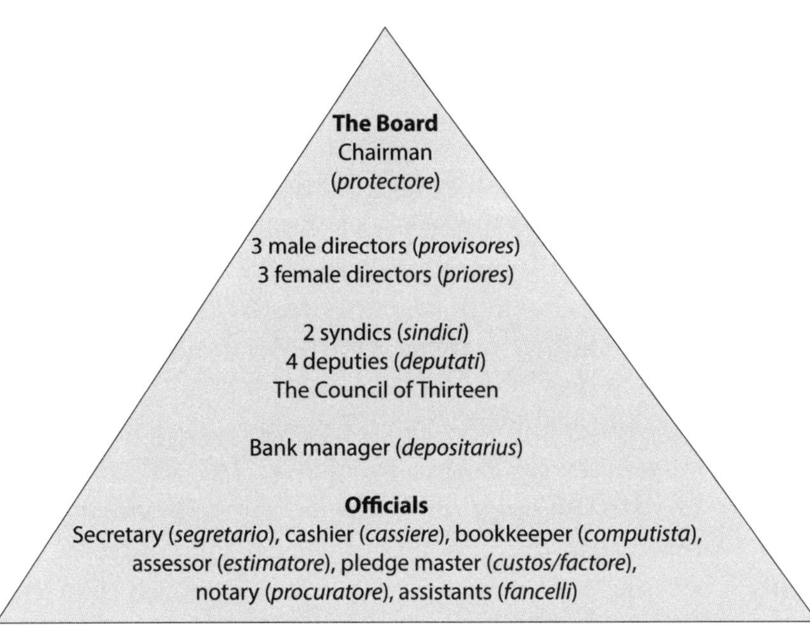

31. Organisation chart for the *monte* in Rome according to the statutes of 1557

who had little but were not helpless. Having few things to call your own was not necessarily regarded as an ignoble way of life. On the contrary, it was seen as perfectly legitimate and key to society's survival, and therefore deserved whatever support it might need. Microloans were not designed for the poorest of the poor, i.e. anyone not in a position to provide for themselves, for whom the idea of being 'helped to help themselves' was a slap in the face. These people – beggars, or those who lived with disabilities or chronic illnesses – were provided for with alms, which were handed out regularly via charitable municipal or Church networks.[31]

The customers of the medieval *monti* were thus not the poorest of the poor. They may have had hardly any savings or cash, and consequently paid no taxes, but they did have clothes, furniture, tools and jewellery, which made pledges the obvious credit instrument. In a society where saving up was considerably more difficult than it is today, and where banks provided little opportunity to grow what savings you did have, pawning property was neither an act of desperation nor short-sighted. Quite the opposite: as we have seen, people bought everyday objects not only to use them, but as insurance for when times were hard. Buying a good item of clothing was an investment in the future, a reserve fund if you like, which you could tap into and turn into cash in case of an emergency.[32]

That the debtors also included members of the better-off classes, whose everyday possessions likewise fulfilled the double function of both use object and store of value, is evident from what we have seen of Bologna's *monte*; in the course of the 1600s, it became so successful that it opened no fewer than four more branches in the city, together with additional warehouses. As Mauro Carboni shows, the expansion of the *monti*'s financial offering and the ensuing mixed clientele also helped to balance out social inequality.[33]

Socks, belts and oven doors[34]

Would-be debtors pledged anything and everything: jewels, tools, bed sheets, belts and especially clothes were commonly taken to banks as collateral. Since the *monti* kept meticulous pledge registers, we have access to a wealth of detail. Muzzarelli has examined lists of pledges from Perugia (1469), Pistoia (1491) and Urbino (1492–3), and shed light on just how broad a spectrum of goods they were dealing with. The lists from Perugia and Pistoia were compiled for an auction of unredeemed pledges, and the Urbino document records the pledges left with the bank.[35] In Pistoia, people overwhelmingly submitted household objects. More than half of pledges, 399 of 680, consisted of tablecloths, sheets and towels, in addition to 164 items of

32. Tools, clothes and jewellery used as collateral

clothing and 52 pieces of jewellery. By contrast, the list from Urbino contains only few clothes. There, a richly decorated belt fetched sixty Bolognese pennies of credit, almost as much as a well-preserved linen coat (*camurra*). The smallest pledge on that list is a pair of worn-out socks, which a maid called Maddalena exchanged for a loan of six Bolognese pennies; another client received eight pennies for a pillow and fourteen for a baking tin.[36]

The list from Perugia contains a total of 703 pledges: again, the majority are items of clothing, followed by cloths, bed sheets, head coverings, belts, underwear and other textiles alongside a few pieces of jewellery, including a gold ring, a coral necklace and a jewel. Here, too, it seems that anyone in possession of jewellery they could pledge was more likely to pay back what they owed. The list also includes a weapon – which the statutes technically did not allow – and an oven door (*porteletto de forno*). The latter was, incidentally, pledged by a baker. The face value of these objects ranged from one florin for a tablecloth or bed sheet to fourteen florins for several dresses.[37]

What the debtors and buyers did for a living gives us an insight into the social structure of the banks' clientele: they were predominantly artisans and merchants – cotton weavers, tailors, haberdashers, smiths, wool merchants, dyers, barbers, masons, spice merchants, butchers, chicken farmers, bakers, cordwainers and furriers. The names of six women appear among the debtors, though none among the buyers – at least not in this early list from Perugia. Are we to conclude that female debtors were more reliable than men even in the late Middle Ages? Since the list only concerns unredeemed pledges, perhaps the reason that it includes so few women in the first place is that they usually paid their loans back on time.[38]

Interest rates, and the fine line between admin fees and usury

Like the MFIs of the twenty-first century, those of the late fifteenth century also drew much criticism. The question of whether interest rates were legitimate or not was a hot topic at the time. Today, 'usury' is associated with excessive or illegal interest; however, medieval ecclesiastical law defined it as any payment at all received in exchange for loans of cash or goods.

The ban on usury originated in late antiquity, and for centuries it was neither questioned nor heeded. In the twelfth century, however, when the Commercial Revolution dawned and as the credit business grew, discussions about the legitimacy of interest rates gained momentum. Betting on interest rates was evidently producing hitherto unheard of profits, leading to a rise in social inequality. The Church tried to put a halt to it, and twelfth-century council ordinances begin to mention bans on charging interest rates; usurers are refused a Christian burial unless they have first paid their interest earnings back to their debtors; and cities are forbidden from issuing licences to moneylenders.

Although the Church's proscription was ignored, it affected many areas of high- and late-medieval business life, from simple consumer credit to more complex business partnerships, trade alliances, and the interest the *monti commune* paid on sovereign bonds. One consequence was that from then onwards, contracts usually avoided the term 'interest' and employed synonyms instead. Yet even theologians and ecclesiastical lawyers disagreed among themselves. Fundamentalists, like Thomas Aquinas in the thirteenth century, cited Aristotle's declaration that money was 'barren', while Aquinas's contemporary, Henry of Segusio (alias Hostiensis), the most famous expert on canon law of his day, argued that it was legal for a creditor to receive interest on a loan if they were a merchant – since they were otherwise unable to profit from the money they had lent, they had a right to compensation for loss of earnings.

The ban on interest threw many an upstanding citizen into a crisis of conscience on their deathbed: did the interest on the loan they had been forced to extend to the Florence's Monte Commune constitute usury, and was it thus an obstacle on the road to Heaven? Was it worth selling your soul for? One man plagued by such thoughts was the Florentine merchant Angelo Corbinielli, who for that very reason included a clause in his will to the effect that his heirs were to refuse all loans in future, lest the Church decide that the interest received on them constituted usury.[39]

Both opponents and proponents of the *monti* carefully analysed these subtle theological arguments concerning the legitimacy or otherwise of charging interest. While some *monti* initially refused all interest payments, others insisted on them from the start, at a rate of 5 per cent (considered a very small percentage at the time), arguing that they were in fact admin fees, necessary to cover the *monti*'s expenses – the cost of storing pledges, office rents, salaries and such. A total ban on interest was hindered by the practicalities of implementing financial services for the poor. MFIs needed staff who had to be paid, offices in which to conduct their business, warehouses for the pledges, etc. The associated expenses had to be covered somehow, and the money had to come from somewhere. But where was the line between covering your expenses and interest? Many thought that even moderate rates of 5 per cent were merely interest disguised as compensation for expenses, and therefore usury. Others justified themselves by pointing out that their business was urgently needed in the face of growing poverty, as well as for reasons of sustainability: if they waived their fees, the pawnbroker's initial capital would have to be used for wages, rents and such, and would quickly disappear.

In the early days, both sides commissioned countless reports, which either confirmed or questioned the legitimacy of these MFIs. To say that the Church was against interest and the cities for it is too simplistic. Rather, the pragmatic voices arguing in favour of moderate interest rates often came from Rome, and even among Franciscan missionaries – those charismatic champions of the *monti* – there was disagreement. Michele Carcano, one of the architects of the first *monte* in Perugia, was a radical fundamentalist and strictly against them, condemning in his sermons anyone who charged interest or even merely tolerated it – without exception, regardless whether they were the manager of a Christian pawnbroker's, a Jewish moneylender, Augustine hermit, town councillor, Christian merchant or poor widow. He even criticised the pope several times for tolerating such things. Other prominent Franciscans, meanwhile, such as Galvano da Padova and Bernardino da Feltre, understood that a bank for the poor can only work in the long run if it can at the very least break even, and argued in favour of moderate interest rates for the benefit of the community.[40]

The moral economy of the monti di pietà[41]

We can see that the creation of these urban MFIs in Italian cities during the Renaissance greatly benefited society. The banks enabled people to take out loans on affordable terms, and sought only to cover their costs, not to make a profit. Many survived until late into the twentieth century, extending small loans to people on the margins of society for hundreds of years.

In many towns and cities they offered other protections to the poor too, in addition to financial support. The buildings belonging to the *monti* enjoyed similar privileges to churches and were places of asylum. In Perugia, for example, they announced that anyone who was on their way to the *monte* with a pledge, or leaving the *monte* with a loan, could under no circumstances be arrested, even if they had previously been expelled from the city. Outside the *monte* in Vicenza they put up a stone tablet which declared: 'Whoever you are, if you are fleeing from justice or from an enemy, when you touch the sacred threshold you are safe.' In Pistoia, too, it appears that you were beyond reach of the city's courts the moment you crossed the *monte*'s threshold.[42]

These practical offers of help, extended to those who were at risk of being left behind by the Commercial Revolution, make it clear that maximising profits was not the aim of the *monti*. History thus provides an example of a socially and economically sustainable business model that lasted centuries, surviving crises, bankruptcies, revolutions and even Napoleon, simply because it fulfilled a crucial function, i.e. providing financial services to the socially and economically weaker members of urban society. The *monti* were never about turning metaphorical dish-washers into millionaires. No, the aim of these medieval MFIs was to enable the metaphorical dish-washer to live a dish-washer's life with dignity. Everyone must be guaranteed access to the market – no matter if they are a pig herder, maid or, well, a dish-washer. The people who founded the late-medieval *monti* understood that, I think. And would no doubt have elected Muhammad Yunus to the board.

Peer-to-Peer Lending

These MFIs were at this time located chiefly in Italian cities – but there were ordinary people everywhere, of course. In

London, too, a cordwainer had to invest in leather before he could produce shoes, and a tailor in Barcelona might not have had sufficient cash to pay for a fresh delivery of cloth. The question is, therefore, how these people got hold of the capital they needed, however little that might have been.

For a long time historians did not give the matter much thought, choosing to focus on the business of merchants and bankers, whom they saw as the first modern, market-orientated humans, and thus as the forerunners of modern business and finance. The old-school view was that the rest of the medieval world happened outside the market, and was economically underdeveloped. At most, we thought, people bartered with each other, or borrowed money from relatives, or incurred debts with their feudal overlord – until, thanks to modern credit instruments, 'little' people, too, were in a position to achieve a degree of financial independence.

This interpretation is now seen as outdated. A few years ago, a new generation of historians decided to take a different approach, examining primary sources and making a number of surprising discoveries in the process. Their goal was to properly explore the monetary needs of ordinary people away from high finance and the narrative of progress, and they tried to find out how people paid for their everyday expenses. They studied sources which, while not new, had so far remained ignored. To cut a long story short, they showed that the loan business was as widespread in the pre-modern world – including among 'little' people – as today; if not more, in fact, given that buying things on tick was common, and cash reserves were far more limited.[43]

The reason we can know this for sure is that credit transactions were recorded in writing, by way of insurance. Many places north of the Alps kept municipal debt books in which the residents registered their credit transactions, including agreed repayment schedules, to avoid any issues later; south of the Alps, in the wider Mediterranean region, you went to a notary whenever you borrowed money. Fascinatingly, it appears that no amount was too small to warrant recording by a notary or municipal court, and you can find entries for as little as a few pennies, or just enough money for a pair of shoes. The reason this is so interesting is that there was evidently an astonishing variety of consumer credit available to people in those days. We clearly have to revise not only our belief that our ancestors were economically underdeveloped, but also our assumption that it was only with the advent of capitalism and the invention of savings and loan banks and credit cooperatives that the 'poor' could open a bank account and thus participate in the financial markets. Might we have had it the wrong way round? Did capitalism in fact lead to the exclusion of a large part of the population from local financial markets?

'Only few venture into the abyss of microloans.' Gabriela Signori[44]

The main reason historians shy away from microloans is that working with the relevant primary sources is not the most fun you could be having. Reading and analysing court records, minutes, judgments, entries concerning expulsions for unpaid debts, notaries' files and other administrative documents is no walk in the park. Once you do venture into them, though, you gain remarkable insights into just how pervasive the urban credit market was. In his account of the situation in the Swiss town of Thun, the historian Simon Teuscher writes, 'You get the impression that nearly everyone might have owed money to nearly everyone else.'[45] This included the local elites, officials and members of the town council, as well as those at the very bottom of the social hierarchy. Barmaids gave credit to domestic servants, farmers owed money to breeders, merchants to carters, craftsmen to their servants, servants to their landlords and citizens to town clerks (possibly for writing out deeds). The network of credit relationships zigzagged through small-town society, and it is clear that people regularly lent money not only to close or extended family, but also to others outside their immediate social circle.[46]

Let us look at some concrete examples from European towns and cities, starting with Basel at the end of the fifteenth century, where – as the historian Gabriela Signori has discovered – peer-to-peer lending transactions were safeguarded by means of an entry made in the municipal debt book by the court. It is thanks to such initiatives that we are now able to obtain detailed insights into the medieval credit business of ordinary people.

Death of a swineherd

The swineherd Antonius died in Basel's hospital in early February 1478. We don't know how old he was, we don't know where he worked and we don't know how he died. Yet because of a list produced by an official at a Basel court on 10 February 1478, we know the precise state of his assets at the time of death.

The swineherd's assets are as modest as you would expect, comprising mainly clothes – two coats, four shirts, headgear, underwear – and basic equipment (pails and knife), and finally cash assets amounting to a penny short of sixteen shillings. He was obviously poor. The fact that he died in hospital is further evidence of this, because to be taken in by a hospital back then you had to be needy more than ill. They did care for those who lived with a disability, but also looked after the aged and the poor, as well as beggars and the homeless. People could, if they wanted to and were wealthy enough, pay their way into hospital, to be looked after there in their dotage – i.e. become a prebendary – but Antonius was doubtless not one of them. Rather, he died in hospital because he had become insolvent during his lifetime.

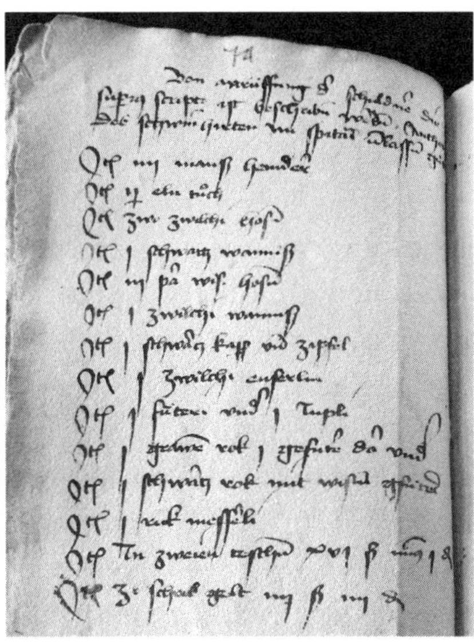

33. Inventory of the belongings of swineherd Antonius, dated 10 February 1478.[47] It reads: 'Pursuant to an application from his creditors made on the above date, this is a catalogue of Antonius the swineherd's estate, as relinquished by him in hospital: item: four men's shirts; item: cloth, 1½ ells; item: two pairs linen hose; item: 1 black jerkin; item: 3 pairs white hose; item: 1 linen waistcoat; item: 1 black cap, pointed; item: 1 pair linen sleeves; item: 1 feeder pail and 1 wooden pail; item: 1 grey coat, lined; item: 1 black coat with white lining; item: 1 penknife; item: in two of his pockets, 16s. minus 1d. Item: scribe's fee of 4s. 4d.'

Why, we wonder, did anyone bother entering an inventory of a poor swineherd's belongings in a municipal register? The first three lines of the list explain why: 'his creditors' had made 'an application', i.e. had presented themselves to the authorities after his death to try to recover at least some of what he owed them from his estate. This is precisely why, in the early 1400s, Basel had introduced a catalogue for the possessions of those who died intestate or insolvent. Antonius may have been both; and due process dictated that his effects were catalogued in order that they could be handed over to his creditors in part payment for any outstanding debts. The clerk's administrative fee for producing the list (4s. 4d.) was simply subtracted from the total and retained by the court.

This brief entry from February 1478 tells us two things: firstly, that from the point of view of the Basel court, even a swineherd who died in the municipal poorhouse was not too poor to settle outstanding debts; the second – and more surprising – aspect of this discovery is that in late fifteenth-century Basel, even a swineherd was deemed creditworthy, otherwise he would not have had creditors. You could speculate that Antonius was rich once, and merely ended up in hospital because he had overextended himself; but it is highly unlikely that he was ever one of Basel's affluent citizens: swineherds were neither upwardly nor downwardly mobile – they were always more or less paupers. Though evidently creditworthy ones.

To understand why this should be the case, we have to go back a tad further. Alongside the 'little catalogue' listing the estate of someone who died insolvent, city courts soon introduced other stand-alone volumes and series of books to record credit agreements (*Vergichtbücher*), the attachment of chattels (i.e. confiscated goods) and income from public trials. All these are in the Basel archive, and Signori testifies to the mind-boggling amount of data they contain.[48] The city was clearly attempting to regulate the various stages of the credit process, from issue to foreclosure and forced auction, in response to an increase in cash and goods transactions. Together, these administrative instruments are evidence that what we today call peer-to-peer lending was everyday practice in urban communities at the time, with court registers acting as legal safeguards.[49]

Peer-to-peer lending in Basel in the late 1400s[50]

Debtors had to solemnly swear before the court, official, sheriff or reeve to keep to the arranged payment schedule. This was particularly important in the case of out-of-towners, who in addition had to promise, in the event that they missed a payment, to immediately present themselves in the city and remain there until they could come to a revised agreement with the creditor.

This is what happened in the case of Martin Kempf and Jakob Spuri from Lahr, who, on 11 January 1480, appeared before Basel officials because the agreed repayment deadline had passed. They extended their contract by a fortnight, but on 9 February, more than three weeks later, both parties appeared once again before the court because, despite the extension, the debt was still not repaid. They agreed a new deadline, this time 25 July 1480. If the outstanding amount was not repaid by then, the debtors were to be forcibly kept at the Zum Schlüssel inn until the debt was settled or the collateral surrendered.

Non-Basel residents were often required to put up 'horse and cart' as security, or, in the case of larger sums, sign a promissory note in which they mortgaged their estate. Guarantors are only rarely mentioned in the registers, and in the course of the fifteenth century fell out of fashion entirely. Anyone who did not pay their debts on time was threatened with expulsion: they were ordered to see the censor (*Unzüchter*), thrown out of the city, and instructed not to re-enter it until they had enough money to settle both the debt and the penalty.[51]

Horses, bread and shoes – what Basel's residents borrowed money for[52]

The *Vergichtbücher* only seldom mention why someone borrowed money, but now and then the purchase of a horse is mentioned as a reason for a loan, and there are scattered references to unpaid bills for things like bread, wood, leather, sheets or shoes. The cordwainer Konrad Oltinger and his wife Katharina, for instance, obtained trade credit from a tanner called Antonius Schmid for leather worth thirty-five Swiss pounds; regular bread deliveries were the reason why the couple who ran the Zum Schwarzen Rüden at Kuttel Bridge got themselves indebted to the baker Hans Tumringer, for which debt they had put up their entire inn, together with eighteen beds, as collateral; and a certain Peter Köhler from Hüningen, a village just outside the city, owed the landlord of Zum Kopf in the borough of St Martin 1,000 faggots of brushwood.

Whenever houses are mentioned, it is often simultaneously as collateral and reason for a debt, because many people could not afford their own home. This was the case for saddler Hans Brunn and his wife Ennelin, who appeared before the court on 4 May 1480, a week after agreeing to buy a small house from the butcher Lienhard Seiler in Spalenvorstadt Street. The selling price was twenty florins, and the two parties had come to court because the couple did not have sufficient funds for the purchase. They agreed a repayment schedule of a florin a year, with the first instalment due on 25 July and the next at Christmas. The repayments were to be continued until the full amount had been settled – i.e. for twenty years. And theirs was not a unique case.

Who took out loans, and who issued them? A review of the year 1480

The simple answer is: anyone and everyone. Most of those who registered their debt at the sheriff's court in Basel were from the city. The creditors as well as debtors included everyone – men and women, tailors, fishermen and butchers, convents and clergy. For the sake of clarity, court clerks added small symbols in the margins to illustrate a creditor's occupation or name: blacksmiths got a horseshoe, butchers a cleaver, Hans Giger a violin (*Geige* being the German for violin), Wernlin Hafengießer a three-legged pot (*Hafen*), and fishermen a fish.

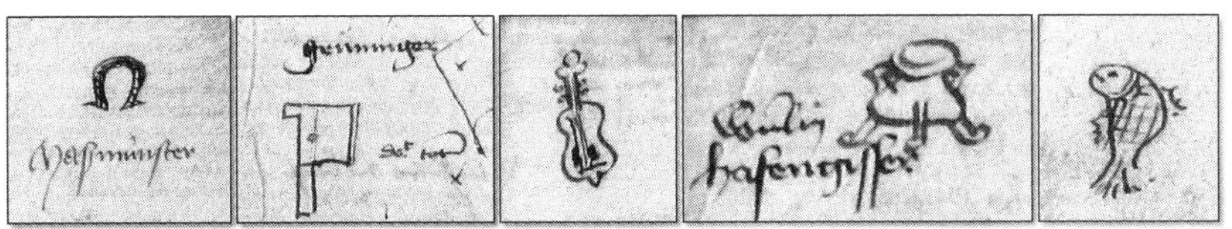

34. Pictograms in a *Vergichtbuch*, illustrating names and occupations

Women: Elsi Tieringer, alias Engelhardin[53]

It was perfectly normal for a woman to be actively involved in the microloan market, whether as a debtor or as a creditor. During the first half of the fifteenth century, more than a third of all transactions involved one or more women, and most acted in their own name, not their husband's. One such woman was Elsi Tieringer, wife of the official Engelhard Tieringer, who was declared insolvent and had her property seized in the summer of 1480. Her case is documented in the court files, which give us a wonderful insight into the microcosm of a municipal enterprise: for this woman, who doesn't appear in any tax registers – meaning that she was too poor to pay tax, and wasn't a member of a Basel guild – had clearly been running a thriving textile business. Among her assets was an unusually large number of coats and skirts, and she also took deliveries of cloths, thread and weaving combs, all of which suggests that she either produced or traded in clothes, perhaps even both. She had an employee called Elsin Franken, and was well connected in the city, especially among the elite. We know this because she did business with highly respected citizens, from the minster's chaplain to the mayor, from leading merchants to the city's famous master papermaker. Unfortunately, we can only view her network from the perspective of failure, but – ah, the irony of fate! – this is also the very reason why we know so much about the many business relationships of this Basel woman in the first place, whom history has otherwise consigned to obscurity. Altogether, fifty of her business partners, thirty men and twenty women, appeared before the municipal court in early November 1480 to stake their claim. By then, however – knowing that she would never be able to settle her debts – Elsi had already taken to the hills.[54]

Transparency creates trust

Was Basel's solution of having debts publicly declared an efficient way to protect credit contracts? Was it chicanery, or did it create an atmosphere of trust? Despite their many inconsistencies, an entry in the city's debt books was evidently a popular safeguarding method for socially inclusive microloans. Then as now, credit created social as well as economic dependencies, but simultaneously also built bridges between the wealthier and less wealthy segments of the urban population. An entry in a *Vergichtbuch* gave you peace of mind, because if your debtor stopped making repayments you did not have to go to great lengths to prove the existence of said debt – it had been acknowledged before a court. The Basel method subsequently proved to be extremely efficient. Nearly all publicly declared debts were paid on time. There is a certain paradox in all this, for when a debtor insists that a loan is officially recorded, they are protecting themselves against the possibility that the creditor will default on the loan; they want to play it safe – which means that they don't trust the other party. At the same time, though, an official record creates the trust necessary to encourage someone to even consider issuing a loan in the first place, thus encouraging the circulation of capital in the city.[55]

Tally sticks: a pre-modern Bitcoin

35. Reproduction of a simple tally stick

As we have seen, everyone owed someone something. In every European city, microloans were a part of everyday social and economic interactions.

Let us return once more to Paris. There, in the early eighteenth century, 65 per cent of wage workers and 60 per cent of staff were in debt when they died; and studies of eighteenth-century Lisbon and Amsterdam throw up similar numbers.[56] From mid-seventeenth-century Lyonnais bakers' estates we also know exactly how much credit they extended to their customers – or, to be more precise, we know this from the calculations made by their heirs, usually the widow. What makes these calculations so special is their materiality: instead of ink and paper, they consist of wood. They are *batons de comptage*, i.e. tally sticks, into which are carved notches that represent the unpaid sums. From these collections of tally sticks we know that a fifth of Lyons' bakers had allowed their customers to amass tabs of more than 1,000 livres for bread and rolls. The numbers for Lyonnais butchers are similar, and one left behind tally sticks recording debts of several thousand livres.

What exactly is a tally stick? You could call it the Bitcoin of the Middle Ages: a cryptocurrency based on analogue signatures and a decentralised accounting system. It is a virtual currency in the sense that, when you use a tally stick as a method of payment, you are recording a transaction of real value in a virtual medium – or let's call it a symbolic one. Its validity is guaranteed by a network of peers with equal rights and obligations. This is how it works. You take a wooden stick and carve the sales value of a product or service into it. When the deal is agreed you split the stick in two, right through the middle of the tallies; one half is retained by the creditor, the other goes to the debtor. When the day for settling the account comes round, the creditor and debtor fit the two halves together to make sure that neither has manipulated the price after the fact. The split sticks can also be used as currency within a network of peers, who guarantee the validity of the currency – meaning that the butcher can use a tally stick received for a roast (i.e. the money owed to him by the customer) to pay the baker for his weekly bread delivery. He can do that because the baker, being an equal participant in the city's market, knows that he can trust both the butcher and his customers. This is commonly known as 'having confidence in a client's liquidity', which is why the currency was reserved for consumer credit transactions with long-standing customers.[57]

The fact that the tally sticks were so widespread, in all European countries and beyond, is evidence that not only debt and credit transactions but decentralised accounting systems involving networks of equals were a common phenomenon. Researchers have only recently discovered this, and it looks like there is hardly a language – or culture – that does not have a word for these tally sticks. In Latin they are called *tessera* or *talia*; in French they are *batons du compagne*, in Italian *taglie di contrassegno*, in Germany *Kerbhölzer*, in Austria *Raithölzer*, in Switzerland *Alpscheit* or *Tesseln*. Not only that, but in many regions these cryptocurrencies remained in use deep into the twentieth century. According to the latest version of the French *Code civil*, they were still recognised as a payment method in 2016.[58]

Why it's not historians' fault that we forgot all about microloans

Historians used to be interested mainly in the story of progress as envisaged by the nineteenth century. And as it says in the Bible, 'Seek, and ye shall find'. So they found progress wherever they sought it, even if it meant passing over this or that detail. The history of the tally stick is a perfect example. The relevant entry in the *Lexikon des Mittelalters*, a key German-language reference work for the Middle Ages, describes it roughly as follows. In the old days, people used tally sticks to make calculations and record debts. With the development of writing systems and the introduction of paper in the thirteenth century their popularity waned, and they were replaced by sealed letters as a more modern and reliable form of documentary proof. The entry only briefly mentions exceptions in mining (an otherwise reasonably progressive sector) and in England.[59]

This harmless entry concerning a completely harmless artefact demonstrates the way that unthought-out, preconceived ideas can prevent us from apprehending and interpreting historical facts. In this case, the author of the article was simply convinced that economics had risen from its primitive beginnings – when, for want of a writing system, people still had to carve notches into a wooden stick to remember a debt obligation – to a more advanced age when people used pen and paper, i.e. wrote proper invoices and promissory notes. From the wooden stick to the account ledger, and from there straight to the modern credit economy – that is the notion which underlies this encyclopaedia entry. It presents the tally stick as an instrument of primitive economies, which had to give way to progress as long ago as the Middle Ages. But the historical data, that is, the facts as they really are, very much speaks against this.

Archaeologists and historians are finding tally sticks everywhere, across the whole of Europe and the Mediterranean basin, from Kyiv to Brittany and from Stockholm to Tunis, dating from antiquity all the way to the twentieth century. This truly lavish haul is all the more surprising when you consider that destruction is built into the logic of the tally stick as a credit protection tool: once you settled a debt – when you had paid your quarterly butcher's bill or your tab at the baker's – the tally stick was snapped into small pieces or burnt.[60] That so many of them are still extant can only be further proof that peer-to-peer lending was a universal phenomenon, and that debts were not always intended to be paid back.

The question that remains is: when and why did we forget all about it? Who is to blame: modernity? Globalisation? The historian Ludolf Kuchenbuch has a different theory, which he sums up as 'the bankification of the consumer': because transactions, including private ones, were increasingly administered by banks, peer-to-peer lending fell out of fashion.[61] Which makes you wonder if, historically speaking, this is such a recent development, things could change again just as quickly; and current endeavours to move towards complementary regional currencies may prove as future-proof as the cryptocurrencies whose prices have been rising so sharply on the world's financial markets.

Rent-a-Cow: When Town and Country Joined Forces

We will end this chapter by looking at 'cow rental' – a form of centuries-old in-kind credit financing with a long and rich tradition, which shows how urban and rural areas can come together to finance the business of agriculture and hedge against the attendant risks. The technical term for the practice is 'livestock leasing', where a lessor hands over one or more animals to a lessee to look after and make use of for a fixed period. Profits and losses are split according to a pre-agreed ratio, usually fifty-fifty. Sometimes the deal is extended to allow a lessee to add their own animals to the communal stock. Livestock leasing probably happened all over Europe, but most scholarly studies have so far focused on Italy, France, Spain, Austria, Germany and Switzerland.[62]

It is a business model that gives us invaluable insights into how to manage and safeguard an economically sustainable farming business; however, it also serves as a cautionary tale, in that we must not give in to excessively romantic notions of a back-to-basics 'good life'. Medieval farming happened in close proximity to nature, yes – but in the first instance, this meant being exposed to nature's vicissitudes.

Livestock lease is analogous to a simple partnership governed by civil law: at its heart is the establishment of an association that enables the parties involved to realise certain business projects. Such partnership agreements were common in those days, particularly in the context of trade in the Mediterranean, where a *commenda* or *societas maris* (lit. 'marine [trading] company') involved two partners, one of whom would invest the capital, while the other acted as the entrepreneur, i.e. executed the business itself, in his or the investor's name. He would use the capital to buy wheat, wine, salt, cloth and such on the market in Marseilles, hire a ship and crew and set sail for Acre or Cairo, where he would sell the cargo and load the ship with goods bought at local markets, to sell on for a profit in Marseilles. You could make huge amounts of money from such trades but they were extremely risky, because you had to hedge against the loss of goods and crew resulting from bad weather, pirates or the actions of rival enterprises. A *commenda* provided you with at least something of a buffer against such risks, because it meant that both profits and losses were shared.[63]

In the case of livestock lease, we are dealing with a *societas ruralis*: a *commenda* agreement relating to the cultivation of land and livestock farming. In this case, the investor (funder or lender) is the lessor, and the capital consists not of money but animals, mostly cattle, although horses, mules, goats, sheep, pigs, chickens and bees are also listed as capital in some livestock partnership contracts. The entrepreneur is the lessee, who is responsible for looking after the cattle and providing them with shelter and food, in exchange for which he can make use of them for the period defined in the contract. The 'use' to which he put this living capital chiefly involved 'pulling power, manure and milk', i.e. he could yoke the animals to a plough or cart, utilise the manure as precious fertiliser for the fields and turn the milk into cheese. In the case of pigs, their use value consisted of their meat; bees provided honey. The biggest wins came from breeding the animals: the cow could give you a calf, the horse a foal, the pig a piglet, a swarm of bees another swarm of bees. Lessor and lessee usually shared any profits made from breeding equally between them.[64]

Both *commenda* and livestock leasing are designed to alleviate risk by allowing profits and losses to be shared. The risks involved in maritime trade may be more obvious than those involved in farming, but the latter, too, was a treacherous business. Long, cold winters could see spikes in the price of fodder, leading to a sharp increase in the cost of keeping the animals through the winter; adverse weather could ruin your harvest; and disease, storms, fires and robbery could eat into your profits. Breeding was also always an uncertain enterprise, because you had little influence on the quality of the offspring – and the birth itself was a dangerous moment too: stillbirths occurred frequently, and cows often died during labour. By sharing losses as well as gains, both parties were able to better cope with such eventualities.

The *contractus ad caput ferreum* (lit. 'iron cattle contract') worked similarly, but provided no insurance against such risks. Found in, among other places, southern Tyrol, it involved a seigneur (such as a monastery or nobleman) giving a tenant cows to look after (usually six or more). Said tenant was usually a mountain farmer, who would keep and breed the cows and pocket all the profits. When the 'iron cattle contract' came to an end, the farmer merely had to return six cows to the lessor.

All the calves belonged to the farmer, and the landlord merely got back his capital investment (as the old saying went, 'iron cattle never dies').[65] Such processes provided Alpine livestock operations with the support they needed, while also encouraging the expansion of farming in the Alps during the late Middle Ages. What at first sounds almost like a system of subsidies was very risky in practice because the lessee was liable for any loss of animals, whether through accident, theft or illness – and the costs could be punishing.

Rights and responsibilities

The lessee promised to treat the cattle with due care and attention (*cum omni cura et diligentia*), to make sure they were well fed, housed in proper stables during the winter months of November to April and grazed outdoors in the summer. It was his duty to watch over and look after them, and if he neglected the cattle or sold any animals without the lessor's prior consent he had to pay compensation. There were certain exceptions, for instance if the loss of an animal was due to an act of God. Legal records usually gave the example of a wolf which takes a sheep or a horse; in such cases, assuming the farmer could provide some form of proof – the carcass of an animal or its fur, or the head or tail – he was excused from paying compensation. In the case of bees, which could abscond during swarming, an empty beehive and its honeycombs were acceptable as evidence. If a farmer committed fraud, such as by slaughtering a rented cow, he had to fully compensate the lessor.

As well as watching over and caring for the animals, the lessee had to treat them appropriately. Wording around this is commonly found in agreements involving working animals: in Rottweil in the Black Forest, for instance, you were not allowed to 'sublet' a draught horse; you, as the lessee, could spread its manure and harness it to a cart to help you sow, reap or drive to the mill or the market, but you were not allowed to yoke it to a heavy plough or to a harrow unless the lessor gave his express consent.[66] Lessees were also duty-bound to regularly report their earnings and pay out the relevant share of profits as per the agreement's schedule.

The lessor, for his part, was responsible for making sure that the animals did not become a burden for the farmer, and had to pay compensation for any 'imbalance'. One medieval statute concerning the leasing of farm animals, for instance, stipulated that chickens must not be allowed to brood for 'half-profits', and calves and foals too must not be taken on for 'half-profits'. These 'half-profits' refer to certain less productive stages in an animal's life cycle, and the idea here was that the animal must not become a burden for the farmer responsible for feeding and caring for it: for example, broody hens don't lay eggs, and cows don't produce milk when they are pregnant – in both cases, they're no use to the farmer. Calves and foals, too, are unproductive: the farmer cannot put them to work yet, and all they do is eat and take up room. Numerous legal texts stipulated that if this happened, the investor had to pay a subsidy to the farmer for his labour and the cost of the extra fodder.

In part, this also goes for feeding animals in winter, when fodder often had to be bought, sometimes at considerable expense to the lessee. The aforementioned Rottweil statutes also provide for a special contribution from the lessor whenever a sheep 'went cold', i.e. could no longer become pregnant, to compensate the lessee for the 'absent' lamb, which constituted a loss. In certain cases, when there was little effort and expense involved in feeding and caring for the animals – e.g. in the case of sheep or goats which remained on the pastures all year round – the lessee had to pay a 'tax' to balance things out. In Ferrara, it was two blocks of sheep's milk cheese per animal fortnightly. Lessees also had to pay a 'tax' if a horse did not foal; the assumption was that the lessor effectively lost his anticipated profits (i.e.

the foal), while the farmer could still use the horse for other things.

Naturally, these mutual rights and obligations sometimes caused arguments, such as when an animal was 'flawed' or suffered from a disease. What was to be done about a lame horse that could not be harnessed to a cart, or a cow that no longer produced milk? Who bore the risk that a cow met with an accident, or died during calving, resulting in a loss of capital? Who paid for the vet? What happened if one of the partners did not keep to the terms of the contract, which was often verbal, and demanded more money or returned less than he should? Who paid the price for acts of God, i.e. if animals were killed as a result of war, rustling or bad weather? These things were all covered either by precedent or by statute, but, as we know, laws are better suited to solving conflict than preventing it. No wonder, then, that what we know about livestock leasing in the Middle Ages stems largely from court proceedings.

Why lease?

For the lessor the advantage was that, instead of having to pay for the expensive business of wintering your cow, or sending her to the slaughterhouse in autumn or early winter, you could lease her to someone and receive not only a 'rental' income but a share of the offspring (i.e. the value of, say, half a calf) on expiry of the agreement. You could, of course, choose to sell the animal – but cattle prices went down in the autumn, because so many owners wanted to avoid the expense of wintering.

For the lessee, the advantage was that instead of buying a cow, you could lease one at a fifth of the cost. Cows not only produce milk but can be used as draught animals, and the contracts therefore frequently define a timeframe that allows the farmer to use the animal for ploughing and tilling in spring and early summer (April to June). The Magdenau parish's *Offnung* (declaration), for instance, provided that cows should be leased on St Vitus's Day (15 June), so that they may 'earn' their wintering – clearly referring to the work they carried out as draught animals during ploughing, sowing and harvesting. Furthermore, there was the offspring to consider: in those days, cows calved in autumn or spring, which added to the number of animals that needed wintering, and the cow would thus have 'earned' her barn and board.[67] Sometimes the lessor added his own cattle or bought additional animals, in a practice called a 'share rental agreement'. All this benefited both parties, who thus shared the high cost of wintering.

Livestock leasing as a credit transaction

The scenes we've just witnessed sound lovely, don't they? You can picture the lessor bringing his cow into the lessee's barn in June and fetching it again a year later, with a calf in tow. However, such cases seem to have been fairly rare. In practice, livestock rental was usually a loan transaction – or an investment involving a peri-urban farm that needed funds for a specific reason, and which in reality meant the transferral of ownership rights to existing stocks.

Let us consider the following example from St Gall in 1422, gleaned from one of the few surviving livestock leasing contracts.[68] It represents an agreement between the widow Guta Landin from St Gall and the farmer Hans Högger from Hörisau, whereby Landin would 'place' six cattle, two horses, a young horse, three foals, four cows, two year-old calves born the previous year and two calves born in 1422 'in his stables', for which she paid 52 (Carolingian) pounds and 16 ½ pennies. However, all this is legalese and not to be taken literally: rather, we assume that the animals were already in the farmer's possession prior to the contract, and that he merely needed a loan. He had approached

Guta Landin, widow of St Gall's former mayor, who frequently acted as financial backer to St Gall's hospital and other causes, and she had lent Högger the money he needed by buying a 50 per cent share of his business, valued at £52 16½d. She would be repaid the original sum in full on expiry of the loan, and on top of that receive half the livestock's progeny by way of interest. The contract also included a protection clause for Högger: Landin could cancel the contract any time she liked, but it would remain effective until 11 November, the usual date when profits were shared out in St Gall; this gave Högger enough time to profit from the loan, but he would not be saddled with the cost of wintering. In short, Högger's livestock continued to belong to him – though only half of them, with the other half acting as collateral. Transactions such as these gave rise to the terms *Halbvieh* (half-cattle), *Teilvieh* (part-cattle), *Zinskuh* (tax cow) and *Rindermiete* (cattle rent).

Peri-urban farming in the 1400s

Such transactions were common not only in the countryside, and aristocratic or monastic seigneurs were not the only creditors. Ordinary townspeople, too, conducted credit transactions with farmers in the surrounding regions, including private investors, merchants, women, and often also Jewish traders, who were only rarely allowed to purchase real estate and therefore lacked sufficiently large pastures and barns. The practice of renting cattle allowed them to expand their business into livestock trade.

Ulrich Meltinger, a merchant living in Basel during the second half of the fifteenth century, represents a particularly well-documented example of how urban cow rental worked.[69] His ledgers show that alongside many other businesses – owning real estate, trading in wool and textiles, metals, wine, spices, fish, grain, paper and rags – he was also heavily involved in livestock leasing.[70] This urban entrepreneur had signed contracts with no fewer than twenty farmers, whereby they would winter his cattle and raise his calves. The entries in his accounts vividly portray the business relationship between the city and the surrounding region. His investments made him a profit, but he also suffered losses. To begin with, acquiring cattle was not cheap: a cow cost between 40s. and 70s. (£2–£3.50), with pregnant ones the most expensive. Because farmers, as the 'producers', had a hard time competing against cash-rich butchers and cattle merchants in the marketplace, it was often strategically better for them to involve potential buyers from the very start, so that they could share the cost of acquiring the animals required for breeding – as well as any risks. The investor wanted the business to succeed, and would if necessary provide the farmer with fodder or cash on reasonable terms.

Between 1474 and 1477, Meltinger's books contain entries that read roughly as follows: 'Bought a black and brown cow and an eight-day-old calf for Erhard Keller, a Neuwiller farmer. He was to look after the calf for me for four weeks and then bring it to me. For that, I paid him £3, cash in hand. That was on St Martin's day. He brought me the calf as agreed, but it was small and worth little. I also leased him a red cow for proportional rights, for which Keller paid me his share in the amount of 30s. [= £1.50]. Alas, the cow died when in labour with the second calf, which calf now (three years later) has her own calf.'[71]

This shows how precarious a business livestock breeding was: the calf of the black and brown cow evidently did not meet the lessor's expectations, and then the cow herself died while giving birth to her second calf. This meant that, after three years, there was no change in his profit and loss sheet, because he found himself still the owner of one cow and one calf. Many other agreements like this are recorded in his ledger. At Ulrich Metzer's, the first of five calves was stillborn; Heinrich Muspach – a farmer who often also acted as Meltinger's negotiator – had two of Meltinger's cows and two of his calves in his barn, and one of the latter died. Dorothee Rippmann, an expert in agricultural history, estimates an average loss of 10 per cent, i.e. that roughly one in ten calves died at birth or before reaching slaughter age.[72] Elsewhere, things went slightly better, such as in Ruedi Wins's barn in Oberwil, where a cow leased by him in 1471 produced a female calf that same year – which he sold for 17s. – then another the next year, and the year after that a bull calf. According to Meltinger's November 1474 accounts, this particular lease agreement earned him a profit of two young cows.

Researchers have interpreted these contracts in very different ways. Some see them primarily as financial instruments that helped create interdependencies, used by townspeople to control or even exploit rural areas. Such contracts constituted a clash of interests between the two parties involved, because the farmers' dependence on capital injections from the city ultimately resulted in their becoming heavily indebted. Yet the case of Ulrich Meltinger suggests that livestock rental was not inevitably a lucrative business for the investor. In his case, the focus was on meat production. Elsewhere, for instance in the great textile centres of Flanders and the Netherlands, it was far more profitable to engage in leasing sheep, whose wool – an extremely valuable raw material – could supplement imports from England.

Ideas for a mutually supportive agriculture

Livestock leasing provides us with invaluable inspiration for how we might interweave town and country in today's food supply chain. Peri-urban farming is in need of models of such joint endeavours: what might the legal and economic terms look like? Are there models other than the currently predominant cooperatives for us to consider? Are there situations where a private-sector-style business makes more sense than an association? Livestock lease supplies us with a few ideas here: contracts involving joint ownership of capital, risk-sharing and involving urban consumers in the cost of business by integrating them into the 'production process'. In the case of livestock, it means sharing the expense of breeding and raising the animals, but the same principles can be applied to the cost of sowing, irrigating, maintaining, weeding and harvesting vegetable plots, where a capital investor receives a part share of the profits.

There is one aspect in which livestock leasing is analogous to those forest management cooperatives we looked at earlier: both institutions were gradually abolished in many European regions over the course of the nineteenth century. In the opinion of that century's 'modern' legal experts, neither was a proper institution founded on solid and consistent principles. Instead, they were simply contracts that appeared in various forms and guises, and whose terms were solely determined by local customs and habits. And for these modernisers, local customs and habits were the enemy – a mere obstacle on the road to finally getting the whole world under control.[73]

When exactly did we forget about microloans?

What we have discovered in this chapter leaves us wondering why Muhammad Yunus had to rediscover microloans in the late twentieth century. Medieval urban and rural communities were clearly in their own way interested in socially and economically sustainable structures, and wanted to make sure that everyone had access to capital. The *monti di pietà* were the northern Italian cities' response to the Commercial Revolution, which resulted in a never before seen economic boom that changed the world in the short space of a century. Enormous profits were made and enormous riches amassed. No one questioned that the gains belonged to those who produced them – i.e. traders, merchants and bankers – but at the same time, everyone saw that long-term economic growth was impossible without people, and that increased wealth goes hand in hand with a growth in social inequality. The rich became richer, the poor poorer, or, to be more precise, the not-rich bulk of the population was pushed into ever greater misery.

Those who became rich sought to counteract this by coming up with ways to redistribute the wealth, founding banks that we now call MFIs, bringing together the necessary capital resources by making generous deposits and supporting the banks' activities on a voluntary basis. The banks did not mention profit among their objectives. They determined the range of clients, defined interest rates, and stipulated that pledges could be used as collateral, thereby guaranteeing that the not-rich could participate in the financial markets. The sponsors of those banks for the poor were, incidentally, the same people who sponsored the art of the likes of Donatello, Leonardo da Vinci, Michelangelo and Raphael.[74] Other places found other solutions: Basel, for example, made a communal effort to encourage peer-to-peer lending by protecting loans by entering them in public debt books. On examination, these show that, firstly, everyone owed everyone else, and secondly, that even a poor swineherd was regarded as a creditworthy member of society. What is remarkable from our point of view is the city's patent interest in loans as a way to facilitate its citizens' financial affairs – or else Basel's administrators would never have worked so hard to manage them – as well as how transparent the urban credit market was.

Furthermore, market participation was more important than alms, and this was true even for debtors who failed to repay their loans and were exiled from the city. Most eventually returned and settled their debts, meaning that they remained part of the community, both as consumers and as potential investors. Finally, the tally sticks of the Lyonnaise butchers and bakers clearly show that debt can act as the glue that holds a society together. Through their mutual indebtedness, everyone was connected to everyone else: the baker recorded the cost of the bread he delivered to the knife sharpener on a tally stick, which he then used to pay the butcher for his Sunday roast, and the butcher in turn used the stick the next time he had his knives sharpened. In a system like that, being debt-free was a curse – for you only truly belonged if your tally stick had notches on it. This is something we often forget, just as we forget the important role played by payment in goods or services rather than cash, as evidenced by cattle leasing.

In short, medieval societies were eager to enable and safeguard market participation for all: everyone owed everyone else, all kinds of credit instruments were available, and the capital markets were surprisingly accessible.

5

MINIMALISM

'All we need is less'[1]

Is 'less' a solution? Is there still time for us to change course? Can we counteract climate change with abstinence? Some believe that we can, and are looking for simpler ways to live – without SUVs, as carbon-neutrally as possible, with little money and much idealism.

'Minimalism' has become a catch-all for lots of very different movements. The term actually comes from architecture, where it signifies a clarity of form and function. Back in the early twentieth century, Mies van der Rohe, the father of modern architecture, made 'less is more' the underlying principle of his work.[2] In his 1973 book *Small is Beautiful*, the economist E. F. Schumacher called for a return to 'the human scale', and argued that Buddhism supplies us with economic principles beyond the mere maximisation of utility that are better suited to humans as well as to nature.[3] That Kris Kristofferson and Janis Joplin scored a hit with a song that included the line 'Freedom's just another word for nothing left to lose' fit in perfectly with the zeitgeist.

But minimalism is ancient news. History provides a wealth of examples of the refusal of property, and most cultures have exhorted their members to periodically abstain from food, sex or celebrations. On top of that, there are those true experts in frugality who, voluntarily or otherwise, have obeyed strict rules of abstinence. This includes not only monks and nuns in medieval monasteries and convents, but a whole spectrum of communities who have eschewed prevailing social norms. Some are religious, like Pierre Maury and his fellow Cathars, and others include the Monte Verità reformists of the early twentieth century, and certain schools of philosophy, as exemplified by the ancient Greek Cynics.

Diogenes of Sinope: Wealth is the Vomit of Fortune

Diogenes of Sinope, the philosopher who lived in a barrel, is perhaps the most famous of all ancient minimalists. He had studied under Antisthenes, who some say was the founder of Cynicism – although Socrates is also often credited with it. This school of minimalist philosophy, which will be the subject of the present chapter, included among its many members Crates of Thebes as well as Hipparchia, one of the oldest-known female Greek philosophers.

To start with, a little background. The Athenians of the fifth century BC were an advanced people. In fact, they thought they were the most sophisticated civilisation on the planet. They did indeed have a good reason for thinking so: politically, they were far ahead of many others. More than two and a half thousand years ago they invented democracy, the rule of the people, where everyone had a vote. Almost everyone, that is, because there were a few, necessary, minor limitations: slaves, women and foreigners (known as 'metics') were excluded from 'the people'. The vote was thus restricted to 10 to 20 per cent of Athens's residents. Still, it didn't do the city's reputation as the inventor of democracy any harm.

Athens's economy was booming too. In the sixth century BC, the great reforming statesman Solon had liberated the peasantry and prohibited bonded labour, thus triggering an economic upswing that turned the city into a flourishing centre of trade and commerce. What the Athenians could be proudest of, though, was that they had invented philosophy. Although a fly did immediately land in the ointment of that achievement, when Socrates (469–399 BC), their first and greatest philosopher, was put on trial by his fellow citizens and sentenced to death for impiety and corrupting the minds of the city's youth.

What does all this have to do with minimalism, you ask? Well, what Athens's virtuous citizens minded most about Socrates was his unconventional way of life. Today, we would call it minimalist: he lived and taught in the marketplace, in full view of the public, chose not to earn a living, and cared for neither wealth nor reputation. He made the Athenians exceedingly uncomfortable. Status, nice clothes and opulent feasts were unimportant to the philosopher, who pursued a very modest lifestyle. He might not sound like much of a criminal, but many of his sermons were interpreted as critical of the Athenian citizens' way of life; and indeed, Socrates wasn't shy to let you know exactly what he thought. He accused them of caring more about property, wealth, reputation and status than about seeking deeper insights into the world, the truth, and focusing on the well-being of their souls.

You might say that Western philosophy was born with the spirit of minimalism, in Athens in the fifth century BC. Socrates' students, chief among them Plato and Aristotle, took his ideas further: Plato (428–347 BC) founded his own academy of philosophy around ten years after Socrates' death, on his property just outside the city walls. It is believed that the Platonic Academy operated for 700 years, and it has been a continuous source of fascination for us for more than two thousand years. During the Renaissance, in 1510, Pope Julius II commissioned Raphael to paint a gigantic seven-metre-wide fresco of the academy's famous alumni on the wall of his private apartment at the Vatican, in the Stanza della Segnatura, where he would sign important documents. At the centre are its founders – Plato, sporting an impressive grey beard, and Aristotle, dressed in a blue *himation* and holding a book.

36. Raphael, *The School of Athens* in the Vatican's Stanza della Segnatura, 1510–11

Diogenes: the minimalist prototype

As your eye scans the assembled philosophers, it can't help but stop at the very centre of the fresco. There, lounging on the otherwise empty steps, is a strange figure: bearded, barefoot, bare-chested, half draped in a blue robe, a beggar's bowl by his side. The old man is engrossed in reading a text of some kind. It almost seems as if Raphael deliberately placed him there as the real, if slightly off-centre, focal point of the roughly semicircular cast of characters directly below Plato and Aristotle.

The man is Diogenes of Sinope, a rare beast among even these rare philosophical beasts. Diogenes represents a radical form of Socratic teaching. Like Socrates, he did not give a fig for status or renown; like him, he exhorted people to care about their souls and true happiness rather than money and possessions. Yet Diogenes was much more extreme: he offended people, and provoked them with his occasionally sensational public appearances. It is said that Plato called him 'a Socrates gone mad'. Diogenes is another person often credited with founding the school of Cynics, literally 'the dogs', a trend in Greek philosophy that we would nowadays categorise as minimalist.

The few reliable facts we know about his life won't take long to summarise. He was born the son of a banker and money changer in the port of Sinope, in northern Anatolia, on the Black Sea. Following a transgression of some kind (the details are unknown), he was thrown out of the city and sought refuge in Athens. There he joined a philosophy college founded by Antisthenes, the first Athenian Cynic. On a sea voyage he was captured by pirates and sold into slavery, and became a private tutor in Corinth. Following his release he lived by turns in Corinth and Athens, where he wrote several works, none of which have survived. He died, presumably in Corinth, in around 320 BC; some believe that he died in 323 BC, on the same day as Alexander the Great.[4]

To balance out the sparse data about his life, we have a wealth of anecdotes about him. He captured people's imagination for centuries, and each generation told its own stories. In the third century AD, i.e. more than five hundred years after his death, a Roman historian of philosophy collected all the tales and legends he could find and wrote them down in a still extant, ten-volume series about the ancient philosophers' life and work. This historian – Diogenes Laertius – conscientiously details all his sources; and we owe him a debt of gratitude for thus ensuring the survival of information that was contained in sources which have since been lost to us.

Diogenes and the origins of the 'tiny house' movement

Why have people been so fascinated by ancient Greek minimalism? The reason is the combination of self-reliance, abstinence and joy that Diogenes embodied like none of its other, later champions. He lived out his ideal of frugality as a sort of philosophical vagrant, going so far as to make his home in a *pithos* in Athens's agora, the central marketplace, when a prospective rental contract fell through. A *pithos* was a bulky, thick-walled, big-bellied storage vessel – some were taller than a grown man. They resembled amphorae, but usually had a flat bottom. These containers were used to store grain, wine, salt or oil and were moved using ropes attached to loops in the top half of the vessel.

The advantage of living in such an unusual home was that it was flexible. It allowed Diogenes to move whenever he thought it necessary.

There is evidence showing that it was indeed possible to find shelter in *pithoi*, and that they sometimes acted as temporary housing. For instance, the ancient comic poet Aristophanes declared that the rural population lived in just such clay vessels when they fled to Athens during the Peloponnesian War. Archaeologists have supplied additional evidence to suggest that you could sleep in them with the discovery that *pithoi* were used as coffins: sixteen specimens containing human remains were found near Sevastopol in Crimea, each around 130 cm tall and just under 70 cm in diameter. Image 38 shows how the dead were positioned in the barrel. It is possible that Diogenes, who once called death the 'brother' of sleep, deliberately evoked the similarity between home and coffin, and that he was staging a tongue-in-cheek performance of extreme frugality by 'living' in a 'coffin'.

Diogenes kept his head above water by begging. But beyond that, he dedicated himself fully to philosophy; he went to where people gathered, made speeches and put on performances

37. Diogenes in his barrel, in conversation with a philosopher

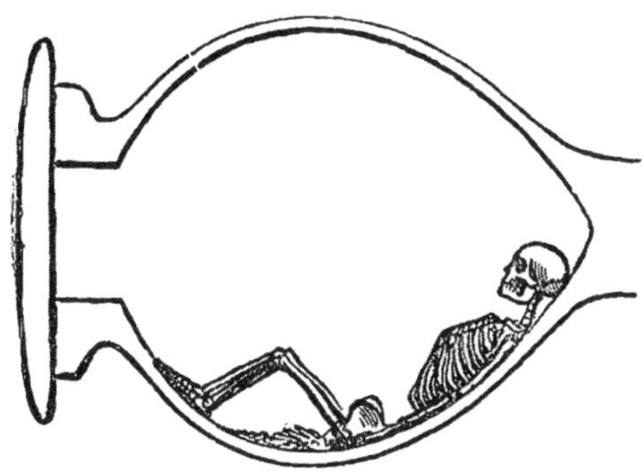

38. *Pithos* or dolium, containing body. From Samuel Birch's *History of Ancient Pottery* (1858)

designed to challenge spectators' preconceptions. He thought that living in tune with nature was the only possible happy life. The gods, he said, have made life so easy for us humans; and yet we insist on making things difficult for ourselves. Why? Because we think we need honey cakes and lotions and other rubbish. And so we started trading stuff, going to a lot of trouble to endlessly exchange one worthless thing for another. Diogenes simply could not fathom why someone would spend a fortune on a marble statue but consider two copper coins too high a price for a bushel of porridge.[5]

The path to freedom begins with frugality

Key to his philosophy was the concept of frugality, which he believed enabled humans to attain maximum and true freedom. When Alexander the Great, the most famous of all Greek rulers, visited Corinth, he assumed that the city's famous philosopher would come and see him. Diogenes, however, made no attempt to introduce himself to the famous king. So Alexander went to him. Diogenes was, as usual, sunning himself by his barrel, and made no move to get up when he saw the ruler approach with his entourage. Alexander was surprised, but didn't let it show. They greeted each other politely, and when the conversation started flagging Alexander decided to show off his generosity. He asked the impecunious philosopher if there was anything he could do for him. Diogenes thought about it briefly and replied: 'Actually, there is something – could you move a little? You're blocking the sun.' Alexander's entourage was shocked. Surely it bordered on *lèse-majesté*? But Alexander showed no sign of being offended. On the contrary, he was deeply impressed by this eccentric philosopher. On the way back, when his companions started making fun of Diogenes, he told them to stop. 'Leave it be,' he supposedly said. 'If I wasn't Alexander, I'd want to be Diogenes.'[6]

Provocation as a tactic

Diogenes' philosophical method was to continuously attack convention, tradition and custom. He wanted to convert people, not, like Socrates, through conversation but by means of sheer provocation. Unlike the Athenian Socrates, Diogenes was a refugee from the Black Sea coast; he neither had relatives in the city nor held public office, and as a result was both more independent and more radical than his predecessor.

These days, we would call Diogenes' attempts to get people's attention a sort of performance art. He knew that they needed scandal and spectacle. Once, the story goes, when he realised that no one was listening to his speech, he started warbling. Immediately a small audience assembled. 'When someone acts like a clown, you come running,' he admonished them, 'but when they try to talk about serious things, you couldn't care less.'[7] Another anecdote describes how, during the Isthmian Games in Corinth, he made a speech about resisting our harmful appetites, concluding with the example of Hercules: just as he had mucked out the Augean stables, said Diogenes, people urgently needed to muck out their souls. To make sure that the spectators would remember his words, he added an unforgettable full stop: he squatted down on the podium on which he had been orating and defecated.[8]

The Greeks saw themselves as thoroughly tolerant, and sufficiently respectful of and relaxed about oddballs and eccentrics; they were therefore not particularly bothered by the Cynics – even if the latter turned their noses up at everything which the smart set considered sophisticated. In fact, the Cynics despised all supposedly 'done' things. While wealthier Athenians had chefs, wore fancy clothes, surrounded themselves with brown-nosers and minions, and kept mistresses rather than visit a brothel or inn, the Cynics always did the exact opposite. They wanted to shock people, and to radically interrogate existing norms and conventions.[9]

Wealth: the 'vomit of fortune'

Many memorable sayings have been attributed to Diogenes; one is that 'wealth is the vomit of fortune'. For him, greed was the root of all evil.[10] He allegedly once explained the true nature of happiness to Alexander the Great thus: 'Not having any money', he told the king, 'is not poverty. There is nothing wrong with begging. But to want everything, and to be willing to use violence to get it – as you do, Alexander – *that* is poverty.'[11] Material possessions are a burden, a prison, but voluntary poverty is (as Crates of Thebes argued) the 'starting point of freedom'. Again and again, the Cynics mocked peers who submitted to the pressures and obligations of private property. Bion, a second-generation Cynic, once said about a rich miser: 'He does not own his wealth, his wealth owns him.'[12] These pronouncements betray an almost naive and irreverent delight in provocation, and the Cynics' minimalist lives lent them a very particular authority. If you have nothing, you can dare anything – because you have nothing to lose.

Asceticism: the art of needing nothing

Rather than insisting on constantly discussing things and studying old books, the Cynics saw their philosophy as a radical practice that required daily exercise. This daily exercise was called *askesis*, and took its name from the training regime of the athletes in the city's gymnasia. The Cynics believed that asceticism was preventative, prophylactic. Every day they trained their bodies in the art of resilience and their minds in the art of concentration. The only difference between them and athletes was their goal: whereas the latter trained their bodies in order to one day win a contest in a stadium, the former trained body and mind to strengthen their willpower and resilience. It was a regimen for a life lived in harmony with nature, on the road to true freedom and the absence of need. Someone who regularly practised drinking only water, sleeping on the ground, dressing plainly and eating simple foods, and who was used to enduring both heat and cold, would be able to bear the vicissitudes of fate with dignity. It was not a matter of self-denial for its own sake, though, or for a higher purpose; rather, it was turning philosophy into practice; they lived freely, wanting nothing, without a homeland, as beggars and vagabonds, a hand-to-mouth existence, from one day to the next.

Crates of Thebes: the mediator

Crates was a prosperous landowner from Thebes, of noble birth, with a numerous staff, who lived in a large house with an imposing entrance hall and was elegantly dressed. At some point, though, he realised that his wealth did not protect him or provide him with any security, that everything was in constant flux and uncertain, and that he did not need any of it to be truly happy. He sold everything he had, shared the proceeds among his fellow citizens, and from then on led a life of radical poverty.[13] Several sources suggest that the reason for his metamorphosis was that he could no longer bear the worries and bother of business, that he wanted to be rid of all his responsibilities, and therefore sought refuge in the philosophy of poverty. Today, we would probably surmise that he suffered from burn-out. The way he changed his life so radically made him a much-sought-after mediator when conflicts arose. He was not interested in unsettling his fellow humans; in fact, he was a good listener. It is said that his peers nicknamed him Thurepanoiktes, literally 'door opener', because he was valued everywhere as someone you could have a sensible conversation with, and every door was thus always open to him. Unlike the hectic, restless citizens of Athens, he had one exceedingly valuable resource in abundance: time. This meant that he could act as peacemaker and umpire. One source describes how, just as Hercules was celebrated by the poets for conquering monsters, both animal and human, and casting them out of this world, Crates fought wrath, envy, covetousness, greed and all the other corrupt desires of the human soul.

Crates of Thebes lived and preached the simple life as an antidote to the miseries of his age. He advised his pupils to 'gather lentils and beans, my friend. That way, you'll vanquish want and poverty!' Elsewhere, he talks of poverty as his friend, not his enemy. He suffered from kyphosis, but practised asceticism and went for a jog every day: 'I run for my spleen, my liver and my stomach,' he said. When he once saw a young athlete feeding his massive body with wine and meat, he told him, 'You are a strange bird. Stop reinforcing the walls of your prison.'[14]

He could be harsh too. He flung some stinging insults at the rich: 'You ought to string yourselves up! You have beans, figs, water, clothes from Megara, are prolific merchants and farmers, yet you are traitors, tyrants and murderers, and commit all sorts of crimes instead of keeping your heads down. We, however, live in peace, because Diogenes of Sinope has liberated us from all evils. We have nothing, but have everything; you have

39. Crates and Hipparchia. Fresco, Casa della Farnesina, Museo delle Terme, Rome

everything, but have nothing, because you are irritable, jealous, fearful and arrogant.'[15]

One of his students compellingly describes how liberated he felt after he transferred from the academy in Athens to Crates' school. At the Athenian academy, worrying about everyday things had almost driven him mad: he had needed sandals, a cloak and servants, and constantly had to shop for food – fancy white bread, good wine and delicacies – for the communal meals. Now that he had joined Crates, however, rye bread and herbs was all he needed, and he no longer required any staff. Life was so much simpler. And whenever he did feel like a little luxury, there were other ways to get it: for instance, if he wanted to take a bath, he went to the public ones, and if he wanted a more elaborate breakfast than usual, he could obtain a nice little meal by going to the blacksmith's and roasting a sprat over the fire. In the summer, he said, he slept in temples, in the winter in bath houses, and his former desire for luxury and fear of poverty had vanished.[16]

Minimalists: the cosmopolitans of antiquity

The Greeks were, by modern standards, extremely xenophobic. They divided the world into 'them' and 'us', Greeks and non-Greeks (barbarians). The Cynics, however, thought such distinctions meaningless. All they cared about was someone's disposition. It didn't matter where they came from, or what language they spoke. They were in fact convinced that they could learn a lot from the same foreigners whom the average Athenian looked down on. The Cynics believed that everyone, Greek and non-Greek, free or enslaved, was connected. Indeed, they went further: their philosophy embraced the whole of nature, animals and plants, in one all-encompassing, comprehensive world view.[17]

What happened next?[18]

The Cynics appeared on the scene at a time when the world was changing. For one thing, the concept of the Greek city state (*polis*) had been turned upside down by Alexander the Great's conquests. Yet many were far from ready to rethink their traditional roles in communal and political life. They stuck firmly to what they thought was the only right solution, namely a system based on small, regional political units. At the very same time, Diogenes was preaching cosmopolitanism. He declared himself as a citizen without a city (*a-polis*) and without a homeland (*a-oikos*): a citizen of the world (*kosmopolites*). Before then, such cosmopolitanism was generally viewed as a negative, which by definition devalued the existing city states. Few could imagine a future without them. They suffered from a fear of loss. Meanwhile, the Cynics argued that we should not be afraid of loss and should stop clinging to old things, and promised a new form of freedom.

Their message was welcomed by many people. Cynicism is the only ancient philosophy that turned into something like a mass movement. We know more than eighty representatives by name, and there is evidence of a further thirty anonymous Cynics.[19] Our fascination with them continued down the centuries, and ensured that their writings were passed down and expanded on. Even though Diogenes of Sinope never created his own academy, the philosophy spread across the entire Mediterranean region and beyond. The Cynics' way of life remained attractive to successive generations, and later appealed also to the Romans: Dio Chrysostom, Epictetus and Lucian were among the most important representatives of Roman Cynicism, and for three years the Roman Empire was ruled by an emperor – Julian (AD 361–363) – who was well disposed towards the Cynics.[20]

St Francis of Assisi: Money is Dung

Francis of Assisi was the Diogenes of the Middle Ages. Just as the Greeks in Athens had to tolerate the sight of the Cynics and their constant provocations, the residents of northern Italy's wealthy medieval cities had to put up with the presence of the Franciscans, young men of working age who eschewed the middle-class life and had no fixed abode, no family, no proper job and instead wandered through the streets, preaching and living off alms. Francis lived up to Diogenes' example in every way – except for the barrel. Instead, he occasionally spent the night in a walk-in baker's oven. Francis also dealt with Emperor Otto IV exactly as Diogenes had with Alexander, and simply ignored him. When Otto happened to be in the area one day,

Francis declared he didn't have time to meet him because he was too busy praying.[21]

Who was Francis of Assisi?

Luckily for us, people in the Middle Ages put a lot more in writing than the ancient Greeks. Francis himself wrote a lot – not only several iterations of a set of regulations for his religious community (the Rule of St Francis), but also letters, poems (including the famous 'Canticle of the Sun') and, finally, his last will and testament. One of his early companions, Thomas of Celano, composed no fewer than three biographies of the founding father of the Franciscan order, each of which focused on a different aspect of his life and work. Others copied him, and wrote about their version of St Francis. Biographies of other members of the order have also survived, as have numerous chronicles, letters and stories; the most famous of these is perhaps the chatty friar Salimbene di Adam's chronicle, a sort of diary about his itinerant life, which took him from the court of the French king to the vineyards of Bordeaux. Thanks to this cornucopia, we know an astonishing amount about the thirteenth century's voluntary poor.[22]

Born with a silver spoon in his mouth

St Francis was born in 1181. His father, the successful Assisan merchant Pietro di Bernardone, travelled a lot. The boy grew up sheltered and wanting for nothing, and his future was assured: there was no question that, at some point, he would take over the family business. He was popular and had lots of friends whom he liked to spoil, and he never missed an opportunity to party. He appears to have been a spendthrift. In the way he dressed, too, he was prone to excess and filled his wardrobe with expensive clothes. His vanity was such that, to catch people's

40. The oldest existing portrait of St Francis of Assisi, painted during his lifetime (before 1226)

attention, he had his tailor combine the finest cloth with the cheapest, i.e. blend materials of very different kinds and quality.[23] For a time, he was something like the ringleader of Assisi's gang of teenagers, which suggests that he possessed a certain charisma even as an adolescent.

When he was around twenty years old, however, something unexpected happened. He went off to war – a small war, with the nearby city of Perugia – and in 1203 was imprisoned for almost a year. It was evidently a life-changing experience. In 1204, he returned home a different man. The boy who had so recently been the local youth's high-spirited leader now avoided human contact, spent most of his time outdoors in the local woods, withdrew from the world and muttered unintelligibly. One minute he wanted to become a knight; the next he decided to join the city's leper community; the next he declared that he would go to Apulia (which he actually did). Were he around today, he might have been diagnosed with chronic depression.

His mother tried to convince Francis to join the family business; eventually, he relented. He went on a business trip for his father, where he sold the entire store of goods he was carrying, as well as his horse – because he wanted to return home on foot, 'free of all burdens' – and offered the proceeds to the priest of the little church of San Damiano, just outside Assisi. The priest refused the money, possibly because he was afraid of incurring Pietro's ire, so Francis threw the coins at him through the window. The great schism between Francis and his father came in early 1207, when Pietro dragged Francis to the local bishop, in the hope that the prelate might bring the young man to his senses. When this, too, failed he publicly disowned his son. A large crowd of Assisi's citizens was present to witness the deed, but Francis stood there unmoved, reacting if anything with relief, demonstrating his willingness to be disowned by stripping and handing every single item of clothing – including his underwear (*femoralia*) – over to his father.

This dramatic moment continues to capture people's imagination to this day, and it is one of the most famous and popular anecdotes from the life of St Francis. Giotto's painting of the scene on the walls of Santa Croce in Florence vividly shows the rage and helplessness felt by Pietro. He is so upset that the bystanders have to hold him back, to prevent him from beating his son up or violently forcing him to come home. A barefoot and naked Francis, meanwhile, finds refuge in the folds of the bishop's cloak.[24]

'This is what I want'

Francis was now free of all worldly possessions and the responsibilities that come with them. He began restoring churches and other buildings. For a year he lived like a hermit, looking like an ancient philosopher with his simple belted robe and staff, and his feet shod in light sandals. He must have been cold a

41. Francis breaks with his father (Giotto, 1318–25)

lot, because although Umbria's winters aren't usually freezing, they are not exactly warm either. Animals sometimes kept him company, and he shared his lodgings – in barns or stables – with them. One day, most likely on 24 February 1208, Francis attended a service at Portiuncula, a small church he had rebuilt. The gospel reading was from Matthew 10:9–10, which describes Jesus sending his apostles out into the world. Francis was enthralled by what he heard, and immediately after the reading asked the priest to explain the text. Thomas of Celano, one of Francis's biographers, turns this episode into the key event in the saint's life. The priest, he writes, patiently explained everything to him, step by step; and when Francis heard that the apostles were allowed to possess neither gold nor silver nor copper, that they must not take a bag with them on their journey, or a change of clothing, or a staff or bread, and that they must only preach the Kingdom of Heaven and repentance, he suddenly knew: 'This is what I want, this is what I ask for, this I long to do with all my heart!'[25]

In Celano's rendering, the moment marks the conclusion of a long-drawn-out and often painful process of transformation, which started with Francis's period of depression following his release from prison in 1204. He saw everything clearly now. He knew what kind of life he wanted to live: one of extreme poverty, free of the burden of property, free from the pressure to earn money and multiply his wealth, free to dedicate himself to nature and his fellow man. Others followed his example, and the Franciscan movement soon gained momentum.

He was an enthusiastic preacher. According to Celano 'his word was like a blazing fire', which penetrated into the hearts of those who heard him and filled them with wonder.[26] Francis truly was a changed man. People felt that he was speaking directly to them, and they sought him out and joined him. In the summer of 1209, he and eleven companions travelled to Rome to obtain Pope Innocent III's blessing. The pope recognised them as a new community based on voluntary poverty and added them to a list of official mendicant movements, which already included the Dominicans, founded by another merchant's son, Dominicus, from Caleruega near Burgos in Castile.[27] The movement proved contagious, and when the Franciscans returned from Rome they acquired more and more followers. Among them was Clara, Francis's close childhood friend, who secretly ran away from home in 1211 to join him. During this period, the community was separated into several smaller groupings of no fixed abode. Several sources describe them sleeping in caves, in the open air or in lodgings provided by hospitable locals. This is also where the aforementioned bakers' ovens came into play, large ovens found in fields outside Tuscan villages, whose stone walls retained the heat from the day's baking and thus provided shelter from the autumn chill.

Celano reports that, in addition to refusing a permanent home, the Franciscans had contempt for anything which they considered superfluous. Their tables were bare, and they had nothing that was not essential, no household 'stuff', no knick-knacks, no unnecessary furniture, books or bed sheets – calling to mind the modern-day Marie Kondo phenomenon. Speaking of bed sheets, Celano adds, Francis categorically refused to sleep on upholstery or feather pillows. In fact, he was practically allergic to them, and even when a host sorted him out with a comfortable bed he would simply lie down on the floor to sleep. He had a similar attitude to non-essential clothing and soft textiles, and regarded fastidious dressing as a sign of an extinguished spirit.[28]

Money is dung – and so is property

Francis despised money and called it 'dung'. He may not, like Diogenes, have believed that wealth was the 'vomit of fortune', but he did believe that it was the biggest obstacle on the road to a good life.[29] Anyone who wanted to join the order had to give away everything they had. Unlike 'traditional' monks, such as the Benedictines – who also took a vow of poverty – the Franciscans eschewed not only private property but also collective property. It meant that the community as a whole, not only individual members, was forbidden from owning tangible things, including houses, and from having any kind of wealth.

It was a difficult proposition, because the movement grew so quickly that it was soon short of accommodation, and additional funds were needed for the everyday expenses that arise when a large number of people live together. The early texts are unambiguous: there was tension. But the movement's founder didn't care. He remained an extremist. When Francis returned to the little church of Portiuncula to speak at a gathering, and heard that the citizens of Assisi had built a house for the brothers to stay in, he immediately climbed up to the roof and started pulling off the slates and tiles. He ordered the others to do the same and to completely demolish the house – or, as Celano puts it, 'this monstrous thing contrary to poverty'. He would have torn it down to its foundations had the watchmen not convinced him to stop, by explaining that the house would not be fully owned by the brothers but continue to belong to the town.

A similar event occurred in Bologna, where the citizens had also built a house for the Franciscan community. Francis refused to enter it, and ordered it to be cleared immediately. Even the brothers who were ill had to leave, he said. Only when Ugolino di Ostia, cardinal-protector of the Franciscan order, explained that the house belonged to the pope, who had merely made it available to the brothers, did Francis allow his fellow brothers to move back in. (Celano could personally vouch for the truth of the tale: he was one of the sick brothers evacuated that day.) As Francis drily observed, 'We can do without ownership according to the form prescribed,' but 'we cannot live without the use of houses.'[30] This, then, is the Franciscan alternative to property: using objects, buildings, gardens and land – but without right of ownership.

International expansion

In the course of the thirteenth century, the movement spread from the town of Assisi across Europe like wildfire. After the order's official launch in 1209 Francis embarked on an itinerant lifestyle, travelling through Italy with a group of companions, preaching the simple life. Assisi became the centre of the order's activities, and as early as 1217 the brothers advanced into Spain, France, Hungary, Morocco and Egypt. Early communities also sprang up in Damietta, Tripoli, Jerusalem and Acre, but were short-lived. When Francis died in October 1226 his movement had reached far beyond Italy's borders, into most countries around the wider Mediterranean region. Two generations later, at the end of the 1200s, there were around 1,500 Franciscan communities across Europe, from Syracuse in the south to Enköping in the north, from Caffa and Riga in the east to Lisbon and Ardfert in the west.[31]

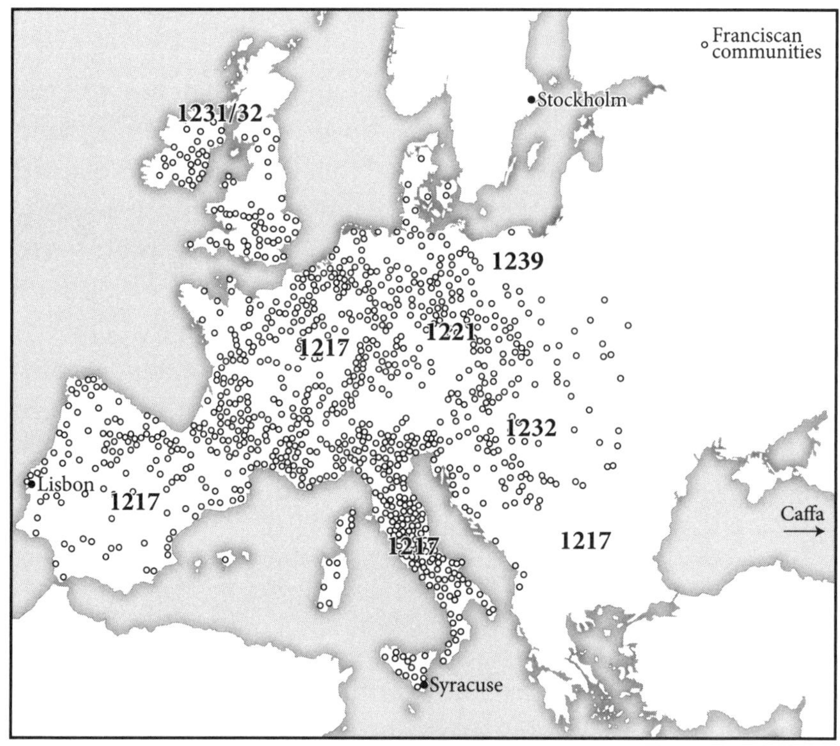

42. Map showing the locations of Franciscan communities in Europe *c.* 1300

Assisi, Whitsun 1217

Francis ceaselessly made travel plans. First he wanted to go to Syria, then to Spain and Morocco, after that to France. Yet he was forced to keep postponing his plans due to illness. May 1217 saw the first annual meeting of friars in Assisi. More than 5,000 are said to have attended what seems to have been a sort of Franciscan Woodstock. There was a proper festival atmosphere – the brothers rejoiced at seeing each other again, and sang and made merry all day long. The brothers slept under the stars, on simple mats of straw; indeed, some sources nicknamed it *il capitolo delle stuoie*, 'the chapter of straw mats'. Even the citizens of Assisi were overjoyed, and catered for the assembled Franciscans.[32]

It was over that weekend that the order first discussed how best to spread word of the new way of life beyond the Alps, and decided to send advance parties to Spain, France, Hungary and Germany. They needed hardly any kit, because the brothers would live from what they could find along the way or obtain from begging. Francis said he himself would go to France – but this journey, too, came to nothing.

Instead, he boarded a ship bound for Syria, only to be blown off course by an adverse wind, ending up on the Dalmatian coast. Disappointed, he unsuccessfully sought passage on board a ship setting sail for Ancona; so he and his companions smuggled themselves on board and completed the voyage as stowaways. A fellow passenger and a sailor provided them with food and drink until they arrived back in Italy, safe and sound.[33] Francis's long-planned journeys only came to fruition two years later, in summer 1219. He finally made it to Syria, where he met the sultan, who went so far as to invite this odd holy man to his palace. Their conversations inaugurated the inter-religious dialogues between Islam and Christianity that were later embedded in the tradition of the Franciscan and other mendicant orders. Altogether, Francis spent a whole year in the Middle East.[34]

Travelling on no money in the thirteenth century: from Trient to Augsburg

The foray into Germany that the friars had planned in 1217 initially came to nothing, and was only carried out four years later. Jordan of Giano, a member of that expedition, reports in his memoirs that Francis suddenly remembered at the 1221 annual meeting that the order still hadn't made headway in Germany. Too ill to make the announcement himself, he delegated the task to Brother Elias, while crouched at his feet like a little child. So it fell to Brother Elias to communicate Francis's wish, which was roughly this: beyond the Alps there was a country called Germany, where lived pious Christians known in Italy primarily for their pilgrimages to Rome in the summer heat, pearls of sweat forming on their brows, with long walking sticks in their hands and wearing wide, shapeless shoes. So far, the brothers who had been sent to Germany had returned each time without success, having had only bad experiences and been chased away for begging and vagrancy; now, though, they would have to pluck up the courage for another attempt.

Twenty-seven men came together in a diverse group: seven Italians, seven Germans, a Hungarian and twelve others of unknown nationality. Among them were Thomas of Celano; John of Plano Carpini, who was multilingual and later composed one of the first travelogues of Asia written by a European; and Jordan of Giano, the chronicler of the order's German branch. The latter recounts that the group first met in Trient in Switzerland, where a wealthy citizen called Peregrinus equipped them all with a fresh set of clothes before selling everything he had and joining them on their journey to Germany; that they paired up, and set off on 29 September, travelling via Bolano, Brixen and Vipiteno; and that they would fall asleep at night on empty stomachs and wake up hungry the following morning. But they walked on, even though half a mile later their knees trembled, their legs failed them and their eyesight became blurry. They ate fruit and herbs they picked along the way – it was never enough to still their hunger, but it felt good to have at least something to eat in their pockets.

Finally, they reached Matrei in eastern Tyrol, where they met two generous people who sold them bread for a couple of coins, which they augmented with turnips. Then they continued walking, heading for Mittenwald in Bavaria, reaching Augsburg a good two weeks later on 15 October. The bishop and his deputy were delighted to welcome them. The latter even put his office building at their disposal, where they could recover from the arduous journey across the Alps. The very next day, however, Caesar of Speyer convened the brothers and dispatched them to Würzburg, Mainz, Worms, Speyer, Strasbourg, Cologne, Salzburg and Regensburg in small teams.[35]

Travelling on no money in the thirteenth century: from Augsburg to Canterbury

On 10 September 1224, nine Franciscans arrived in England. This party, too, was remarkably diverse and international: Agnellus of Pisa, Richard of Ingworth, Richard of Devon, a very young William of Ashby, Henry of Treviso from Lombardy, Laurence of Beauvais, a craftsman, William of Florence and the probationers Melioratus and James Ultramontanus. The friars had embarked at Fécamp in France equipped with a few basic necessities, and after landing at Dover travelled onwards to Canterbury. There they initially put up at the hospital for poor priests, but later found a small chamber in the nearby schoolhouse, where they would spend their evenings sitting by the fire, drinking home-brewed beer and discussing the events of the day.

The first to join the party in England was Brother Solomon, who was consequently cast out by his family. The second, William of London, was a London tailor; the third, Joce of Cornhill, was a cleric who soon departed for Spain, where he lived (and worked) until his death; the fourth, John, later went to Ireland. Others, such as Vincent of Coventry, Adam of Exeter and Richard Rufus of Cornwall, were scholars; and it seems that numerous knights and noblemen also joined up. The knight Richard Gubiun, for instance, supported the community in Northampton by donating parts of his estate; though his benevolence and generosity vanished the moment his own son decided to become a Franciscan brother. That was taking things too far, thought Gubiun, and he ejected them from his lands and demanded his son's return. The 'guardian' of the house, Peter the Spaniard, proposed that the boy should choose for himself, and when the latter, without hesitation, chose voluntary poverty, his parents were so moved that they changed their minds and henceforth supported their son and his community however they could.

We even have membership numbers for this early period: Thomas of Eccleston notes that, at the time of writing – i.e. around 1255–6 – there were 1,241 brothers in England and Wales, spread across forty-nine settlements.[36] This means that each community comprised on average about twenty-five members. In the following years they added another thirteen houses, bringing the total to sixty-two. In 1539, during Henry VIII's Reformation, every single one of them fell victim to the dissolution of monasteries.

The architecture of a life without possessions

Because the Franciscans refused any and all property, many of their houses were handed over to the relevant parish. The community gained supporters all over England. One of them was the Countess of Leicester, 'who in all things cared for them even as a mother cares for her sons'. In London, a certain John Iwyn bought a piece of land and gave the Franciscans right of use; he himself later entered the order.[37] William Joynier, lord mayor of London, built them a chapel and small house with his own money, and made regular donations; Peter de Helyland gave them £100 for an infirmary at their London base; Henry de Fowie and Salekin de Basing had water pipes laid for them, with the generous support of the king himself. A merchant called Robert de Mercer gave them a house to use in Oxford, where so many students, graduates and noblemen joined the community that they soon needed a larger dwelling. Thankfully, a local miller called Richard transferred the deeds to a piece of land, together with a house, to the city for the brothers' use. In Cambridge, they at first lived in the old synagogue next door to the prison. In Shrewsbury, a burgher named Lawrence Cox built them a house on a plot of land donated by the king; when he realised, too late, that the stone walls did not meet the requirements of voluntary poverty (which stipulated that the walls should be made of wood or lime and straw), he had it torn down and rebuilt from mud.[38]

The cosmopolitans of the Middle Ages

Mobility was as much a hallmark of medieval minimalism as it had been of its classical predecessors. Being independent of a family, flexible and self-sufficient gives you more room to manoeuvre, and means that you can make your home more or less anywhere. It is unsurprising, therefore, that in the 1200s – half a century before Marco Polo – members of the mendicant orders were among the first Europeans to travel to Asia. Their plan was to reach Karakorum and eventually Beijing.

The Franciscan friar John of Plano Carpini is a wonderful example of this mobility. The Italian was part of the expedition to Germany in 1221, and became warden (*custos*) of Saxony, whence he oversaw the order's spread across Bohemia, Poland, Hungary, Denmark and Norway. He was appointed minister of the province of Germany in 1228, briefly spent time in Spain in 1230, and then returned to Saxony in 1231 to manage the new province. He knew the eastern European borderlands well, which is why he was selected for a mission to Asia at the 1245 council of Lyons. Together with Brother Benedict from Poland, who became his companion and translator, he left Lyons on Easter Sunday – 16 April 1245 – to visit Batu Khan, Genghis Khan's grandson, in Karakorum. He was curious about the Mongols, who had so effortlessly vanquished the Polish army in the Battle of Legnica in April 1241, and wanted to find out more about their culture and way of life.

Hoping to get to know these potential enemies in the east, he travelled across the width of Europe and Asia, and saw places and people whose landscapes and existence no European knew anything about. The pope had done well to choose John. Although he was over sixty and by all accounts somewhat rotund – far from ideal, one would have thought, for such an adventurous and strenuous journey into the unknown – he also had a wealth of experience and was extremely adaptable, intelligent, and clever in his dealings with strangers, whether stable boy or ruler. Salimbene di Adam knew him personally, and describes him as friendly, curious, educated, highly experienced and a skilled orator.[39]

Criticisms

However, this fascinating success story wouldn't be a proper story if there was no other side to it. The truth is that these mendicant brothers had their critics from the start.[40] Their peers accused them of contravening their own rules, arguing that their extreme poverty may have existed in theory, but that in practice no one really kept to it. Some said that the Franciscans were in the Church's pocket, accepted money from rich friends and patrons, and frequented town halls, bourgeois palaces and royal courts. Many people were angry. How can someone who has taken a vow of poverty sit at the same table as high society, at the same table as the rich and powerful – especially the latter?

Others didn't like the fact that the friars did not live surrounded by the walls of a monastery, and regularly used meeting houses (convents) that were also used by non-Franciscans.[41] Another point of contention was their refusal to work. Why should young, healthy men who were fit for work live off other people's charity? Even within the movement itself, there were the same serious tensions we see between 'fundamentalists' and 'pragmatists' in modern-day political parties and other organisations. The former demanded an extreme form of renunciation, the others moderate consumption. The conflict intensified in the late thirteenth century, and the order repeatedly threatened to split into factions.[42]

The thirteenth-century boom in voluntary poverty

How to explain the comprehensive success of this minimalist movement? Their detractors notwithstanding, these mendicant orders were society's answer to the period's economic changes. The Commercial Revolution was creating not only winners, but also countless losers, and the gulf between rich and poor kept widening. The minimalists have been interpreted by some as a protest movement – for instance by the historian Johannes Schlageter, who believed that the reason why minimalism was such a success was that the voluntary poor refused to seek property, status or power over others. Instead, they turned towards those who had lost out in the game of progress, the people who were being marginalised by urban society. The friars' settlements were usually located just outside the city walls, near the poor and the lepers, and represented 'an alternative not only to the prevailing economic and social structures, but to the prevailing mentality, culture and religion, and therein lay their success'.[43]

Between heresy and holiness

Of course, St Francis was not the only option.[44] Many other minimalist movements were born during that period; there was Peter Waldo's community of Waldensians in Lombardy, for example, and the Cathars in southern France. These two were declared heretical, while others – the Humiliati, Dominicans, Carmelites and Hermits of St Augustine – were integrated into the Church. The history of the beguines, who were also founded during this time, is proof that there could be a compromise of sorts too, between tolerance, condemnation and acceptance. The reason why these movements were so generously supported by the inhabitants of towns and cities was no doubt that they advocated emancipation, got actively involved, tried out new ways of life beyond traditional family structures, and offered new forms of togetherness and relationships that stretched beyond city walls – in short: inclusivity. Whether heretical or incorporated by the Church, what united these movements was not this or that theological nicety, but their shared ideal of simplicity.

The 'disenchantment of the world'

Most of these minimalist movements couched their mission in religious terms, which tends to make them seem alien today. Most, too, were created in the context of the Church and framed as a critique of the Church's increasing worldliness and wealth. Yet both the ecclesiastical and the secular sphere were being transformed. After all, the increasing inequality affected the whole of society. Everyone and everything was changing. The historian Stefan Weinfurter describes it (*pace* Max Weber) as the period when the world became 'disenchanted', and the religious and secular powers, pope and emperor, lost their halos during both the Investiture Wars.[45] As far as social changes were concerned, they were all in the same boat. Interestingly, however, it was the Church that protested most against them; perhaps because its commitment to continuous reform had, over the centuries, produced a culture of systematic critique within the Church itself, which reached a peak in the writings of twelfth-century scholars and became the subject of academic research proper in the thirteenth century. Ecclesiastical scholars even declared pragmatic dissent a form of scholarship, and the French philosopher Pierre Abelard suggested that doubt itself was a path to truth.

For love of learning: poverty and the universities

Along with the mendicant orders, the final decades of the twelfth century and first decades of the thirteenth brought with them the universities.[46] There already were higher education institutes, of course. Plato's academy in ancient Athens was the original model; in the early Middle Ages, convent schools played a crucial part in educating the young; and with Europe's increasing urbanisation, cathedral schools took on an ever more prominent role in the larger cities during the 1100s. Then came the universities. Surprisingly, we know almost nothing about how they started. The search for clues as to who invented or founded the earliest such institutions has ended in bitter disappointment, because in those days there were no foundation charters, no written commissions for university buildings. All we have are clues suggesting that, starting in the mid-1100s, a new type of organisation began to emerge in places like Bologna and Paris.

They were essentially private associations of students and graduates, guilds of sorts, described in papal letters and elsewhere as *vestra universitas*, which gave rise to the term 'university'. The term has nothing to do with any claims to universality, but merely signifies a collective: a group of students who formed a *studium*, a 'study', and hired a teacher whom they paid with donations (*collectiones*) or even, frequently, 'in kind'. Both students and teachers eschewed a regular income, status and wealth, and dedicated themselves entirely to their love of knowledge. In Paris, for instance, as Abelard became ever more famous and, pugnacious intellectual that he was, made many enemies, students flocked to his lectures, keen to listen and debate, including well-known figures such as John of Salisbury and Otto of Freising. Eventually they moved out of the city, to the hill of St-Geneviève, which is now the site of the Panthéon.[47]

These colleges later gave birth to universities, and in his 'Privilegium scholasticum' addressed to the students of Bologna's law school – which lays claim to being the oldest university in the world – Frederick I Barbarossa somewhat pompously praises those who 'exile themselves through love of learning [and] prefer to wear themselves out in poverty rather than to enjoy riches, and those who expose their lives to every peril, so that, defenceless, they must often suffer bodily injury from the vilest of men'.[48] It is likely that Bologna's legal scholars themselves drafted the document for the emperor to sign – which perhaps explains the slightly exaggerated wording. Still, the emperor consented to their plea for protection. He valued these new communities of students and scholars, who willingly gave up at least a few years of making a living for the sake of their studies, and who were usually strangers in the city, far away from home.

We can be certain that the earliest universities – Salerno, Bologna, Montpellier, Paris, Oxford, Cambridge – were not created on the orders of a monarch or pope, but by the communities themselves. Strictly speaking, they were associations of people whose lifestyle we would today describe as minimalist: in the Middle Ages, students were very much the 'voluntary poor' and were supported largely by donations and stipends. In subsequent years they received additional endowments from both secular and religious rulers: for example, the university founded in Paris by Robert de Sorbon – now better known as the Sorbonne – had its statutes officially recognised by the pope in 1215, and the French king later funded places for twenty poor students.

The historical roots of the environmental movement

The thirteenth-century minimalists redefined the relationship between humans and nature. Thomas of Celano's biography of St Francis includes two particularly interesting stories in that regard. The first describes how, one day, Francis, who was on his way into town, met a man with a sheep. He asked him what he was doing with the animal, and the man replied that he was taking it to market, to sell to a butcher. Francis was seized by pity, and could not bear the thought of the animal being slaughtered. He offered the man his cloak in exchange for the sheep, and the man agreed. Francis was delighted. The sheep joined the community, following the friars around and eating, drinking and sleeping with them, until Francis finally gave it to a farmer to look after.[49] In the second story, Celano recounts that Francis once bought freshly caught fish at a port, only to throw them back into the water and save their lives. His sermons to the birds are famous too, of course. Francis did many things that your average person wouldn't, and even Pope Gregory IX, who was probably well disposed towards this thoroughly eccentric saint, occasionally called him 'Brother Simpleton'.[50]

The Franciscan communities were usually vegetarian. When a physician once prescribed Francis chicken broth for medicinal reasons he drank it, but then spent the next several days feeling guilty, going so far as to ask one of his brothers to publicly punish him for harming the creature. Dominicus, the founder of the Dominican order, is said to have stopped reading books because their binding and pages were made from parchment, i.e. animal skins, and he couldn't stand the thought of all the animals that had to die for their sake. He refused to wear clothes and shoes made of leather, and several sources mention that the sight of people wearing furs was unbearable to the friars.

Yet their rejection of luxury never stopped them from being convivial. Quite the contrary: because they needed so little, they had the most remarkable experiences. Celano says that when Francis one day invited his physician to join him for a meal at short notice, he remembered only as they were approaching the house that there was hardly anything to eat. Miraculously, at that very moment his neighbour came by; she had just cooked a

43. Sermon to the Birds (Giotto, *c.* 1295)

meal and wanted to share it with the brothers, and had brought fish, lobster terrine, and grapes and honey for dessert. They cheerfully ate their fill. We also know that Francis, despite his asceticism, did have one great love, a favourite food whose taste filled him with pure joy. And that food was parsley.[51]

Ecology and the Franciscans' love for nature

A wonderful story – a parable, really – passed down to us by a friar with a poetic bent, illustrates the Franciscans' freedom and affinity for nature using the image of lovers at a picnic. Francis and his companions (goes the parable) are madly in love. They desperately search for their beloved lady, the Lady Poverty, who personifies the absence of need. A wise old man tells them where to find her: Lady Poverty can only be found in nature, in the wilderness. So they walk to a strange place, where no man dares to tread, and there submit to nature, to the unknown. After days and weeks of searching and uncertainty, they finally find Lady Poverty. She is lonely and upset. At first she refuses to go with them, having had bad experiences with humans. But at some point she senses that Francis and his companions are serious. Overjoyed, they climb the mountain and reach the pinnacle of happiness. Afterwards, exhausted by the difficult ascent, they sit down to a picnic. Lady Poverty asks for water and a towel to wash her hands. The companions bring her water in a cracked jug, and offer her their robes for a towel. By way of food, they serve a few bits of bread; the grass is their tablecloth, and instead of a warm stew they pour water into a bowl and dunk the bread in it. Wild herbs add sophistication to the menu. There is no salt or wine, and instead of knives they use their teeth.

After this satisfying meal, Lady Poverty lies down for a nap. They fetch her a stone for a pillow and give her the meadow for a bed. She lies down 'naked on the naked earth'. After a short rest she feels refreshed, and asks to visit the brothers' home, their abbey. They gladly take her by the hand and lead her up the mountain. From the peak they show her the whole world: 'That', they say, 'is our abbey.'[52]

It is only a story, of course. A story they used to tell to each other in the order back in the day. A story that expresses, in the thirteenth-century terms of courtly love, the fact that man belongs to nature. Francis's relationship to Nature was indeed special: he loved her.

Nature is to be loved, not mastered

Interestingly, Lynn White, who is perhaps the most frequently cited twentieth-century technology historian, saw Francis as the embodiment of a turning point in history and acknowledged him as a saint. In 1967, *Science* published a fascinating piece by White about the historical roots of the environmental crisis, in which he used the past to shed light on the most pressing modern-day ecological issues.[53] In his view, the religious stories of Judaism and Christianity, in particular the creation myth and the Old Testament's declaration that 'man shall have dominion over all the earth', were to blame for the rise of the West, for the mechanisation of the world, for our subjugation of nature, and finally also for the Great Divergence. The latter is also known as the 'Why Europe?' question: in the course of the 1800s, thanks to technological advances, the West left the rest of the world behind, especially Asia.[54] The question is, how was the West allowed to conquer the entire world, colonise and exploit it, destroy nature, trigger globalisation, export pollution, and so on and so forth?

In his 1967 article, White focuses on culture and the link between religion and ecology. He argues that the 'dominion' sentence in the Bible was a key factor, and that – unlike orthodox Christianity, Judaism and Islam – the Western Christians took God's exhortation seriously, which eventually led to our subjugation of nature through technological advances. White, as a technology historian, was arguing that Western Christianity was to blame for creating an imbalance between humans and nature. It had replaced the old animistic religions, which had an immense respect for nature and ascribed a soul to every shrub and cloud, with an exclusively anthropocentric religion. It was an interesting theory, not least because it turned the prevailing ideas of his time on their head. In 1967, Christianity and the Catholic Church were considered the biggest obstacles to progress, and White was suggesting that the opposite was true: that Christianity had been the main driver of progress – as well as our ruthless conquest of nature.

For White, Francis was the only exception, a counterbalance, a Christian antidote. He argued that Francis was a representative of the Church who had miraculously managed not to end up being burnt at the stake, even though his views were deeply heretical. Instead of dominion over nature, he preached harmony; he treated nature with kindness and love, and praised Mother Earth, Brother Sun, Sister Moon, Brother Wind and Sister Fire as great, exalted powers. When a young hare came to Francis for shelter, it did so because Francis had a 'tender love' for nature, as well as *pietas*, pity and reverence. Francis felt he was part of nature, not a guest in it, that man and nature were partners, not opponents.[55] White ended his piece with the suggestion that Francis should be made the patron saint of environmentalists, and on 29 November 1979 Pope John Paul II did just that.[56]

White drew a lot of criticism for his thesis. Some said that he might be an expert on the history of technology and economics, but that he knew nothing about theology or religious studies. Or was that exactly why he saw things more clearly than his peers?[57] In the meantime, the dust has settled. Both the environmental movement and academics have learnt new things. White's faith in animist religions has cooled a little, as has the romantic notion that natural religions promote an idyllic harmony between man and nature. Buddhism does prohibit the killing of animals, but most forests in India in China have survived only because their former rulers were keen hunters and granted them special protection as royal hunting grounds.

On closer inspection, the supposedly holistic vision of the natural religions – the soulful natural world with its sacred trees and copses – has revealed itself as little more than a pious dream. The Indologist Axel Michaels has demonstrated that the worship of trees did not inevitably lead to environmental protection. The logic behind it suggests precisely the reverse: a tree was usually sacred because of its singularity, because it was simply the only one left.[58] The magical fog around nature-loving Mother Earth cults has also lifted. The idea that indigenous North Americans and their gods mutually agreed to treat nature with great care fails the fact-check too. All you have to do is consider the reality of mother–child relationships: biologically speaking, reproduction almost always exacts a price from the maternal animal's organism – nature predicates that mothers are by definition exploited. The metaphor of Mother Earth, and its associated idea of humans living in harmony with nature, is therefore pretty flawed. Furthermore, when you think of how combative mother–child relationships can be, and that they can, at best, only turn out well if the child successfully detaches from the mother, the Mother Earth myth provides us with only extremely shaky support in our struggle to protect the environment.[59]

Regardless of our cultural and religious views, there is no doubt that we humans have violently, and on a massive scale, interfered with the ecosystem of our habitats. No matter which continent we settled in during the past 100,000 years, we sooner or later secured the extinction of every single large mammal – long before Christianity was invented.

Perhaps White was mistaken, then. If he was, we ought to remove Francis from his pedestal of Christianity's great nature-loving exception of a saint. Yet his extraordinary connection with nature is a quality that has future potential. The latest anthropological and ecological theories increasingly question the distinction between humans and nature, a distinction that was cemented by the modern age. The proposition that humans are part of nature and culture is part of human nature constitutes a far more interesting hypothesis, perhaps, and recent theories have been inspired by the interplay of the various agents within a given ecosystem.[60]

Perhaps we should update St Francis, and turn him into the patron saint of the minimalist movement. He unashamedly celebrated the freedom that comes with wanting nothing, and not being afraid of depending on others. This directly affected his understanding of the relationship between man and nature: he did not in the least desire to control nature and lived, rather, in a kind of continuous conversation with it. He loved devoting himself to nature, and clearly did not want to exert power over it. The parable of Lady Poverty evokes the image of an almost erotic partnership, a relationship that flourishes in an austere wilderness and leads to the very apex of freedom. In Francis's world, there is no line between man and nature – in his courtship of poverty, his talks with the birds, his eulogy to Brother Sun and his conversation with his own body (which he often called 'Brother Ass'), he almost lustily celebrates man and nature dissolving into each other.

Pierre de Jean Olivi: Minimalism and Economic Theory

The thirteenth-century minimalists were not unworldly dropouts, but exercised a decisive influence on social and economic life in towns and cities. They got involved. As we saw in the chapter on MFIs, the Franciscans – alongside members of other mendicant orders, especially the Dominicans – used their sermons to convince those around them of the pressing need for banks for the poor. They were medieval influencers with a high impact factor. The townspeople greatly valued their expertise, and sought them out as consultants and experts, particularly in the realm of finance. They knew what was what, and it was no coincidence that the Franciscan friar Luca Pacioli has gone down in history as the father of double-entry bookkeeping. In the late fifteenth century, he collated the prevalent accounting practices into a sort of textbook, and doubtless owed his understanding of the field to the mendicant orders' centuries-old preoccupation with economic matters.[61]

Their feel for economics was evident from the beginning. They did not shy away from worldly affairs; indeed, they preached in churches only rarely, preferring to go where people naturally

44. Portrait of Luca Pacioli, 'father of double-entry bookkeeping', by Jacopo de' Barbari (1495)

congregated: the marketplace. There are plenty of records of marketplace sermons conducted at international markets and annual and trade fairs (*in nundinis*) or at the weekly market (*in mercatis*). The historian Jörg Oberste has meticulously examined the sermons that have survived and found that, almost right from the start, mendicant preachers were very interested in what went on in the markets.

Humbert of Romans, a Dominican friar, opened one of his marketplace sermons by asking: what are markets good for? The answer, he said, was simple: no country was capable of providing its people with everything they needed, and trade was thus both useful and necessary. Consequently, markets are good because, firstly, they make countries humble, because they remind them that they depend on others; secondly, they create relationships and friendships between countries; and thirdly, they make an important contribution to the survival of humankind by providing it with goods.[62]

As Oberste explains, the mendicant sermons of the thirteenth century deviated from the tradition of discriminating against mercantile professions which had dominated public discourse since antiquity. Humbert, for instance, was keen to remove the whiff of unseemliness, of corruption, attached to markets and their participants. He hypothesised that merchants had a choice, and that each could choose for themselves between honesty and deception. In line with the contemporaneous ethics of intentionality, which interrogated both human motives and the circumstances of each case, Humbert distinguished between the many participants who conscientiously respected the rules of the market passed down by their predecessors and those who carelessly ignored God's commandments. In short, he appealed to the conscience of each individual merchant.

The mendicant friars' curiosity about the affairs of the market, the openness that these religiously motivated medieval minimalists displayed towards economic issues, cannot be explained away by a desire for riches. The mendicant orders, unlike old-school Benedictines, never accumulated wealth. They had no sudden ambition to be rich. No: what we can discern is a genuine interest in the *practicalities* of life without, or with little, property. We might say that their notorious arguments about the true shape of poverty is what made them experts in wealth, whose negative consequences they were determined to avoid. For example, they had intense exchanges about the difference between property (*proprietas*, absolute sovereignty over something), possession (*possessio*, having something at one's disposal) and enjoyment or usage rights (*usus*). They debated the price of goods and services, such as whether the value of a preacher's work could be equated to a baker's. They were also fascinated by what constitutes a fair distribution of riches, and thus became well versed in the field of markets, finance, ownership rights and credit. The Franciscans regarded poverty, want and deprivation 'not as a void to fill but as a starting point for measuring values, wages and prices'.[63]

Mendicant friars played a further role, too, which is worth examining in this context: as a result of living in the midst of urban society, preaching and ministering to the towns' and cities' inhabitants, they also took on the function of confessors. We might compare them to modern consultants or coaches. They had their finger on the pulse of the age, understood the problems people faced, and recognised the challenges that economic growth brought with it: namely, increasingly byzantine mercantile practices, contracts and business models, businesses that kept growing, merchants who kept getting more successful, and more and more money in circulation. (In England, for instance, the number of silver pennies in circulation increased tenfold between 1180 and 1280.[64])

Monetisation, urbanisation, economisation and expanding markets influenced all aspects of life in Europe, and no one was exempt. Not only that, but they created much doubt, because it was frequently unclear whether and how the accumulation of private profit could be reconciled with the public good. Over the course of the thirteenth century, the common good, the *bonum comune*, was increasingly designated the goal of all business and finance, while usury was seen as a major problem and declared its arch-enemy. But where did usury begin and end? At what point did making a profit cross over into greed? The question posed a serious challenge to Christian merchants, who, after all, did not want to play fast and loose with their souls, and so the father confessor became their most valued advisor.

Within the Church, too, there was great uncertainty, and responsibility for judging a contract's sinfulness or otherwise was delegated to the conscience of the individual. Personal responsibility became increasingly important, with the result that instructions for how to spot the sin of usury started appearing in early thirteenth-century confession manuals, the *summae confessorum*.[65] As a father confessor, you were jointly responsible for recognising and exposing sin, but in order to judge whether the penitent was guilty of the sin of usury you had to understand business practices and contracts. As Joel Kaye puts it, 'One unintended consequence flowing from the logic of the usury prohibition was that those who would judge and enforce it, even those clerics most suspicious of the corrupting effects of commerce and the pursuit of monetary gain, had no choice but to pay ever closer attention to the details of economic life.' And as confessors and preachers, the members of the mendicant orders found themselves in the front line. The very champions of a simple life without possessions turned into the most important economic theorists of the late Middle Ages, who developed guidelines for traders, merchants and entrepreneurs on how to balance profit with the common good, identified the pricing paradox, formulated early thoughts on marginal utility, and defined the properties of capital.[66]

The Narbonne school and the economics of need

The school of Franciscan economics included medieval scholars such as Alexander of Hales, Jean de la Rochelle, Bonaventure, Richard of Middleton, Pierre de Jean Olivi, Duns Scotus and, later, Bernardino di Siena. The economic historian Raymond de Roover has called them some of the 'greatest economists of all time'.[67]

Their most original thinker was no doubt Olivi – which is why I refer to the Narbonne school, named after the place where he wrote his 1295 treatise on contracts. In this seminal work he developed the conceptual terminology for analysing market mechanisms, based on observations from the business practices of his fellow countrymen in southern France, which he translated into the learned discourse of contemporary academia. Instead of simply parroting the recently rediscovered works of Aristotle and his dogma of the sterility of money – i.e. that it cannot multiply, and when it does it is 'against nature' – Olivi describes current economic practices concerning the flow of money and goods, and explains, among other things, that credit transactions are unavoidable (a view not uncommon even then), and that capital, such as the trading capital of an overseas merchant, has the inherent potential to germinate (*ratio seminalis*). His thoughts on pricing are considered groundbreaking and have won him a reputation as the father of the 'subjective theory of value'.

Pierre de Jean Olivi: the contrary Franciscan

Sylvain Piron, a history professor at the École des Hautes Études en Sciences Sociales in Paris and probably the world's foremost expert on Olivi, describes him as 'one of the most adventurous, exciting and prolific of all medieval thinkers'.[68] For a taste of his originality, we need look no further than his will. He died peacefully on Friday, 14 March 1298 at the age of fifty, in the Franciscan convent of Narbonne, surrounded by his brothers. He was buried there, and left behind a last will and testament that ends with these words:

> I say that it is useful to write and recite contrary opinions without stubborn approval of any particular alternative so that it will become apparent that neither is held as the faith and that neither is unshakably held; and also so that, through comparison of these opinions, the understanding of the advanced reader (as well as those upon whom it is incumbent to advance) can be exercised more fully.[69]

With this earnest plea for intellectual flexibility and openness, Olivi concluded an extraordinarily rich intellectual life's work. Theo Kobusch has given him the epithet 'the contrary Franciscan' for his tireless defence of the right to disagree, and for doing more than perhaps anyone else at the time to promote a culture of open debate and intellectual freedom. Moreover, Olivi innately mistrusted authority: the argument of tradition has no place in philosophy, he declared, and to say that 'Aristotle said so, therefore it must be so' was, frankly, a syllogism.[70] Declarations and opinions such as these contradict everything we thought we knew about the Dark Ages. Who was this man? Where did he come from? What drove him? How did he, a thirteenth-century mendicant friar, end up an expert in finance?

Occitanie: an epicentre of thirteenth-century intellectual life

Olivi was born in France in 1247 or 1248. His parents lived in Sérignan, ten kilometres south-east of Béziers, now a popular seaside resort, and his mother tongue was Occitan – the language of the troubadours, the language of the south, the *langue d'oc*, where you said *oc* for 'yes' (unlike the *langue d'oïl* of the north, where you said *oui*). We know nothing about his childhood. Although he was a remarkably prolific writer and many of his works have survived, there is no clue in them to his family background, except that he was the son of a man called Jean.

He grew up in a world that was changing dramatically. At the time of his birth, all was still well with medieval Europe. Popes, emperors, kings and knights kept the wheel of history turning. In 1248, the French king Louis IX led a crusade to the Holy Land, and Ferdinand III of Spain conquered the Muslim rulers of Seville following the unification of the kingdoms of Castile and León. Meanwhile, the bitter power struggle between Pope Innocent IV and Emperor Frederick II dominated policy in the Holy Roman Empire and Italy, and Henry III of England reformed the country's coinage and finances. Across Europe, the big cheeses were in charge.

Eighteen years later, in 1266, when Olivi was sent to Paris to study, the world seemed to have become unhinged: Louis IX's army had returned in 1254 after suffering humiliating defeats in the Holy Land, and the age of the crusades was coming to its end. The last Hohenstaufen emperor, Frederick II, died from diarrhoea in Castel Fiorentino on 13 December 1250, and Germany's princes couldn't agree on his successor. The Holy Roman Empire was losing its shine. On the Iberian peninsula, the newly founded emirate of Granada was growing stronger (it would retain power until 1492). And in England in 1258, the very system of monarchy itself was at risk when the barons, led by Simon de Montfort, rose up and demanded a properly representative parliament. The foundations on which the medieval world order had been built were crumbling.

Only a generation earlier, the first major battle of the twenty-year-long Albigensian crusades had hit the residents of Béziers hard: its entire population, men, women and children, were murdered in 1209 by plundering crusaders intent on annihilating the heretical Cathars (also known as Albigensians, after their headquarters in Albi). It is reported that when, shortly before the battle, a crusader asked how he would be able to tell right-thinking Christians from heretical Cathars, his commander replied: 'Kill them all. God will know his children.' It is not unreasonable to think that Olivi's grandparents or other relatives were among the victims. People's memory of the event was still fresh, and you certainly would not have been an outlier in the Languedoc for voicing doubts as to the Church's authority.

Alongside political and religious unrest, people's lives were dominated by Mediterranean trade too. From the late twelfth century onwards, trade in the region expanded massively, initiating the Commercial Revolution. It began with the Italian and French ports along the Mediterranean coast, where Venice,

Genoa and the towns on the south coast of France became major hubs on a trading route that took in Mallorca, North Africa, Egypt and the Levant.

Scholarship and the art of dissent

In Olivi's time, Paris witnessed an academic revolution,[71] a new form of scholarship which Frank Rexroth has called 'learnt obstinacy'. It followed its own logic and defined its own ends, and is better known as 'scholasticism'. What motivated its students was not that it was useful or improved their job prospects, but the will to truth itself. Doubting and questioning became the ultimate scholastic method. Abelard had pointed the way when he called his twelfth-century magnum opus *Sic et non* – which literally means 'yes and no', but is perhaps better translated as 'thus, and also otherwise'. Everything that is may conceivably be other. Every thesis is worth interrogating. Every assertion warrants an objection.

The public reading of a text (*lectio*) lost relevance and gave way to the *disputatio*, academic debate, as the key teaching tool. A topic – usually known in advance – was posited in the form of a question (*quaestio disputata*), and the scholars would consider various possible responses and arguments pro and con (*argumentum/sed contra*). The topic was filleted and carefully dissected into sub-topics (*distinctiones*), which were debated in turn, before the whole thing was put back together again in a conclusion (*responsio*).

For Olivi, this approach was maybe less alienating than for some of his fellow students, given that he had grown up in a world where dissent was the norm. By 1266, when he went to study in Paris for seven years, he had already spent time at the Franciscan school in Narbonne. Joining a mendicant order to have access to education was common practice in those days, and the orders offered both the infrastructure and the financing necessary for a solid education. After completing their basic training in the provinces, particularly gifted students were sent to the major university towns of Bologna, Paris, Oxford, Cologne and elsewhere. This is where the orders' most important centres of study were located, the *studia generalia* that acted simultaneously as catalysts and colleagues of the, as yet rather young, universities – the University of Paris, for instance, started appointing mendicant friars to important professorships not long after its creation. The mendicant orders were associations of intellectuals, so to speak, which flew the flag of scholarship and introduced the necessary infrastructure – stipends, accommodation, textbooks, libraries, tutorials – and gave access to circles of learned men. Olivi became a devoted student of Thomas Aquinas, the most famous scholar of his age, who himself had studied in Paris under Albertus Magnus in 1245–8 and had – after sojourns in Cologne, Naples, Orvieto and Rome – returned to Paris to take up a professorial chair and compose his magnum opus, the *Summa theologiae*. Olivi avidly studied Aquinas's theories, and historians of philosophy believe that he may have been Aquinas's most original and interesting student.

In 1273 Olivi returned to Narbonne, where he lectured until 1279. Around Easter 1279 he was invited – probably to Assisi – as an expert on the subject of poverty, to help draft a papal bull. That same year he moved to Marseilles to become a *lector biblicus*, and in the three years that followed formulated several commentaries and *quaestiones* as well as a treatise on poverty (*De usu paupere*). Things were going splendidly for Olivi: his prospects were excellent, he was still in his early thirties, he had studied in Paris and lectured in Narbonne and Marseilles, and could point to an impressive list of publications. True, he only had a bachelor's degree, but he was not the only one; even celebrated lecturers like Bonaventure taught for years before finally getting a master's or a doctorate. We can therefore safely assume that Olivi, too, would have had a great career, and would at some point have followed in the footsteps of his famous teachers and ended up working at one of the prestigious universities of his time, probably in Paris. One of his specialisms was moral philosophy – specifically, the field of what we now call economic ethics. His work focused on the question of what makes for a 'good life', particularly as regards the proper way to implement the vow of poverty prescribed in the constitution of his own Franciscan order. Olivi believed that a life without property was both possible and good for you. Moreover, he saw in it the way of life that most closely met the spirit of the Rule of St Francis.

Academic cockfights

In 1283, however, Olivi's career abruptly stalled. The reason may sound trivial: there was no scandal, no accusation of plagiarism, no #MeToo revelation – merely a row between intellectuals, an academic dispute involving Olivi and a certain Arnaud Gaillard which grew into a long-drawn-out controversy.[72] There was a backstory to this. Gaillard, a fellow Franciscan, was Olivi's elder, but they had been in Paris at the same time and later met again as lecturers in Narbonne and Montpellier. Olivi might even briefly have been Gaillard's student in Paris. It is possible that Gaillard was one of those teachers who can't bear it when a student not only disagrees with them but is better than they are. The fact that Olivi left behind a body of work comprising more than fifty monographs, whereas only two short sermons of Gaillard's have survived, suggests that the younger man perhaps had the more creative brain, and defended positions that later generations still thought worth considering. It appears, then, that Gaillard may have had good reason to be envious of Olivi. Whatever the case, the affair concerned philosophical and theological issues, specifically the matter of Franciscan poverty, Olivi's field of expertise. When, in 1279, the pope set about preparing his position paper on the internal dispute about poverty that was troubling the

Franciscan order, he invited Olivi to join the commission tasked with formulating it. The resulting statement formed the basis of the *Bulle exiit qui seminat*, which officially recognised the right to voluntary poverty as a way of life.

Did Jesus and his apostles live in absolute poverty?

We do not know what exactly happened, but from Olivi's letters we learn that in spring 1283 Gaillard sent a list of accusations against Olivi to the order's minister general. Everything we know about the individual accusations comes from Olivi's written defence, which reveals that they consisted in the main of objections to his commentary on Revelations and his writings on the subject of poverty. The questions debated at Montpellier at the time included the following. Could one state with certainty that Jesus and his apostles lived in absolute poverty? Was it legitimate to encourage young men who were fit for work to survive on alms? How sure can we be about the Apocalypse?

It seems that – as is common in such conflicts – Gaillard extracted individual sentences from their context and presented them as Olivi's theses, in order to make him look bad in front of the minister general. Olivi believed that right was on his side, but was unexpectedly prohibited from further teaching. A commission was set up, and the administrative mills of academia started grinding. Slowly. Very slowly. Olivi was frustrated. In a letter to a friend, he wrote: 'I have been deprived of all things, including my writings.'[73] He had to wait until May 1285 for an opportunity to properly defend his position.

Ultimately, the affair ended in a whimper. Nothing happened, except that two years later Matteo d'Acquasparta, the minister general, appointed Olivi lecturer at the prestigious Franciscan academic centre of Santa Croce in Florence. In 1289 Olivi returned to Montpellier, and in 1292 he finally got the opportunity to present and explain his views on voluntary poverty to the chapter general. He was subsequently appointed once again to a post at Narbonne, where he taught and wrote countless more works until his death on 14 March 1298. His biography would not be complete without a mention of his afterlife. Several years after his death he fell victim to a sad fate when some of his texts, in particular his writings on apostolic poverty, were deemed heretical. His remains were disinterred and burnt in 1319 and his writings banned.[74]

Should we allow markets to set prices?

Let us now turn to Olivi's economic theory. This man, who lived his whole adult life without possessions, who had no home of his own or even clothes he considered his private property, who never needed to worry about his finances, simply because he wasn't interested in having anything one might call 'finances' – this man was intensely preoccupied by contemporary questions about fair economics.

'Is it rightful to buy goods for less than their worth, or sell them for more than their worth?' With this question Olivi begins his 1295 *Treatise on Contracts*.[75] Translated into modern jargon, the question becomes, 'Should we let the market set the price?' The treatise gives us a wonderful insight into how the subject was discussed in thirteenth-century scholarly circles, and you feel as if you're right there in the medieval seminar room, among the students heatedly debating the question and brainstorming ideas. On the left-hand side of the blackboard appear the pros:

1. Yes, otherwise everyone who buys or sells anything is constantly acting wrongfully, which can't be the case, because everyone wants the same thing – to buy low and sell high.
2. Yes, because a seller is legally allowed to charge whatever they please. No law can force them to

sell their goods at a price fixed by someone else. Conversely, no one is forced to buy goods at a price they deem too high. So if the contract of sale has been entered into freely, we can conclude that both parties have freely agreed to the price. As they say, 'A thing is worth what someone will pay for it.'[76]

3. Yes, because it is beneficial to the common good when prices are freely agreed by buyers and sellers, rather than dictated from above or otherwise fixed. It also minimises the risk of fraud.

On the right-hand side of the blackboard, are listed the cons:

1. Deception, compulsion and fraud violate natural law and the law of friendship. We must not do unto others what we would not have them do unto us.[77] And to knowingly charge too much or pay too little constitutes fraud.
2. Commutative justice stipulates that each should be given their due, so the two things that are exchanged have to be equivalent.[78] To knowingly charge too much or pay too little violates the principles of equality and justice.

'Value' vs 'use value'

Olivi believes that the interplay between supply and demand is central. The arguments he drafts into battle are to this day considered integral components of classical pricing theory. After the initial brainstorming session, he introduces the distinction between value and use value.[79] The first is a measure of 'the real goodness of [a thing's] nature', and by that measure a mouse is worth more than a loaf of bread because it has 'a soul, life, and the ability to perceive'.[80] However, a loaf of bread is worth more to us than a mouse because we need bread every day, while we would rather do without mice; and because goods are bought and sold with a view to their usefulness, it is as a rule their use value – their function and utility – that matters. From this, Olivi extrapolates three factors that determine the price of goods:[81]

1. Usefulness (*utilitas*): the natural qualities of a thing that make it more or less suitable or effective for our purpose. A good loaf of bread made from wheat is therefore worth a lot more than a dry loaf made from barley, and a strong horse is much more useful (for work or in battle) than a donkey or a mule.
2. Availability (*raritas*): is one product more important to us than another because it is rare or difficult to produce? A shortage increases demand (or the desire for the relevant product – *indigentia*), and at the same time reduces our chances of obtaining and using the product. For instance, a certain type of grain is worth much more in times of shortage and famine than in times of abundance. Or take the four elements, water, earth, air and fire. For most people they are cheap, because they are available always and everywhere, unlike e.g. gold or precious lotions; and this despite the fact that water and air are indispensable to our survival and thus de facto more important than gold and perfumed luxuries.[82]
3. Subjective value (*beneplacitas voluntatis*): we value something according to how much or little it delights us, or how much or little we desire to have it. In this context, 'using' something means subjecting yourself to it, or possessing it and disposing of it as you please. The pleasure you take in something – i.e. the degree of satisfaction you associate with using and owning this or that – is therefore a not inconsiderable factor in

> determining its price. A horse, for example, will give one person far greater pleasure than another. And so one person will pay a very high price for something that is utterly worthless to someone else.

Why is a diamond worth more than water?

If a representative of the late nineteenth-century Viennese school of neoclassical economics had read Olivi's treatise, they would have blanched. In the 1800s, scholars thought that the objective theory of value had for centuries been the prevailing explanation for how prices were set. According to the objective theory of value, the usefulness, i.e. the use or exchange value, of a given product was the chief factor in determining its price. Depending on availability, there were two kinds of goods: non-finite commodities, whose production could simply be increased as demand for them increased, and whose price remained relatively stable as a result; and finite commodities, i.e. rare goods, whose supply could not be easily increased, such as the work of a famous artist or a rare diamond. The price of rare goods depends on how much demand there is for them, i.e. the intensity of a buyer's desire to possess it.

This is where the objective theory falls short, because objective prices only reflect a product's exchange or use value, which does not account for the exorbitant sums fetched by works of art and diamonds. This problem is known as the 'paradox of value' or the 'diamond–water paradox'. Objectively speaking, water has the highest conceivable use value because we need it to survive, but it costs almost nothing; whereas a diamond or a work of art has a low use value, but people will pay unimaginably high prices to possess them. And this is true even though they are all finite resources. It was not until 1870 that the concept of marginal utility introduced a new dimension to the theory of values and prices, and made up for the limitations of the objectivist model.

Olivi integrates all three factors into his pricing model from the start. The first, usefulness, describes the price arising from the utility of a thing; *raritas* introduces the distinction between finite and infinite commodities; and *beneplacitas voluntatis* brings subjective value into play as a decisive factor. The fact that a late thirteenth-century economic theorist had, without batting an eyelid, listed all the factors involved in pricing, treating them as if they were practically self-evident – and, to top it all, included subjective value among them – considerably dims the halo of the Viennese school's supposedly ultra-modern economic theory.

Fairness and transparency

There is no need for us to style Olivi the progenitor of 'modern' subjective value theory.[83] All he was doing was discussing issues that went viral in the late thirteenth century. His *quaestiones* stick closely to popular topics, his arguments are similar to those of Thomas Aquinas and Alexander of Hales[84] and his *Treatise on Contracts* largely corresponds to the prevailing economic theories of his day. Olivi was neither an outsider nor a revolutionary. His analyses, however, are extraordinarily sharp-sighted, and he perhaps describes some things in more precise terms than his colleagues at the University of Paris. It is also possible that he was more familiar than they with current market practices, and might have spent more time in the actual places where goods were sold and deals struck. He does employ a remarkably large number of terms taken from everyday business jargon. In addition, he highlights how difficult it is to formulate the laws of pricing, because pricing happens within the infinite spectrum of human ways of measuring. Uncertainty, ambiguity, fashion, estimate and opinion play a big part in it, and it's therefore impossible to determine or fix an absolute, final price for anything.[85] In his conclusion he declares that, all in all, it is legitimate to sell something for more or buy something for less than it is worth, provided that the price remains within the boundaries of propriety. The widely accepted value (*pretium iustum*, 'just price') is key, and should not be exceeded or undercut by more than half.[86] So if a jug normally priced at 10d. is sold for 16d. the price is not fair. Transparency also plays an important role: if the 'injured' party, i.e. the buyer of the overpriced jug, knows that it is overpriced, ignores the fact and buys it anyway, the transaction is legitimate, because it was entered into freely. By the same token, anyone can give their goods away for nothing if they want to, just as young Francis of Assisi did, and there is nothing unfair about it.

Price as incentive

The students in our seminar once again examine the question of what determines prices, and adopt and expand their initial list of determinants. The rule of thumb is that the factors which influence value should not be manipulated, as long as they are in tune with the general estimation of a product's value. At this point, Olivi brings the collective estimate of a product's public-good value (*communic taxacio boni communis*) into play. What does this mean? It essentially means that prices reflect the general requirements of society at a given point in time. Today, we would say that if you take into account the *taxacio communis*, the price lies roughly at the point where supply and demand meet. This position was generally accepted among Olivi's fellow scholars too. Yet Olivi argues the case from an unusual perspective: if there is a shortage of grain in a particular region, the price should be allowed to rise accordingly. For instance, if the price for a measure of grain is normally (according to the *taxacio communis*) £10 and then rises to £20 during a famine, it constitutes a flagrant deviation from the communal estimate, but is nevertheless legitimate. Why? Firstly, because sellers have to pay a higher price for their wares too; secondly, because if prices are not allowed to rise, the common good is at risk – because anyone in possession of useful products has no incentive to sell them to those who need them, which will cut off their supply to the community at large.[87]

Odd Langholm, a political economist who has devoted half his life to medieval economic theories, highlights the importance of this proposition.[88] Olivi believed that the price of a product was not merely the result of an interaction between material circumstances, human needs and moral values, but also a cause – or as we would put it, an incentive. Prices act as stimuli on suppliers and create effects that benefit society. Langholm points out that this thesis created a dilemma even for medieval scholars, because it clearly contradicted the traditional Christian idea that brotherly love alone guarantees the well-being of humanity. Olivi and his contemporaries were pragmatists, though, and were theorising for a humankind after the Fall, in its 'postlapsarian' condition. That is, they argued on the basis that we are who we are and not how we should be, and market regulations need to fit in with human reality. What makes Olivi's thinking unusual is his logic: instead of invoking natural justice, he produces examples that pursue a clear, analytical line of reasoning. He argues that, while food prices should be allowed to rise during shortages in order to incentivise suppliers, the same does not apply when it comes to individuals who are in need.

In such cases, the current market situation (i.e. the product's use value) must not determine its price. For example, when someone is dying of thirst, you must not sell them a glass of water at a price that is based on how badly they need it; if someone is ill and can only avoid certain death by taking a specific medicine, you must on no account price it based on its 'real' value (in terms of its usefulness to the buyer). Life is priceless. In such cases, the law of common good overrides a seller's personal interest. Emergency situations and hardship thus limit the freedom of the market.

Production costs, prices and wages

Finally, Olivi argues that, in addition to demand and supply, prices are determined by the effort that goes into producing and providing the goods, which he sums up as 'labour', 'risk' and 'industry' – or, perhaps more accurately, 'cleverness' (*labor, periculum, industria*).[89] Risky and labour-intensive production processes and high transport costs raise the price of goods, which is why products from regions far removed from central France or the eastern Mediterranean (Languedoc's main trading partners) were more expensive than goods from nearby regions. The cost of goods and services also rises in line with the knowledge and brainpower required to provide them. Hence a builder earns less than the architect who instructs him, despite the fact that the builder spends all day doing physical work and often has better practical knowledge and a better skill set. This is generally true of higher-ranking jobs, which are associated with a larger salary, because they require 'greater' skills and intelligence and mean a 'greater' mental burden (i.e. responsibility). In addition, the expertise needed to carry out the more demanding professions requires a long and arduous period of study, as well as experience and hard work. Studying is expensive too, and risky. At the same time, not all that many people are suited to major, important tasks, which is why their work is valued more highly.

Just as the price of goods is partly determined by market factors (demand and supply), wage levels are likewise determined by market conditions. Regardless of whether it's doctors, lawyers, soldiers or builders, if there are a lot of them they'll get paid less; and when there is a shortage of workers, wages rise. Langholm defines this as the early stage of a groundbreaking new development in the theory of value: what Olivi is doing is explaining the value of goods and services partly in terms of their rarity and usefulness, and partly in terms of production costs, including wages, and the risks taken by suppliers.[90]

Capital needs to circulate

Imagine that, after an extremely dry summer, Florence is facing the prospect of a famine. Its inhabitants know from experience that the grain stores will last till Christmas, and they can maybe just about make it through January and February; but by March at the latest they will run out of food. If the city wants to pre-empt a famine, it has to stock up on grain. There are two options: raise taxes to generate income with which to buy grain, or ask (or tell) local grain merchants to sell all their grain to the city. To avoid the downside of raising taxes – it affects everyone, including the poor – Florence decides to buy grain from the merchants, ideally immediately after the harvest, when prices are still reasonable. However, for precisely the same reason the merchants want to wait to sell their stores until prices start rising. Should the city agree to buy grain in the autumn, but at the price it is likely to fetch in the spring?

Olivi, who had lived in Florence for two years, chose this as the basis for his discussion about the legitimacy of charging interest. In his view, the Florentine scenario is comparable to a compulsory loan or overdraft: both mean a potential loss of profits (*lucrum cessans*), for which it is reasonable to demand compensation. This opinion, incidentally, was already voiced in 1253 by Henry of Susa, cardinal bishop of Ostia, in his *Summa aurea*. However, forty years later Olivi is the first to mention the term 'capital' in the context of economic theory. Using what he has learnt from his conversations with merchants and what he knows about contract law, he counters Aristotle's dogma of the sterility of money. He declares that there are two kinds of money:[91]

1. Money as a simple medium of exchange, whose basic function is to measure value and price, which makes it possible to compare dissimilar goods – for example, a loaf of bread and a horse (*pecunia numerata*)

2. Money that a merchant uses to make a commercial investment in order to make a profit. According to Olivi, money here takes on a different guise, similar to that of a piece of land, becoming 'fruit-bearing' and non-finite.

Olivi here literally describes money has having a 'seminal' quality, which the merchants referred to in their contracts as 'capital'. It was clearly an everyday term among them, and comes from the Occitan language.[92] Olivi underlines this fact, describing traders in the harbour talking about *capitale* when talking about investing in the cargo of a merchant vessel, which might earn a huge return if everything went as it should. Invested wisely, money had the potential to increase. Perhaps he chooses the idea of fruitfulness, *ratio seminalis*, to neutralise Aristotle's dogma of the sterility of money; either way, he uses the ability money has to multiply in order to explain the need to raise interest, arguing that when a merchant lends his money to another, he is forgoing potential income and has a right to seek compensation without being accused of usury.[93]

Olivi's focus is entirely on the common good, which is why he is so keen on this. If we don't take into account the ability of money to function as capital, there is no incentive for anyone to invest in things that benefit society at large.

A minimalist who saw new possibilities

On the one hand, Olivi's treatise is a typical example of the sort of discussions people had about economic theory towards the end of the thirteenth century; on the other, though, it is quite remarkable. His insights run deeper than other people's, and what is particularly striking is his understanding of how to push the boundaries. In this sense, he was a true genius: he found a way to go beyond those boundaries, and his arguments reveal not merely the limits of what was possible in his time but suggest a line of flight on the horizon of the imaginable world which extends the conceivable beyond the limits of tradition.[94] The concept of the common good, which gained prominence during the 1200s, provided the framework for Olivi's theory that economic exchange is subject to a dynamic equilibrium. One result of this was our growing appreciation of the social function fulfilled by merchants as the distributors of goods. They played an ever more important role, and were even seen as altogether indispensable to common good; and when they gained, everyone gained.[95]

6

A TAILWIND FROM THE PAST

What Would Our Ancestors Suggest?

Now that we are coming to the end, let us turn the tables for a moment. If they were around today, our ancestors would definitely be surprised by many things. They would envy us a lot too, and not only for our advances in dentistry. They would be amazed by how comfortable our lives are.

Or so we assume. In fact, we can't be sure that they would be happy in our overheated living rooms; they might feel trapped, and miss the fresh air coming in through the draughty windows. Perhaps they would be exhausted by our constant need to shop. Long-haul flights might not be quite to their taste either, because pre-modern humans were not used to spending hours and hours hemmed into a small space, unable to stretch their legs – everyday life was a lot more mobile, and the chair only became a truly democratic piece of furniture in the nineteenth century, thanks to Michael Thonet. Before then, people sat on benches that were constantly carried hither and thither, or on the floor, or ... well, moved around. Even churches did not have benches until the 1500s, when the Reformation introduced a more disciplined attitude to churchgoing than people were used to in previous centuries, which were full of hustle and bustle, including in the house of God. The speed of everything would most likely irritate our forefathers and the range of goods on offer would astonish them: fresh strawberries all year long, meat every day? They would pinch themselves, and think the dream of the Land of Cockaigne had finally come true.

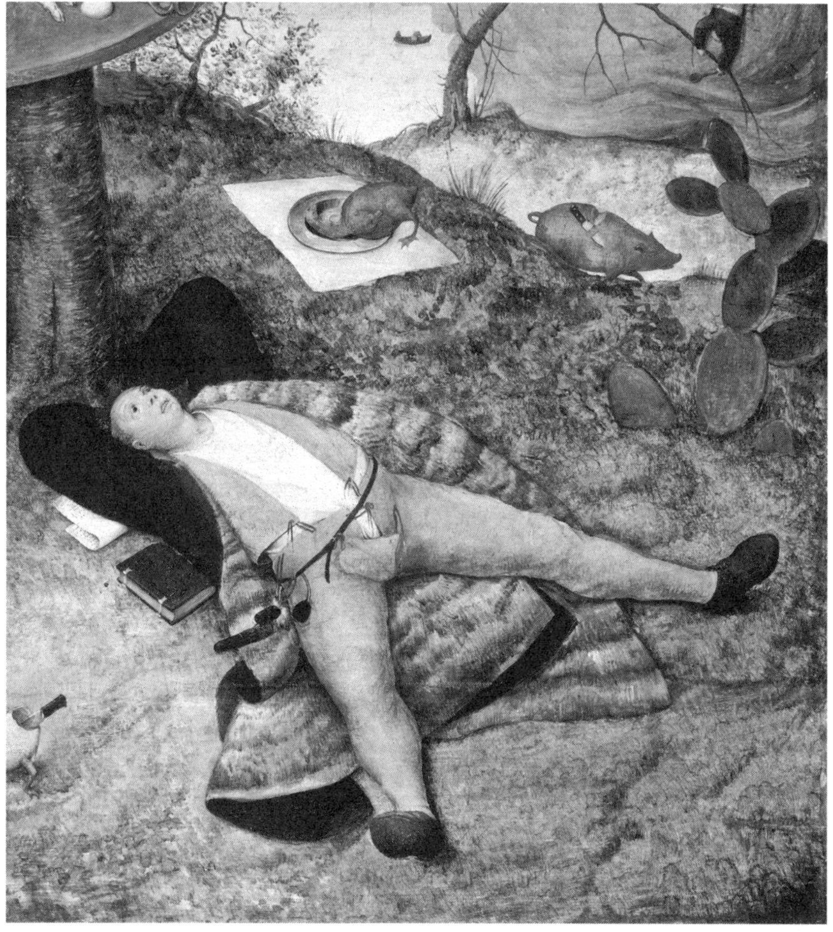

45. Pieter Bruegel the Elder, *The Land of Cockaigne* (detail), 1566

That said, in the Middle Ages many people thought Cockaigne the stuff of nightmares, not dreams. Our voracious appetite is not our most attractive quality, and Pieter Bruegel the Elder's famous imagery brilliantly represents Cockaigne as a profoundly farcical world. Bruegel's human, having stuffed his face, lies there, exposed to the observer, with legs akimbo and flies ajar. Nearby, a boiled egg stalks past him on amphibian legs. On the right, in the background, a droll little mannikin dangles from a mountain of porridge, exhausted from the effort of having to eat his way through it using a wooden spoon, only to arrive on the other side looking utterly ridiculous, tumbling like a toddler down the slope. Elsewhere, a goose voluntarily lies down on a plate, ready for roasting, and a hog trots about calmly with a knife in its loin. Our sheer insatiability is paraded here in all its grotesque glory.

It is quite possible that our ancestors would scoff at our unashamed greed. However, they would probably be happy for us too, because of everything that modernity has achieved – our astonishing transformation over the past 500 years, and how we've managed to tame nature, straightening rivers, scaling mountains and advancing into both air and space. And when we tell them about climate change, they might not be particularly perturbed. They would perhaps smile reassuringly, lean back and tell us that we will surely find a way. We, who have changed so much, can surely change once more to surmount the challenges we face in the twenty-first century?

So they would be all the more bemused when we tell them that, for the past fifty years, ever since the Club of Rome's *The Limits to Growth*, we've been like rabbits caught in headlights. All this time, we have known that humanity is working towards its own demise. All this time, we have understood that, if we carry on this way, we'll have a catastrophe on our hands. Fifty years ago, the report told us that

> if the present growth trends in world population, industrialization, pollution, food production, and resource depletion continue unchanged, the limits to growth on this planet will be reached sometime within the next hundred years. The most probable result will be a rather sudden and uncontrollable decline in both population and industrial capacity.[1]

We knew then that we could change current growth trends and 'establish a condition of ecological and economic stability' only if we took rapid and decisive action. That fifty years have passed in which we have done nothing consequential about it – during which, in fact, we have turned the dial on the growth machine up by several notches – our predecessors would find very hard to believe. But you're so *modern*, they would say. You're so flexible and incredibly creative. You have technology we could only dream of in our day, you have the state and democracy, you can make your own laws and make sure that something is done about the root causes of these problems. You are rational; you discovered the principles of reason during the Enlightenment. You could simply apply the fault principle and bring whoever is liable to account. Surely you can do that? It is your responsibility to ensure that the planet remains habitable by humans. All you need to do is change, as you have done so often in the past. All you have to do is adjust your expectations and your value system, reorientate your productivity and your economies, build the cost of environmental destruction into your business plans, tax pollution appropriately, create financial incentives for protecting the ecosystem and thereby ensure that the planet's limits are respected. All you have to do is rethink your world. So where's the problem?[2]

And if we tell them that it's just not that easy, they would start wondering. Is it possible, they would ask, that despite all the changes you have gone through, you're still the same? Is it possible that you actually can't cope with all the freedom you've won for yourselves? Because otherwise you would simply do what needs to be done. What you need are limits. In our day, we had sins: in the marketplaces they told us that some things were forbidden, pure and simple, and we were constantly reminded that much is possible, but not everything is good. The mortal sins were the worst. Gula, for example – gluttony, lack of restraint – was frowned upon, and we didn't spend all year eating meat day in, day out: we had times of abundance and times of abstinence. But tell us, they would ask, who preaches to you? And then, when we show them what people in the twenty-first century hear and see all day long, almost without pause – adverts – they would stop wondering. Well, they'd say, when you preach to your fellow humans every day about where to find the cheapest steak or the most affordable flights to Thailand, it's no wonder that you are where you are. People practise what you preach, and you preach that they need as much as possible as cheaply as possible, and unless you stop nothing will change.

And when we tell them that it's all because businesses have to compete with each other – that they can only increase their return on investment if they are cheaper, tougher and sneakier than their international rivals when it comes to plundering resources, reducing transaction costs and exploiting legal loopholes – our ancestors would simply ask: so why don't you change all that? Don't you know that envy erodes society? Envy is also the least fun mortal sin. It makes you ill. You are creating a collective unwellness. Excessive competition makes society ill, unhappy and tired. Why don't you just stop? Do you need a Father in Heaven again, who forbids you to make each other unhappy?

They would give us one final piece of advice: don't underestimate indolence. We used to call it 'acedia', today you call it 'status quo bias'. You have to give people a kick up the proverbial, especially those stuck in their boss chair, insisting that the world should play by their rules. People like that frequently suffer from a superiority complex – which we call pride, *superbia* – and it is usually the most piteous of all people who are caught in that trap. They just can't help it. Their self-esteem is so fragile that they have to constantly suck the marrow out of the rest of the world, and they will, if need be, drag it into the abyss with them. For some inexplicable reason, men are particularly liable to it. Our forebears will probably be somewhat sorry to hear that, because 50 per cent of them were men. They might advise us to let women do the steering for once. In the Middle Ages, it was not unusual for a woman to head up a business. The Fugger dynasty, for instance, rose to power during the fifteenth century under the leadership of women.[3]

Maybe it's time you learnt to set yourselves limits.

Would they advise us to reintroduce the death penalty? Most likely not, because they, too, loved freedom better than anything. But what stops us from setting clear boundaries? Proscriptions can clarify matters. They make life simpler. As Maja Göpel has said, 'I think many such proscriptions would make a lot of people feel liberated.'[4]

Bertha Benz would be surprised too

Let's go back to the beginning of this book. Can our adherence to old ideas be accounted for as a sort of collective developmental disorder? Why is it practically impossible for us to get rid of modernity's paradigms, even though we know that they were created for the world of our grandparents and great-grandparents and are no longer useful to us?

The best illustration of this is perhaps the combustion engine, without a doubt a brilliant nineteenth-century invention. It was built in 1876 by Nicolaus August Otto and Gottlieb Daimler of the Deutz gas engine factory and launched by Bertha Benz in 1888, with a pioneering, almost thirteen-hour-long drive from Mannheim to Pforzheim in the legendary Benz Model 3. No one can doubt that this invention revolutionised and enriched life for twentieth-century humans. But Bertha Benz is from our great-great-grandmothers' generation, who lived a century and a half ago, and she would surely be surprised to hear that it took her descendants more than a century to invent something new.

Cognitive dissonance and the unwillingness to change

Paradoxically, we want things to improve yet stay the same. People often do the strangest things to prevent change, eschewing neither effort nor expense to ensure that their world view remains intact. How else to explain our attachment to the combustion engine? In the same way, we are attached to advancement, growth and increasing our wealth. The arguments for the status quo are all too familiar and plausible: it's worked well so far, why panic now? There will always be some unintended consequences. Friction loss is inevitable, so global injustice is something we just have to grin and bear, and we can't prevent climate change anyhow.

Why change is so difficult remains a mystery, especially given that humans are, historically speaking, such experts in it. We can do things differently. We're brilliant at it, in fact. But we only rarely decide to do so of our own accord. Most of us only respond to external pressure and will agree to something new only when forced to, despite the fact that we like to think of ourselves as fundamentally quite innovative and modern. Behavioural psychologists call this problem 'cognitive dissonance'. Every year when Christmas is over, we swear we'll eat less chocolate next year and do more exercise. Then, inevitably, there we are, two weeks later, with not enough time on our hands, and then we read somewhere that chocolate is good for the nervous system and so we put our plans to change on hold again, for the time being. We always want some kind of change and we get the need for action, but, when push comes to shove, we decide that things are OK the way they are. The same scenario plays out year after year. Humanity has somehow made itself comfortable in a world where everything has to change and improve constantly, but at the same time we want everything to stay just the way it is. Cognitive dissonance: a chronic illness marked by a strange yet familiar discomfort with the present day.

The pattern of cognitive dissonance also defines our behaviour regarding sustainability. In this case, though, it is about more than just losing a pound or two. It's about overcoming climate change and its consequences. You and I know that everything will change, and we know that we have to change. We want to do our bit, but also don't want to overdo it. We should proceed carefully. Not all that needs doing can be done, and we ought to be satisfied with doing the possible. It starts with our personal lives: everyone knows that flying is bad for the environment and that we urgently have to reduce CO_2 emissions. Nevertheless, you can't ask us to forgo our annual holiday abroad. Flying once in a while isn't all that bad, really. Also, we buy organic stuff all the time, and hardly use the car. And we're OK with that, and we feel good – because we believe that, anyway, radical change is utopian and therefore impossible.

Do you want to leave change management up to crises?

Crises – having a serious illness diagnosed, fate dealing us a nasty blow – are famously good change managers, at least if and when we have overcome their first and perhaps most critical stage. Our reflex reaction to a crisis is refusal and denial. We don't want to believe that someone we love has died. There's been a mistake. It can't be true. It is an inevitable stage of crisis management; you have to live through it and at some point it'll be over. If things go really badly, the traumatised person remains stuck in this stage and will never overcome the consequences of the catastrophe, the death of their loved one. At worst, they will spend the rest of their life in a clinic.

Over the past fifty years, since the Club of Rome's first report in 1972, we've collectively lived through and concluded this first stage – the shock, the not-wanting-it-to-be-true. 'It's not the end of the world,' we said. 'Things like that happen all the time, so don't believe what the media tries to tell you. And anyway, there's no scientific proof.' Now, however, we have entered the next stage, when we face up to the crisis, confront it and work out how to use it constructively. The Covid crisis has taught us that change is possible; if we didn't know it before, we know it now.

In April 2020, a microscopic virus brought almost all air traffic to a standstill. The sky above Beijing was blue again, and many of us discovered that a summer holiday at home can be unexpectedly lovely. All of a sudden we were able to do things differently, because we had to, and this despite the fact that the crisis ruined more than our holiday plans. Drastic cuts, job losses, unrest and social divisions can't be overlooked. They demonstrate that a serious crisis can have extreme and far-reaching consequences, but also the potential to change the world. Already, though, it's clear that in twenty years' time we'll smile at the threat posed by Covid-19, in light of the by-then tangible consequences of climate change – the rise in the Earth's temperature and sea levels, more frequent floods, more intense droughts, more extreme weather events, more marine dead zones due to a lack of oxygen in the water, more refugees and more pressure on democratic governments – because crises make us more susceptible to conspiracy theories and self-anointed saviours.

Does this mean that the crisis has to get a lot worse before we'll allow change to happen and willingly take the next step? In this book I have tried to show that there are alternatives. We don't have to wait for the worst to happen. Change is possible. But here, too, the general laws of successful change management apply. The first is: there is no panacea. Each crisis has to be lived through personally by those affected. You can't delegate the process, just as you can't outsource learning a language or a musical instrument. I can't pay you to learn Mandarin for me; similarly, I can't expect the past to solve my problems here in our present. Each generation has to find its own path. Nevertheless, I can profit from other people's experience. It's useful to learn more about how others have dealt with cataclysms, how they've coped with having their lives turned upside down, how they have defended themselves against major threats. It helps us carry the burden, it gives us hope, expands the horizon of our imagination and thus gives us more room to manoeuvre. This is precisely what history offers us: a path out of paralysis.

Silencing the Sound of Inevitability

One of the secrets of modernity's success is the magic formula 'There's no other way.' People say that capitalism is the only economic model that works. They say that free markets are clearly the best way to distribute goods; that socialism has failed and there are no alternative economic models in sight. Well, that may be true, but if markets really are the best of all possible ways in the best of all possible worlds, we have to make sure that they work properly. We need to reduce their adverse side effects.

Armin Falk, a behavioural economist, once drew comparisons with medicine: if we really know and are sure that we have a brilliantly working pharmaceutical, it is in everyone's interest to limit its adverse side effects. The same goes for markets. They are the best tool we currently have for organising our economies, distributing goods and providing us with the things we need, and for that reason it is all the more urgent that we fix their weaknesses and balance their deficits. The solution to our problems cannot consist of constantly either damning or defending capitalism. As long as there is no alternative system, we have to try to limit the problems it creates. It is quite possible that we end up with something very different.

In order to minimise the unintended consequences of market capitalism we need more research, by academic economists who are more open, less defensive and, especially, non-normative. In the past, business students were more or less indoctrinated; like nineteenth-century theologists, professors instructed them in dogma rather than critical thinking. This has changed in recent years, as a new generation of economists has taken over and students call for greater pluralism in academia. Sustainable economics has become established as a new branch of economic sciences, and welfare economics is also increasingly taught at university. Meanwhile, behavioural economists, the new discipline of institutional economics, and Nobel Prize winners such as Amartya Sen, Joseph Stiglitz and Elinor Ostrom are demanding economic theories fit for the twenty-first century, ones that do not orientate themselves on paradigms of the past. Kate Raworth, for instance, an economist at the University of Oxford, has proposed a 'doughnut economy', which replaces short-term thinking for maximum gain with managing resources in such a way that 'no one falls short on life's essentials'.[5] The economic sciences are in the process of once again taking the lead, and are creating an alternative roadmap for the future. The interesting thing about it is that they are spearheaded by women. They are perhaps less afraid of change, maybe because they have less to lose – after all, modern economies have for the past century systematically denied them the opportunity to participate, at least in leadership positions.

But let's return to the supposed lack of alternatives: of course, there will always be situations without an exit route. If my child is drowning, I have to jump into the water. There's no other way. But in 'future planning' the single-option model doesn't work, because if there is no other option we can't make plans. So let's say goodbye to the single-track thinking of the last 200 years and look further back, to the way pre-modern humans managed their lives and resources. There, we can indeed learn practical lessons from the past.

Cooperating makes us happier than selfishness

Cooperation does everyone good, us as well as our planet. Immediately, though, there's an objection from the back row:

wasn't our exploitation of the planet's resources over the course of the twentieth century the result of brilliant teamwork? Let's not glorify cooperation – our gift for it has led to wars and concentration camps too. But what is being argued here is that good things can be achieved if we cooperate. All we need to do is want them enough.

In the first chapter of this book, I showed how communal resource management in medieval monasteries and convents worked for more than a millennium and a half; naturally, people experienced failure back then too, but they tried again and again. Knowing that, as the Bible says, 'man does not live by bread alone', we created ways of life that systematically integrated spirituality into the everyday. It doesn't mean that all was hunky-dory. On the contrary, what we are able to reconstruct from the history of these communities that lived and worked together is that they went through all sorts of departures, high points, crises and collapses. We have learnt how people back then tried to balance the inevitable tension between individual and society, and minimised the disaffectedness that results from living too much in each other's pockets by establishing clear rules; and how, from generation to generation, they kept changing and rearranging themselves with controversial reforms.

Equally, what clearly emerged from our case study of the monasteries is the realisation that communal economies can work – without exploitation, without slavery. True, most monasteries had lay brothers who took on the day-to-day manual labour, but they were proper members of the community. Nowadays we could describe them as full-time, permanent employees. The role of monasteries as landowners, too, has frequently been misunderstood. The folk who lived in the villages and estates belonging to the monasteries were no serfs in the eighteenth-century sense. They were not enslaved, like those forced to work sugar plantations in America. They were people who put their labour at the disposal of their landowner or employer on clearly delimited working days in return for land, protection and membership of the community. It is possible, then, to work together for a secure future. We can take inspiration from this, and redefine the aims of economic management: do we want to hoard our gains, or drive economic sustainability and take care of each other? Do we want to enjoy the fruits of our labour as a community? How about pursuing a caring economy, instead of exploitation?

Sustainability is our only viable survival strategy

We are capable of managing our economies without destroying the planet's assets. Our ancestors knew ways in which to use communal resources sustainably. Of course, we exploited nature then too, but humans have never done as much damage to nature as they have in the past 200 years. When the mining administrator Hans Carl von Carlowitz introduced the term 'sustainability' in the 1700s, he was responding to the over-felling of trees that resulted when, in an age of absolute monarchs (then considered rather modern), the sovereign ordered the intensification of mining efforts. Before then we shared public resources like forests, soil, bodies of water and mountains without destroying them, and built the cost of the effect on our surroundings into our plans – in the form of waived earnings, fishing quotas, bans on forest clearing, fallow years, and so on. Ostrom's rules for the sustainable shared use of communal resources essentially represent a rediscovery of empirical historical knowledge. A common objection is that people back then, such as Lake Constance's fishermen, weren't at all interested in ecological issues or environmental protection in today's terms. But that is exactly the point: sustainability is not a 'nice to have', it isn't a modern invention. Sustainability is the only survival strategy we have. The fishermen on Lake Constance knew that, and when they managed the lake, the source of their livelihood, so carefully they were acting in their very own interest. It makes you wonder: when did our capacity for long-term thinking and acting in the interests of our descendants disappear? When did we forget how to keep an eye on the well-being of the next generation, and the one after that?

We looked at the Palatine forest associations, the *Haingeraiden*, which worked successfully for centuries. It was only with the seventeenth century's desire for ever more intensive exploitation that this form of forest management disappeared. These old associations (also known as *Markgenossenschaften*, literally 'communal woodland fellowships') were all about the principle of sustainability, which perforce limited the extent to which the woods could be exploited. In the Siebelding Valley, the members of the local association tried to protect their forest from unnecessary felling – merely for the sake of the French king's military interests – by hiding the lumberjacks' tools. Through this joint action they were able to stop the destruction of their forest. Yet they were unable to stand up to the paradigms of increased efficiency and maximisation of utility in the long run. Slowly but surely, the associations were uprooted and finally entirely abolished, as obstacles standing in the way of modernity.

The history of the medieval beguinages, meanwhile, demonstrates how autonomous urban communities of women held their own for centuries, as experts in sustainability. These women took an active part in economic life; as in Marseilles, for instance, where they supplied the financial markets with credit, providing young couples with start-up capital. We find inspiration here, too, for agricultural projects, for example the beguine of Douai's watercress farm and the still-extant urban farm of the sisters of Sint-Truiden.

'All we need is less'

As far as the circular economy and recycling are concerned, history offers us not so much inspiration as crystal-clear guidelines. If one takes a historical view, linear economies are a recent phenomenon; and the problems we feel so acutely now have been created by ourselves. Recycling was the norm well into the early twentieth century, and the second half of the 1900s will in future be notorious for a sad achievement: it was the period when we filled the planet with waste. During the final four decades of the twentieth century, as the markets were flooded with cheap oil, a spectacular waste creation machine was set in motion. With unbelievable speed, it produced nothing but short-lived consumer goods – consumer goods and disposable goods, the overwhelming majority of which were used once and never again, such as plastic packaging for our lunchtime sandwiches. The 'rubbishing' of our planet was accompanied by a dramatic change both in consumption and in our eating habits. We have forgotten what 'fresh' tastes like. A mere forty years ago, most of us would have refused to eat ham that had been lying around on some shelf for weeks, sealed in plastic. A lot is changing now in that regard, but we are still producing 407 million metric tons of plastic every year, of which more than a quarter is packaging. The average plastic bag is used for twenty-five minutes.

The fact that it took us just five decades to get used to this nonsense, however, gives us hope too. It shows how quickly we can get used to something new, that habits are stubborn but not unbreakable. Back then, merely fifty years ago, when single-use packaging was first invented, no one thought that it would lead to microplastics contaminating not only the Earth's oceans and groundwater, but the very food we eat. Whoever is liable for creating the waste should pay for it. The price of plastic must be adjusted to include the cost of disposal and clean-up. The user should not have to deal with the problem. The OECD's new accounting standards are one step in that direction. All kinds of advances are being tried out in the sustainability departments of large corporations too, and it is incumbent upon consumers and lawmakers to urgently support these.

Something else we have forgotten is how integral a part of economic life second-hand markets and repair professions used to be – not least because historians have mainly focused on production and financial markets, and thus lost sight of the huge contribution the recycling sector made to medieval economies. It is clear that our tax systems should support menders. The cost of waste disposal should no longer be borne by the community. This is particularly true of the flourishing online trade: cities should no longer be forced to effectively subsidise Amazon and other online sellers by shouldering the expense of disposing of packaging waste. Here, too, it is only fair to bill the creator. It isn't right that costs are constantly nationalised but gains privatised.

If you let go, your hands are free. This is what we learnt in the last chapter, on the minimalists of yore. What has motivated us humans across the millennia is not only the desire for more – expansion, profit, power: no, what has also driven us is the desire for simplicity and freedom. The question, then, is this: might the pendulum now, after the twentieth century's continuous high of untrammelled consumption, finally swing in the other direction? What happens if more and more of us discover, like Diogenes, the joy of the simple life, and politely beg all those great commanders coming up to us, trying to sell us power and riches, to please move out of our sun? What happens if more and more of us want less and less?

Don't misunderstand me: my question is not a plea for a retreat into isolation. On the contrary. Our lasting fascination with the minimalists of antiquity proves how powerful an idea can be – but ideas need people, they need communities to carry them, to bring them to fruition. All the alternatives suggested here need their visionaries, people who'll carry the desire for change through the city streets, as the mendicant friars did in the thirteenth century. They were able to influence others, they changed the future, took a stance in their sermons, condemned injustice, shaped the markets, offered support to the founders of MFIs and composed analyses of the prevailing market processes that were far ahead of their time. Why not be inspired by these models?

All for one and one for all

The invention of microfinance in the late Middle Ages was born of a concern for the well-being of everyone who lived in the prosperous cities of northern Italy. Here, too, the question arises of how we managed to forget microloans, given that they were once ubiquitous. Why did Muhammad Yunus have to reinvent the concept in the late twentieth century? In the Middle Ages, the financially successful were capable of solidarity too: the cities made a communal effort and invested in the freshly founded banks, and members of the urban elite allowed themselves to be drafted into running the banks for free for a year. The basic idea to be deduced from this, as well as other examples of how earlier societies dealt with microfinance, leads us to conclude that we must ensure that everyone, no matter what their social and financial background or circumstance, has access to the financial markets. Excluding anyone from participation in the market, or – in what is an emerging trend – reducing our participation to the role of mere consumer, dramatically affects the common good. This also suggests a possible objection to a universal basic income: would it not threaten to further reduce us to the role of consumer? Should we not, instead, enable market participation by expanding the spectrum of opportunities?

The fact that every single one of us matters cannot be emphasised enough. History is made by people: the women and men, young and old, rich and poor who take responsibility for their world, singly and collectively. One person may have a bright idea, but it takes a whole village to raise the proverbial child – to support the idea, lend it authority, provide the wherewithal to implement it and to embed the result. Mutual support and teamwork are crucial. The whole is greater than the sum of its parts – Aristotle's ancient observation bears remembering. In such cases, too, working together is a lot more fun than struggling along on your own like a well-intentioned lone wolf.

We must not leave our problems for future generations to sort out

A twelfth-century writer once listed the downsides of old age. Chief among them were stubbornness and grumpiness, querulousness and sluggishness, over-attachment to the past, in-my-dayism and resignation. He also admonished the old not to turn away from the young, and the young not to act like clever clogs and condescend to the old. He reminds the young that 'we are what they once were; and some day we will be what they are now'.[6] This awareness of how intrinsic a part we are of the generational cycle was, in the Middle Ages, deeply anchored in a society that saw itself as a community of both the living and the dead. Our connectedness was a key concept, passed on as cultural legacy from one generation to the next in the shape of a concern for our salvation and prayers for the dead. Papal indulgences secured the flow of money from one age to the next, funding communal and charitable local projects. Their logic may seem decidedly odd to us now, and needless to say we are no longer afraid of purgatory, but we may have thrown the baby out with the bathwater: behind the concept of purgatory lies the notion that what we do survives us. If I know that my descendants can pray for my soul in limbo, it is very probably in my interest to act in theirs.

We call it 'generativity' now – this idea of caring about future generations and acting for the benefit of the humans of the future, who will inhabit a world where we no longer exist. Instead of 'After me, the flood', we say, 'After me, the future'. Hopefully, we will once again manage to anchor the art of transgenerational thinking and acting firmly in our collective consciousness, and society as a whole. The Fuggerei in Augsburg is inspirational here: this social housing project was initiated in the early sixteenth century and still exists 500 years later, still offering a fresh start to those who have fallen into poverty through no fault of their own. Good deeds have consequences too.

Don't Fear the Future

I hope that this brief history of sustainability has provided some inspiration for how we might go about remodelling our outdated short-term economy into a long-term one. This hope is based on the fact that there were times when we humans knew the limits of our planet better than we do now. We can't help but be encouraged by the thought that we can learn from their experience. They lived in a different world, yes, but the crises they overcame were surely no less existential than ours, and swapping experiences helps.

The future isn't out of options. We have a choice. It is up to us to decide. Pierre de Jean Olivi, the thirteenth-century French economic theorist, wrote not only those famous lines about capital, but also a treatise on freedom.[7] While his contemporaries followed Aristotle and defined human freedom as our ability to direct ourselves towards an end that reason tells us is worth pursuing, Olivi dug deeper. To him, freedom was something that we experience directly, every day, with every decision, as we are constantly torn between two options, between regret and excuses, between courage and exhaustion.

For Olivi, this proves that we have the freedom to choose. He uses the term 'attentiveness', which has been used since antiquity to describe our capacity for apprehending our inner voice, our impulses and feelings. According to Olivi, attentiveness is the first and most noble mark of freedom, and freedom of the will is what makes us more than an intelligent animal. We can make decisions and reflect on our actions. Olivi describes our feeling and taste (*affectus et gustus*) for good, our perception of sweetness (*dulcor*) when someone does the right thing, and believes that our will is indomitable. It transcends all else in creation. Not even God can compel it. Olivi's faith in free will makes humanity the author of its own fate. We have a choice. We can decide whether to leave the future to chance or, trusting in our power, finally take matters into our own hands; whether to let things carry on the way they are, or get together and use our combined strength to back all the great ideas that people are coming up with all over the world. It does us good to converse with the old now and again. The past can take away our fear of the future. If we want to, we can do things differently. The experiences of our forebears – that, at least, is the hope that runs through my book – can whet our appetite for the sweetness of what is good, and inspire us to at least try something new.

ACKNOWLEDGEMENTS

Who would have thought that the Middle Ages gave us not only knights, crusades and castles, but also all kinds of expertise in sustainability?

Thank you to the Middle Ages team at the Institute for History at Mannheim University, chief among them Tanja Skambraks and Stephan Nicolussi-Köhler for the focus and energy with which they have propelled recent research into medieval economics. Thank you also to Maria-Magdalena Rückert, Hiram Kümper, Verena Weller and Katja Gutzmer for their support. I am grateful to the German Research Foundation for their financial support, which helped to create an environment that made it possible for me to rediscover long-lost experiences of sustainable behaviour in history. A very special thank you to Lena Liznerski for her invaluable help in putting together the manuscript and the list of illustrations, to Sophie Henle, Laura Grabarek and Nico Marin Franco for all the time they spent researching the literature, to Christa Petermann for her corrections and benevolent curiosity, and to Philipp Gassert and Angela Borgstedt for providing spiritual support from the perspective of contemporary history. I am also very grateful to Jochen Streb (Mannheim) and Bernd Schneidmüller (Heidelberg) for their both critical and constructive first reading and indispensable advice.

Organised jointly with Talke Schaffrannek (Director of Circular Economy, BASF) and Laura Maria Edinger-Schons (Professor of Sustainable Economics, Hamburg University), the first interdisciplinary teaching sessions – the 'Scientists for Future' lecture series and the 'Sustainability: Lessons from the Past for the Future' seminar – took place in spring 2020. I thank them and the students for the lively discussions, which forced me to be precise and concrete in my thinking about the relationship between sustainable development goals and what our ancestors knew about sustainability. For generously supporting the project in many different ways – with their curiosity, incisive questions, invitations, expert eye, encouragement, by listening – thank you to Christa Schlepper (Vienna), Nicolas Jaspert (Heidelberg), Gerhard Fouquet (Kiel), Sabine von Heusinger (Cologne), Christina Andenna (Graz), Nora Berend (Cambridge), Daniel S. Smail (Harvard), Thomas Ertl (Berlin), Simon Teuscher (Zurich), Silvia Negri (Zurich), Ludger Lieb (Heidelberg), Ursula Beck (Karlsruhe), Sascha Doering (Heidelberg), Rosemarie Tracy (Mannheim), Gabriela Signori (Konstanz), Johannes Paulmann (Mainz) and especially Friedemann Schrenk (Frankfurt/Karonga).

A huge thank you to my editor, Moritz Volk, who first condemned me to radical cuts and then judiciously edited the whole. The book is all the better for it. Any remaining blunders are my own.

I am for ever indebted to Lyndal Roper (Oxford) for setting the ball rolling on a dreary November day in a café in Bloomsbury Square. Last but not least, my deepest thanks to my agent Nina Sillem who, with a truly extraordinary mix of concentration and ease, launched the project and put it on the right track, and who has been by my side throughout the entire effort of writing it.

It never occurred to me while writing this book that it might one day be translated into English, and I am thus all the more grateful to Gesche Ipsen for her careful rendering. The text has gained something in the process. Thank you also to Andrew Franklin and Georgia Poplett at Profile Books and Sue Berger Ramin at Brandeis University Press for their judicious support and constructive suggestions for cuts, and for the smooth and good-humoured collaboration. Finally, thank you to my colleague Sabine von Mering at Brandeis University for her irresistible drive to change the world.

I had to write this book because I want to support the Fridays for Future generation with a tailwind blowing from the past, as we struggle together for the future of our wonderful planet. I dedicate it to my beloved children, Paul, Klara, Friedrun and Lotte, and to my grandson Nelio.

Mannheim, April 2021/Munich, March 2024

LIST OF ILLUSTRATIONS

Tiangong Kaiwu, in Peter Tschudin, *Grundzüge der Papiergeschichte* (Stuttgart, 2002), p. 78.

21. How the art of papermaking spread across Europe. Tschudin, *Grundzüge der Papiergeschichte*, p. 98.
22. Illustration of a paper mill in Comenius's *Orbis sensualium pictus* (Nuremberg, 1658), Chapter 92 'Papier', hs-augsburg.de/~harsch/Chronologia/Lspost17/Comenius/com_0092.html.
23. Black-poplar catkins with seeds. Jacob Christian Schäffer, *Versuche und Muster ohne alle Lumpen oder doch mit einem geringen Zusatz derselben, Papier zu machen* (Regensburg, 1765), Plate 1.
24. Wasps' nests provided the inspiration for wood-based paper. From Schäffer, *Versuche und Muster*, Plate 2.
25. Device for transporting antique columns, late fifteenth century. Francesco di Giorgio Martini, *Opusculum de architettura*, London, British Library MS 197.b21, fol. 27 r. © The Trustees of the British Museum.
26. Aachen's cathedral, by Albrecht Dürer (1520). Reproduction, private archive, Jorg Mühlenberg.
27. Armrest of the throne of Charlemagne, Aachen cathedral. Drawing by Josef Buchkremer (1899). Photo: Wikimedia Commons/ACBahn (CCBY-SA 4.0). Katharina Corsepius, 'Der Aachener 'Karlsthron' zwischen Zeremoniell und Herrschermemoria', in Marion Steinicke and Stefan Weinfurter (eds), *Investitur- und Krönungsrituale. Herrschaftseinsetzungen im kulturellen Vergleich* (Cologne, 2005), pp. 359–75, image 6.
28. Bologna's Palazzo del Monte di Pietà, next to the Cattedrale di S. Pietro (detail). Photo: Wikimedia Commons/Mariaorecchia (CC-BY-SA-3.0), upload.wikimedia.org/wikipedia/commons/6/6b/Il_monte_di_piet%C3%A0_e_la_Cattedrale_di_San_Pietro_a_Bologna.jpg. Used with the kind permission of the Chiesa di Bologna.
29. Pawns taken to the monte, 1550–1700 (ten-year average). Mauro Carboni, 'Converting Goods into Cash: An Ethical Approach to Pawnbroking in Early Modern Bologna', in Nicholas Terpstra and Mauro Carboni, *The Material Culture of Debt*, Centre for Reformation and Renaissance Studies (Toronto, 2012), p. 67.
30. An institutional pawnbroker – the Banca di Faenza – as depicted by Giovanni Battista Bertucci in his sixteenth-century painting

c. 1300. Author's own, following L. Bourdua; Aubrey Gwynn and Neville Hadcock, *Medieval Religious Houses: Ireland* (Harlow, 1970), pp. 235–62; David Knowles and Neville Hadcock, *Medieval Religious Houses: England and Wales* (London, 1971), pp. 221–30; John B. Freed, *The Friars in German Society* (Cambridge, 1977), pp. 173–223; Richard W. Emery, *The Friars in Medieval France* (New York, 1962), p. 6; Richard Southern, *Western Society and the Church* (London, 1970), p. 285.

43. *Sermon to the Birds* by Giotto. Fresco, Basilica di S. Francesco, Assisi, *c.* 1295. Photo: Wikimedia / Public Domain, commons.wikimedia.org/wiki/File:Giotto_-_Legend_of_St_Francis_-_-15-_-_Sermon_to_the_Birds.jpg.
44. Portrait of Luca Pacioli, 'father of double-entry bookkeeping', by Jacopo de' Barbari, 1495. Photo: Wikimedia / Public Domain.
45. Pieter Bruegel the Elder, *The Land of Cockaigne* (detail), 1566, Alte Pinakothek, Munich. Photo: akg-images.

NOTES

1. Was Everyone Poor Until We Invented Capitalism?

1 Adam Smith, *The Wealth of Nations* (London, 1904), p. 23f.

2 See Frank Rexroth (ed.), *Meistererzählungen vom Mittelalter. Epochenimaginationen und Verlaufsmuster in der Praxis mediävistischer Disziplinen* (Munich, 2007).

3 Deirdre N. McCloskey, *If You're So Smart: The Narrative of Economic Expertise* (Chicago, 1991), p. 1.

4 Joshua Greene, *Moral Tribes: Emotion, Reason, and the Gap Between Us and Them* (London, 2013); Lajos L. Brons, 'Othering, an Analysis', *Transcience: A Journal of Global Studies* 6(1), 2015, pp. 69–90.

5 Steven Pinker, *The Better Angels of Our Nature: The Decline of Violence in History and Its Causes* (London, 2011).

6 Juliet B. Schor, The *Overworked American: The Unexpected Decline of Leisure* (New York, 1991).

7 E. P. Thompson, 'Time, work-discipline, and industrial capitalism', *Past & Present*, 38(1) (December 1967), pp. 56–97.

8 Gerhard Fouquet, 'Brücken. Bau und Bauunterhalt im späten Mittelalter und in der frühen Neuzeit: Das Beispiel der Weidenhäuser Brücke in Marburg', in Kurt Andermann and Nina Gallion (eds), *Weg und Steg. Aspekte des Verkehrswesens von der Spätantike bis zum Ende des Alten Reiches* (Ostfildern, 2018), pp. 47–73 (68).

9 Ulf Dirlmeier, Gerhard Fouquet and Bernd Fuhrmann, *Europa im Spätmittelalter 1215–1378* (Berlin, 2010), p. 15.

10 Ulf Dirlmeier and Erich Maschke, *Untersuchungen zu Einkommensverhältnissen und Lebenshaltungskosten in oberdeutschen*

Städten des Spätmittelalters. Mitte 14. bis Anfang 16. Jahrhundert (Heidelberg, 1978), p. 357.

11 Statistisches Bundesamt, 'Global animal farming, meat production and meat consumption', 2020 data, https://www.destatis.de/DE/Themen/Laender-Regionen/Internationales/Thema/landwirtschaft-fischerei/tierhaltung-fleischkonsum/tierhaltung-fleisch.html.

12 Ibid., pp. 445f, 439 and 428.

13 What follows is taken from 'Raum, Wirtschaft und Menschen' in Dirlmeier, Fouquet and Fuhrmann, *Europa im Spätmittelalter 1215–1378*, pp. 6–94. For information on demographics and climate change see ibid., p. 18.

14 Dirlmeier, Fouquet and Fuhrmann, *Europa im Spätmittelalter 1215–1378*, p. 74.

2. Sharing

1 Michael Tomasello, *Why We Cooperate* (Cambridge, MA, 2009). However, let's not be tempted to romanticise things: our ability to cooperate and share has not only made us better at hunting and collectively caring for the sick, but also led to wars, concentration camps and such.

2 Robin Dunbar, *Grooming, Gossip and the Evolution of Language* (Cambridge, MA, 1996).

3 Jan-Otmar Hesse, 'Wie neu ist die Share Economy? Anmerkungen zur Geschichte einer Wirtschaftsform', in Julian Dörr, Nils Goldschmidt and Frank Schorkopf (eds), *Share Economy: Institutionelle Grundlagen und gesellschaftspolitische Rahmenbedingungen* (Tübingen, 2018), pp. 21–37 (26).

4 Interview with Gunther Schnabl from the Institute for Economic Policy at Leipzig University, Susanne Heinrich, 'Der schwarze Pudel', in *Futur II* (2018), https://futurzwei.org/article/1030.

5 Chris J. Martin, 'The sharing economy: A pathway to sustainability or a nightmarish form of neoliberal capitalism?', *Ecological Economics*, 121 (2016), pp. 149–59; see also Russell Belk, 'You are what you can access: Sharing and collaborative consumption online', *Journal of Business Research*, 67(8) (2014), pp. 1595–600: 'The old wisdom that we are what we own, may need modifying

to consider forms of possession and uses that do not involve ownership.'

6 Harald Baer et al. (eds), *Lexikon nichtchristlicher Religionsgemeinschaften* (Freiburg, 2010).

7 *St Benedict's Rule for Monasteries*, trans. Leonard J. Doyle (Collegeville, MN, 1948).

8 *The Rule of the Master*, trans. Luke Eberle (Collegeville, MN, 77).

9 George Lawless, *Augustine of Hippo and His Monastic Rule* (Oxford, 1987), p. 81.

10 Ibid., pp. 93–5. See Luc Verheijen (ed.), *La règle des saint Augustin*, Vol. 1: *Tradition manuscrite* (with a critical analysis on pp. 417–37); for the distribution of clothes see Vol. 2: *Recherches historiques* (Paris, 1967), Chapter 30; every brother is to receive according to his personal need (Chapter 3); whoever needs less is more fortunate, because further along on his path (Chapter 17); superiors are to hand out clothes and whatever else is needed to those who need them (Chapter 32); admonishment not to grumble (Chapter 38); books (Chapter 39); that clothes and shoes shall be handed out as and when needed (Chapters 39 and 40). Cf. also Adolar Zumkeller, *Das Mönchtum des heiligen Augustinus*, 2nd rev. edn (Würzburg, 1968). The Desert Fathers, too, advised against owning expensive clothing and wearing brand-new clothes; see John Wortley, *The Anonymous Sayings of the Desert Fathers* (Cambridge, 2013), pp. 592.11 and 592.13.

11 Georg Jenal, *Sub Regula S. Benedicti: Eine Geschichte der Söhne und Töchter Benedikts von den Anfängen bis zur Gegenwart* (Vienna/Cologne/Weimar, 2018), pp. 25–56.

12 There is no doubt, though, that private property did exist in monasteries. See Christine Stöllinger-Löser and Bernhard Dietrich Haage, 'Privatbesitz im Ordensleben' in *Verfasserlexikon* 11 (Berlin, 2004), cols 1269–70.

13 Singing is a 'body technique', and the bodies of people who sing together become synchronised – something that is now being rediscovered by scholars. The seminal study is Karl Bücher's *Arbeit und Rhythmus* (Leipzig/Berlin, 1909; first published 1896); cf. Peter Senn, 'Music and Economics: Reflections Inspired by Karl Bücher', in Jürgen Backhaus (ed.), *Karl Bücher: Theory, History, Anthropology,*

Non Market Economies (Marburg, 2000), pp. 73–112, especially pp. 77–86 on 'work and rhythm'; Shigenari Kanamori, 'Karl Bücher and Japanese Labour Songs', ibid., pp. 155–62; and Fritz Reheis, 'The Creativity of Slowness', ibid., pp. 163–76. See also Martin Held and Karl-Heinz Geißler (eds), *Von Rhythmen und Eigenzeiten. Perspektiven einer Ökologie der Zeit* (Stuttgart, 1995).

14 Ernst Tremp, *Der St. Galler Klosterplan. Faksimile, Begleittext, Beischriften und Übersetzung* (St Gallen, 2014). Cf. Pascale Bourgain, 'L'imaginaire du jardin médiéval', in Viviane Huchard and Pascale Bourgain, *Le jardin médiéval. Un musée imaginaire. Cluny, des textes et des images, un pari* (Paris, 2002), pp. 85–125.

15 Projekt Campus Galli is in the process of actually creating this 'monastic town' based on the proposed design, using ninth-century construction methods (https://www.campus-galli.de/klosterplan/).

16 Winfried Schich, 'Die Wirtschaftstätigkeit der Zisterzienser im Mittelalter: Handel und Gewerbe', in Kaspar Elm (ed.), *Die Zisterzienser. Ordensleben zwischen Ideal und Wirklichkeit* (Cologne, 1981), pp. 217–37 (218–20).

17 Ibid., pp. 228 and 235. The term 'monastic consumer communities' used by Schich was coined by Hektor Ammann.

18 United Nations, *Report of the World Commission on Environment and Development: Our Common Future*, 1987, https://sustainabledevelopment.un.org/content/documents/5987our-common-future.pdf; for 'global commons', see Chapters 10–12.

19 Ulrich Grober, *Sustainability: A Cultural History* (London, 2010), pp. 159–81 and *idem*, 'Nachhaltigkeit – die Geburtsurkunde eines Begriffs' in *Denkströme. Journal der Sächsischen Akademie der Wissenschaften* 10 (2013), http://www.denkstroeme.de/heft-10/s_77-93_grober; Hans Carl von Carlowitz, *Sylvicultura Oeconomica. Haußwirthliche Nachricht und Naturmäßige Anweisung zur Wilden Baum-Zucht* (Leipzig, 1713), https://digital.slub-dresden.de/werkansicht/?id=5363&tx_dlf%5Bid%5D=85039&tx_dlf%5Bpage%5D=23. Cf. Paul Warde, *The Invention of Sustainability: Nature and Destiny, c. 1500–1870* (Cambridge, 2018).

20 Grober, 'Nachhaltigkeit'.

21 Ibid., p. 165ff.

22 Ibid.

23 Ibid., p. 84.

24 See Joachim Allmann, *Der Wald in der Frühen Neuzeit. Eine mentalitätsund sozialgeschichtliche Untersuchung am Beispiel des Pfälzer Raumes 1500–1800* (Berlin, 1989), pp. 263–86.

25 Stefan von Below and Stefan Breit, *Wald – von der Gottesgabe zum Privateigentum. Gerichtliche Konflikte zwischen Landesherren und Untertanen um den Wald in der Frühen Neuzeit* (Berlin, 2016), pp. 34–55 (32f, 41).

26 Allmann, *Der Wald*, pp. 268–78 (Regional Archive, Speyer, B 2 344/2).

27 *Rheinisches Intelligenzblatt*, 1819 (119), cited in Hans Ziegler, 'Die Auflösung der Haingeraiden', in *Pfälzer Heimat* 20 (1969), pp. 20–23.

28 Tine de Moor, *The Dilemma of the Commoners. Understanding the Use of Common-Pool Resources in Long-term Perspective* (Cambridge, 2015). See also Daniel Schläppi and Malte-Christian Gruber (eds), *Von der Allmende zur Share Economy. Gemeinbesitz und kollektive Ressourcen in historischer und rechtlicher Perspektive* (Berlin, 2018), pp. 33–7 for a list that also includes non-material goods such as political activity, citizens' rights, pastoral care, Church property and symbolic resources – crests, flags, certain types of buildings – and myths and legends whose function was to instil a sense of community.

29 Garrett Hardin, 'The Tragedy of the Commons', *Science* 162(3859) (13 December 1968), pp. 1243–8 (1244), http://dx.doi.org/10.1126/science.162.3859.1243.

30 Aristotle, *Politics*, in *Aristotle in 23 Volumes*, Vol. 21, trans. H. Rackham (London, 1944), 1261b.

31 Alain Marciano, Brett M. Frischmann and Giovanni Battista Ramello, 'Tragedy of the Commons after 50 years', 11 September 2019, http://dx.doi.org/10.2139/ssrn.3451688; and Matto Mildenberger, 'The tragedy of "The Tragedy of the Commons"', *Scientific American* (13 April 2019).

32 Hardin, 'The Tragedy of the Commons', p. 1248.

33 Elinor Ostrom, *Governing the Commons: The Evolution of Institutions for Collective Action* (Cambridge, 1990).

34 Ostrom, 'Beyond Market and States', p. 422.

35 Tine de Moor, 'The silent revolution: A new perspective on the

emergence of commons, guilds, and other forms of corporate collective action in Western Europe', in *International Review of Social History* 53 (2008), pp. 179–212; and Schläppi and Gruber, *Allmende*.

36 Tine De Moor, *The Dilemma of the Commoners: Understanding the Use of Common-Pool Resources in Long-Term Perspective* (Cambridge, 2015).

37 This section presents and summarises Michael Zeheter's insights into the subject; see Zeheter, 'Eine Tragödie der Allmende? Die Bodenseefischerei 1350–1900', in Günther Schulz and Reinhold Reith (eds), *Wirtschaft und Umwelt vom Spätmittelalter bis zur Gegenwart. Auf dem Weg zur Nachhaltigkeit* (Stuttgart, 2015), pp. 133–52. Zeheter, Michael, 'Managing the Lake Constance Fisheries, ca. 1350–1800', in Abigail P. Dowling and Richard L. Keyer (eds), *Conservation's Roots: Managing for Sustainability in Preindustrial Europe, 1000–1800* (New York, 2020), pp. 154–77.

38 Ibid., p. 134f, which provides details around ownership and a list of further reading on the fishing business.

39 Ibid., p. 141.

40 Alas, we no longer know what this measurement equates to. The same goes for a *Konstanzer Zwillichelle*.

41 During Germany's 'mediatisation' – the restructuring of the states and dispossession of the monasteries under Napoleon – Baden, Bavaria and Württemberg expanded their territories all the way to Lake Constance. New fishing laws were subsequently passed that did not suit the lake's specific context and it was partly exempted from them, meaning that the old rules – created by the guilds and former regional sovereigns – continued to hold sway, despite the fact that there was no longer anyone around to monitor them. The fishermen complained about this state of affairs but the powers that were ignored them, as well as the resulting decline in fishing. In 1890, the fishermen decided to take the initiative and opened negotiations that ended with the 1893 Bregenz Agreement, which governs all fishing on the Upper Lake to this day. Its stakeholders include fishermen, governments and representatives from academia (limnologists).

42 Roger Sablonier, 'Innerschweizer Gesellschaft im 14. Jahrhundert',

in Historischer Verein der Fünf Orte (ed.), *Innerschweiz und frühe Eidgenossenschaft*, Vol. 2 (Olten, 1990), pp. 11–236 (83f).

43 Ibid., p. 72.

44 Helmut Jäger, 'Transhumanz', in *Lexikon des Mittelalters*, Vol. 8 (Munich 2003), cols 942f; and Gisbert Rinschede, *Die Transhumance in den französischen Alpen und in den Pyrenäen* (Münster, 1979).

45 Emmanuel Le Roy Ladurie, *Montaillou: Cathars and Catholics in a French Village 1294–1324*, trans. Barbara Bray (London, 1980), p. 135.

46 Charlotte Hallavant and Marie-Pierre Ruas, 'Pratiques agraires et terroir de montagne. Regard archéobotanique sur Montaillou (Ariège) au XIIIe siècle' in *Archéologie du Midi médiéval* 26 (2008), pp. 93–129 (94f), http://www.persee.fr/doc/amime_0758-7708_2008_num_26_1_1661.

47 Le Roy Ladurie, *Montaillou*, pp. vii–xvii. In the event, Guillaume Fort, a Cathar from Montaillou, was executed, together with four Waldensians from Pamiers. The Cathars were radical dualists; they called themselves the 'good', i.e. 'correct', Christians. According to them, the world was divided into good and evil: everything material was evil, especially the human body, which was the prison of the angelic soul and had to be subdued. They believed in the transmigration of souls, were strict vegetarians, and were opposed to sexual intercourse and procreation, arguing that Adam and Eve did neither while they lived in the Garden of Eden. Membership was bestowed in a sacrament called the *consolamentum*, a lengthy ritual that involved fasting and asceticism, culminating in a 'baptism in the Holy Spirit'. In some cases, to speed up the soul's deliverance, they were not averse to drastic measures, withholding food to ease the soul's departure from the evil body. This practice of targeted starvation was called the *endura*. For us today, many of their ideas are hard to comprehend.

48 Hallavant and Ruas, 'Pratiques agraires', p. 128.

49 Le Roy Ladurie, *Montaillou*, pp. 49–50.

50 Ibid., p. 84.

51 Ibid., and see p. 84 and n. 2.

52 Some shepherds were independent too – see ibid., pp. 116–17.

53 Ibid., p. 117.

54 Ibid., p. 133.

55 Ibid., p. 98.

56 Ibid., p. 106: 'In Montaillou, the Pays d'Aillon or Sabarthès there was no communal organization of flocks in the period 1300–25.' However, the situation was slightly different for cows: 'Not far from this area there was a communal herding of cattle [...] [and] there is every reason to believe that the tradition [of collective dairy farming] goes back to the fourteenth or even the thirteenth century. Raymond Sicre of Ascou relates: "[...] *I was leading a heifer of mine to the mountain* [...] *and when I saw that it was beginning to snow I sent my heifer to join the herd of common cows of the village of Ascou, and I went back to the village.*"'

57 Hallavant and Ruas, 'Practiques agraires', p. 128f.

58 Le Roy Ladurie, *Montaillou*, pp. 354–5.

59 Silke Helfrich and David Bollier (eds), *Frei, fair und lebendig: Die Macht der Commons* (Bielefeld, 2019).

60 Schläppi and Gruber, Introduction, pp. 37–41.

61 Scholars have started to look at this more closely; see Marco Veronesi, conference report, 'Cash-Flow im späten Mittelalter. Kirchliche und kommunale Bauvorhaben zwischen Konflikt und Konsens' (organiser: Gerald Schwendler), 23–4 March 2017, in *H/Soz/Kult*, 24 April 2017, https://www.hsozkult.de/conferencereport/id/tagungsberichte-7133.

62 Suzanne van Aerschot and Michiel Heirman, *Les Béguinages de Flandre un patrimoine mondial* (Brussels, 2001), pp. 97–102 and 185–226. Cf. the illuminating account by Letha Böhringer's 'Beginenhöfe', in Jörg Sonntag et al. (eds), *Geist und Gestalt. Monastische Raumkonzepte als Ausdrucksformen religiöser Leitideen im Mittelalter* (Münster, 2013), pp. 341–65 (349).

63 Leuven is a great example of a 'blended' beguinage. The sketch shown is a simplified one, but you can see how the houses are arranged both around a central square with a church and cemetery and along streets (Aerschot and Heirman, *Les Béguinages*, p. 99).

64 Unesco World Heritage List no. 855: Flemish Béguinages, http://whc.unesco.org/en/list/855. See also Aerschot and Heirman, *Les Béguinages*, pp. 185–226, for a description of each of the beguinages: Hoogstraten, Turnhout, Lierre, Malines (Mechelen), Sint-Truiden (Saint-Trond), Tongeren (Tongres), Dendermonde (Termonde),

Ghent (Gand), Sint-Amandsberg (Mont-Saint-Amand), Leuven (Louvain), Brugge (Bruges), Diest and Kortrijk (Courtrail).

65 Ibid., p. 213.

66 Walter Simons, *Cities of Ladies: Beguine Communities in the Medieval Low Countries, 1200–1565* (Philadelphia, PA, 2001). Simons is from Ghent and has been Professor of Medieval History at Dartmouth College in New Hampshire for many years; see Böhringer, 'Beginenhöfe', p. 349. The most useful recent studies of beguinages in general are Jörg Voigt, Bernward Schmidt and Marco A. Sorace (eds), *Das Beginenwesen in Spätmittelalter und Fraüher Neuzeit* (Stuttgart, 2015), including Sorace, 'Beginenhöfe im Spätmittelalter: Perspektiven der Architekturund Kunstgeschichte', pp. 308–13; Andreas Wilts, *Beginen im Bodenseeraum* (Sigmaringen, 1994); Frank-Michael Reichstein, *Das Beginenwesen in Deutschland. Studien und Katalog* (Berlin, 2001); Hannah Hien, *Das Beginenwesen in fränkischen und bayrischen Bischofsstädten* (Würzburg, 2013); Jörg Voigt, *Beginen im Spätmittelalter. Frauenfrömmigkeit in Thüringen und im Reich* (Cologne, 2012); Letha Böhringer's 'Beginenhöfe'; Jürgen Wiegert, 'Die Geschichte des Beginenhofes in Kamp' in *Jahrbuch des Kreises Wesel* 37 (2016), pp. 123–6; Amalie Fößel and Anette Hettinger, *Klosterfrauen, Beginen, Ketzerinnen. Religiöse Lebensformen von Frauen im Mittelalter* (Idstein, 2000); and Walter Reese-Schäfer (ed.), *Handbuch Kommunitarismus* (Wiesbaden, 2018).

67 Simons, *Cities of Ladies*, p. 108; he suggests that women also donated to medieval nunneries, but they constituted a smaller portion – between 10 per cent in England and at most 30 per cent in northern France.

68 Böhringer, 'Beginenhöfe', p. 350.

69 Hedwig Röckelein, 'Hamburger Beginen im Spätmittelalter – "automone" oder "fremdbestimmte" Frauengemeinschaften?', in Marina Wehrli-Johns and Claudia Opitz (eds), *Fromme Frauen oder Ketzerinnen* (Freiburg, 1998), pp. 119–38 (132).

70 Kaspar Elm, 'Vita regularis sine regula. The Meaning, Legal Status, and Self-Understanding of Late-Medieval and Early-Modern Semi-Religious Life', in James D. Mixson and Kaspar Elm (eds), *Religious Life Between Jerusalem, the Desert, and the World: Selected Essays* (Leiden, 2016), pp. 277–316. Jörg Voigt prefers to describe

them as 'worldly-spiritual'; see Voigt, 'Der Status Beginarum. Überlegungen zur rechtlichen Stellung des Beginenwesens im 13. Jahrhundert', in Voigt, Schmidt and Sorace, *Das Beginenwesen*, pp. 41–67. Ecclesiastical law deemed their way of life neither fish nor flesh, neither clerical nor properly lay. This is why they remain difficult to categorise. Beguines were definitively not 'half-nuns', but women who sought to integrate a lived, communal spirituality into their everyday lives. Beguinages usually forged close links with local parishes and any neighbouring – usually Cistercian or mendicant – monasteries. Crucially, they were endowed with legal rights and obligations.

71 Herbert Grundmann, *Religiöse Bewegungen im Mittelalter* (Darmstadt, 1970), p. 48.

72 *Die Colmarer Annalen*, MGH SS XVII, 1861, p. 235, as cited in Reichstein, *Beginenwesen*, p. 31f.

73 For more on the various attempts at an explanation see Reichstein's overview in ibid., pp. 18–30.

74 Simons, *Cities of Ladies*, p. 60. In St Omer in 1322 (population: 35,000–40,000) there were around 395 registered beguines in 22 beguinages, constituting 1 per cent of the town's population; Ghent (pop. *c.* 64,000) 7 per cent; Diest (pop. *c.* 6,000) 3.2 per cent; Liège, in the mid-thirteenth century (pop. 20,000–25,000) 4.4 per cent; Dendermonde, in the late fifteenth-century (pop. 4,500) 5.5 per cent; Mechelen, late sixteenth-century (pop. *c.* 26,000) 6.5 per cent. Herentals recorded the highest proportion in the late fifteenth century, with 3,450 or 7.7 per cent of the total population.

75 Rolf Hackstein, *Der Aachener Beginenhof St. Stephan im Mittelalter* (Aachen, 1997), which includes the statutes of 1246 (28–32), 1333 (32–8) and 1350 (38–3). The prohibition against bathing with men is on p. 35.

76 Private correspondence with the author. See also Böhringer, 'Beginenhöfe', p. 344, and *idem*, 'Beginen und Schwestern in der Sorge', in Artur Dirmeier, *Organisierte Barmherzigkeit: Armenfürsorge und Hospitalwesen in Mittelalter und Früher Neuzeit* (Regensburg, 2010), p. 154; cf. Wilts, *Beginen im Bodenseeraum*, p. 12f, which also highlights their heterogeneity.

77 From Simons, *Cities of Ladies*, p. 131:

'You talk, we act.
You learn, we seize.
You inspect, we choose.
You chew, we swallow.
You bargain, we buy.
You glow, we take fire.
You assume, we know.
You ask, we take.
You search, we find.
You love, we languish.
You languish, we die.
You sow, we reap.
You work, we rest.
You grow thin, we grow fat.
You ring, we sing.
You sing, we dance.
You blossom, we bear fruit.
You taste, we savor.'

The Latin text is from Jean Théobald Welter, *L'exemplum dans la littérature religieuse et didactique du Moyen Âge* (Paris / Toulouse, 1927), pp. 236–44; for a French version see Alfons Hilka, 'Neue Beiträge zur Erzählungsliteratur des Mittelalters (die Compilatio Singularis Exemplorum der Hs. Tours 468, ergänzt durch eine Schwesterhandschrift Bern 679)' in *Jahresbericht der Schlesischen Gesellschaft für vaterländische Cultur* 90 (1913), pp. 1–24 (3) in Berne, Bürgerbibliothek, MS 679, fol. 14 v–15 r, *c.* 1300, here taken from Hilka, 'Altfranzösische Mystik und Beginentum' in *Zeitschrift für romanische Philologie* 47 (1927), pp. 121–70 (160), which cites a further version from the fifteenth century (Tours, Bibliothèque municipale, MS 468).

78 Witt, 'Beginenhöfe', p. 39.

79 Röckelein, 'Hamburger Beginen', p. 131f.

80 Simons, *Cities of Ladies*, p. 195, n. 159 (AMD, FF 661, September 1270, ed. Espinas, *Vie urbaine*, Vol. 3, 409–10, No. 543; ADN, 30 H 18, No. 284 [8 December 1313]). Cf. Böhringer, 'Beginenhöfe', p. 353, n. 45.

81 See, for example, Simons, *Cities of Ladies*, p. 51, n. 97 with reference

to Bruges, citing Dirk Desmet's 'Het begijnhof "DeWijngaerd" te Brugge. Onderzoek naar het dagelijks leven rond het midden van de vijftiende eeuw' (master's thesis, Katholieke Universiteit Leuven, 1979), pp. 60–76.

82 Simons, *Cities of Ladies*, p. 85, n. 159.

83 Fernand Braudel, *Sozialgeschichte des 15.–18. Jahrhunderts. Der Handel* (Frankfurt, 1986), p. 72.

84 Claus Kropp, 'Lebendige Karolingerzeit: das Experimentalarchäologische Freilichtlabor Lauresham an der UNESCO Welterbestätte Kloster Lorsch' in *Geschichtsblätter für den Kreis Bergstraße* 50 (2017), pp. 327–38; see also Dieter Hennebo, *Gärten des Mittelalters* (Hamburg, 1962), pp. 26–40 for the description of the gardens in the St Gall monastery plan.

85 See for example https://www.ludwigshafen.de/nachhaltig/engagement/interkulturelle-gaerten/hack-museumsgarten. Cf. Christa Müller, (ed.), *'Urban Gardening'. Über die Rückkehr der Gärten in die Stadt* (Munich, 2011).

86 See Frank Lohrberg, *Stadtnahe Landwirtschaft in der Stadtund Freiraumplanung: Ideengeschichte, Kategorisierung von Konzepten und Hinweise für die zukünftige Planung* (Stuttgart, 2001), p. 5; for the supposedly 'naïve-utilitarian' relationship with nature see Gerhard Richter, *Handbuch Stadtgrün. Landschaftsarchitektur im städtischen Freiraum* (Munich, 1981), p. 17f, and for Hallerwiese see Alexandra Foghammar, '"*Allen inwonern zu lust und ergetzung*". Die Hallerwiese ist Nürnbergs älteste Grünanlage' in *Nürnberg heute* 70 (2001), pp. 50–55.

87 Florence Wilhelmina Johanna Koorn, 'Von der Peripherie ins Zentrum. Beginen und Schwestern vom Gemeinsamen Leben in den nördlichen Niederlanden', in Wehrli-Johns and Opitz, *Fromme Frauen oder Ketzerinnen?*, pp. 95–118 (101): 'Den Verdienst zu teilen ist nicht typisch für das Beginenleben. Im Gegenteil wird die finanzielle Autonomie der Beginen immer wieder unterstrichen.' ('It was unusual for beguines to share their earnings. On the contrary, their financial autonomy is repeatedly emphasised.') As far as the available evidence shows, it is not until the late fifteenth century that convent laws were introduced which compelled the beguines to share their entire income, e.g. in Deventer, where

many of them worked as spinners. Koorn speculates that income-sharing was instituted in the beguinages during that period thanks to an influential new form of piety (*devotio moderna*). It appears that the beguines enjoyed less autonomy in convents than they did in beguinages (p. 102).

88 Böhringer, 'Beginenhöfe', p. 351.

89 Röckelein, 'Hamburger Beginen', p. 127; cf. Monika Boese and Katrin Tiemann, 'Der Beginenkonvent im spätmittelalterlichen Hamburg' in *Zeitschrift des Vereins für Hamburgische Geschichte* 82 (1996), pp. 1–28 (for accounts see p. 10ff), https://agora.sub.uni-hamburg.de/subhh/digbib/view?did=c1:3093&p=13.

90 Stephan Selzer and Klaus-Joachim Lorenzen-Schmidt, *Rechnungen des Konvents der Blauen Schwestern (Beginen) in Hamburg. Die Mittelalterlichen Rechnungen 1481–1515* (Münster, 2017), for the buildings and toilets see p. 16.

91 Klaus-Joachim Lorenzen-Schmidt, 'Beginennachlässe des frühen 16. Jahrhunderts in Hamburg (1535–1537)' in *Rundbrief des Arbeitskreises für Wirtschafts- und Sozialgeschichte Schleswig-Holsteins* 102 (2010), pp. 32–5. http://rundbriefe.arbeitskreis-geschichte.de/Rundbrief_102.pdf 2020-03-25. An inventory for a 1536 estate sale following the death of a beguine called Geschen Sprenger – which fetched a total of '21m. 8s. 2d.' – lists sheets (which included both bales of cloth and the bed sheets or tablecloths cut from them), a quilt, expensive woollen cloth from Arras, sleeveless capes, pillows, seat and other cushions, cupboards, bowls, a salt shaker, pots and such. The regular estate sales also demonstrate that in those days everything that could still be used was in fact reused or recycled (see the next chapter, 'Recycling').

92 Böhringer, 'Beginenhöfe', p. 344.

93 Simons, *Cities of Ladies*, p. 85l; see n. 158 for documents from Ghent. Cf. Bücher, *Arbeit und Rhythmus*, and Senn, 'Music and Economics', pp. 73–112, esp. pp. 77–86 on 'work and rhythm'. Kanamori, 'Karl Bücher', pp. 155–62 and Held and Geißler, *Von Rhythmen und Eigenzeiten*, are also especially interesting.

94 Simons, *Cities of Ladies*, p. 85f.

95 Böhringer, 'Beginen und Schwestern in der Sorge', p. 140f. Cf. also Vera von der Osten-Sacken, *Jakob von Vitrys 'Vita Mariae*

Oigniacensis'. Zu Herkunft und Eigenart der ersten Beginen (Göttingen, 2000), pp. 196–229, '*Mulieres religiosae* als Krankendienerinnen'.

96 Simons, *Cities of Ladies*, p. 271.

97 Röckelein, 'Hamburger Beginen', pp. 127f, referencing Boese and Tiemann, 'Der Beginenkonvent in Hamburg'. See also Klaus-Joachim Lorenzen-Schmidt, 'Umfang und Dynamik des Hamburger Rentenmarktes zwischen 1471 und 1570' in *Zeitschrift des Vereins für Hamburgische Geschichte* 65 (1979), pp. 21–52 (42). For the beguines and the Hanover rental market see Olaf Mußmann, 'Beginen – "Kommunardinnen" des Mittelalters? Die "*via media*" in Hannover', in Angela Dinghaus (ed.), *Frauenwelten* (Hildesheim, 1993), pp. 19–32 (28). Röckelein believes, however, that Mußmann perpetuates untenable clichés concerning justice and power in late-medieval cities (Röckelein, 'Hamburger Beginen', p. 251, n. 9).

98 Louis Blancard, *Documents inédits sur le commerce de Marseille au Moyen Âge*, Vol. 2 (Marseilles, 1885), pp. 371–83, 'Les commandites commerciales des Béguines de Roubaud'; Isabel Genecin, '"In the world but not of the world"? Doucelina, Felipa, and the Beguines of Marseilles', undergraduate senior thesis (supervisors Charles Amstrong and Adam Kosto), Columbia University, 2015.

99 Sylvain Piron, 'L'apparition du resicum en Méditerranée Occidentale, XIIe-XIIIe Siècles', in E. Collas-Heddeland (ed.), *Pour une histoire culturelle du risque. Genèse, évolution, actualité du concept dans les sociétés occidentales* (Strasbourg, 2004), pp. 59–76.

3. Recycling

1 Jens Lienig and Hans Brümmer, 'Recyclinggerechtes Entwickeln und Konstruieren', in *idem* (eds), *Elektronische Gerätetechnik. Grundlagen für das Entwickeln elektronischer Baugruppen und Geräte* (Berlin/Heidelberg, 2014), pp. 193–218, illustration 7.2.

2 Hermann Stern, *Die geschichtliche Entwicklung und die gegenwärtige Lage des Lumpenhandels in Deutschland* (Leipzig, 1914), p. 2.

3 For what follows see Reinhold Reith, 'Recycling im späten Mittelalter und in der frühen Neuzeit. Eine Materialsammlung' in *Frühneuzeit-Info* 14 (2003), pp. 47–65; Günther Schulz and Reinhold Reith, *Wirtschaft und Umwelt. Vom Spätmittelalter bis zur Gegenwart:*

Auf dem Weg zu Nachhaltigkeit? (Stuttgart, 2015); and Roland Ladwig (ed.), *Recycling in Geschichte und Gegenwart* (Freiberg, 2003).

4 Christian Pfister (ed.), *Das 1950er Syndrom. Der Weg in die Konsumgesellschaft* (Bern, 1995).

5 Reinhold Reith, 'Recycling im späten Mittelalter und in der frühen Neuzeit. Eine Materialsammlung' in *Frühneuzeit-Info* 14 (2003), pp. 47–65 (47).

6 Karl Bücher, *Die Berufe der Stadt Frankfurt a. M. im Mittelalter* (Leipzig, 1914). For more on medieval professions see also Reinhold Reith, *Das alte Handwerk. Von Bader bis Zinngießer* (Munich, 2008), and *Lexikon des Alten Handwerks. Vom späten Mittelalter bis ins 20. Jahrhundert* (Munich, 1991). Bücher was born in 1847, the son of a brushmaker, studied history in Bonn and Göttingen, and briefly worked as a teacher and as a journalist at the *Frankfurter Zeitung*. He became increasingly interested in macroeconomics, and obtained his professorship in Munich in 1881. From 1892 to 1917 he taught statistics and macroeconomics at Leipzig. He is the author of numerous acclaimed works, including a history of economic anthropology. He became professor emeritus in 1917. He continued to work in journalism alongside his academic career, founded Germany's first print media institute at Leipzig University, and has been called the father of communication and media studies.

7 Bücher, *Berufe der Stadt Frankfurt*, p. 16f: 'I concluded my examination of Frankfurt's demographic statistics in 1886 having counted a total of 338 types of jobs. Even that could not fail to be regarded as an astonishingly high number, but now [1914] that I have produced an alphabetical list I find that there are almost five times as many.' He believed this was because they experienced 'little technological advancement [and] people could thus only satisfy their constant need to increase productivity by narrowing the scope of what they produced and the services they rendered'.

8 Ibid., p. 17.

9 Ibid., p. 18f.

10 Sabine von Heusinger, *Die Zunft im Mittelalter. Zur Verflechtung von Politik, Wirtschaft und Gesellschaft in Straßburg* (Stuttgart, 2009), pp. 316–32; on women see pp. 324–6 and the list of sources.

11 Bücher, *Berufe der Stadt Frankfurt*, p. 100; see also p. 18.

12 Ibid., pp. 38 and 104. While *Deschenmecher* made bags (it appears that, from 1320 onwards, the majority were women), *Deschenplecker* repaired them. In 1359 there were fourteen bag producers in Frankfurt; in 1421 a bag mender is mentioned by name and described as 'a poor man'. The mayor's books of 1447 also mention the city's cutlers and blade sharpeners in the context of the decision that they and the shoemakers' guild were to move into the Werthe House together.

13 Ibid., p. 24.

14 In 1420, for example, '*die altgewendere zu den Barfußen und andere altgewendere, die uff der strassen stehen ... gibit iglicher sehs hellir und geben darczu den Luseczoll*'; Bücher, *Berufe der Stadt Frankfurt*, p. 23.

15 Ibid., p. 23f; see also Karl Bücher and Benno Schmidt (eds), *Frankfurter Zunfturkunden*, Vol. 1 (Frankfurt, 1914), p. 507f.

16 Bücher, *Berufe der Stadt Frankfurt*, p. 69f.

17 Valentin Groebner, *Ökonomie ohne Haus. Zum Wirtschaften armer Leute in Nürnberg am Ende des 15. Jahrhunderts* (Göttingen, 1993), pp. 181 and 217f, citing Merry E. Wiesner, *Working Women in Renaissance Germany* (New Brunswick, NJ, 1986), pp. 134–47, and Jutta Zander-Seidel, *Textiler Hausrat. Kleidung und Haustextilien in Nürnberg von 1500 bis 1650* (Munich, 1990), pp. 387–97.

18 Dieter Kramer, 'Vom Flickwerk zur Nachhaltigkeit', in Siegfried de Rachewiltz (ed.), *Flicken und Wiederverwerten im Historischen Tirol* (Weitra, 2015), pp. 67–86.

19 Laurence Fontaine (ed.), *Alternative Exchanges: Second-hand Circulations from the Sixteenth Century to the Present* (New York/Oxford, 2008), p. 1.

20 Louis-Sébastien Mercier, *Tableau de Paris*, Vol. 1, Chapter CLXXXII, pp. 448–50. See Laurence Fontaine, 'The exchange of secondhand goods between survival strategies and "business" in eighteenth-century Paris', in *Alternative Exchanges*, pp. 97–114 (100).

21 Bernard London, *Ending the Depression Through Planned Obsolescence* (New York, 1932), p. 6.

22 See the iFixit manifesto at https://www.ifixit.com/Manifesto and https://kylewiens.com.

23 VDPm Global consumption of paper and cardboard 2006 to 2017

(in million metric tons). Statista, 2018, https://www.statista.com/statistics/270319/consumption-of-paper-and-cardboard-since-2006/.

See also dpa Globus, http://www.agenda21-treffpunkt.de/archiv/17/daten/170609-glo-11782;_Papierverbrauch-Welt-1980-2015.htm; Pipa Elias and Doug Boucher, *Planting for the Future: How Demand for Wood Products Could Be Friendly to Tropical Forests*, Union of Concerned Scientists, October 2014, https://www.ucsusa.org/sites/default/files/attach/2014/10/planting-for-the-future.pdf.

24 For the following descriptions I have relied in part on Peter Tschudin's *Grundzüge der Papiergeschichte* (Stuttgart, 2002).

25 Carla Meyer-Schlenkrich and Rebekka Sauer, 'Papier', in Thomas Meier, Michael R. Ott and Rebecca Sauer (eds), *Materiale Textkulturen* (Berlin, 2015), p. 357, citing Pan Jixing, 'Review on the debate of paper history during recent 30 years in China' in *International Paper History* 15 (2011), pp. 6–12.

26 *Hou Hanshu*, Chapter 108, cited in ibid., p. 73, n. 20.

27 Ibid., p. 74.

28 Meyer and Sauer, 'Papier', p. 360. Carla Meyer-Schlenkrich's *Wann beginnt die Papierzeit? Zur Wissensgeschichte eines hoch- und spätmittelalterlichen Beschreibstoffs*, Materiale Textkulturen 31 (Berlin/Munich/Boston, 2021) is the most recent study on the age of paper. See also Carla Meyer-Schlenkrich, Sandra Schultz and Bernd Schneidmüller (eds), *Papier im mittelalterlichen Europa. Herstellung und Gebrauch*, Materiale Textkulturen 7 (Berlin/Munich/Boston, 2015).

29 For what follows see Julia Becker, Tino Licht and Bernd Schneidmüller, 'Pergament', in Meier, Ott and Sauer, *Materiale Textkulturen*, pp. 337–47.

30 Lothar Müller, *Weiße Magie. Die Epoche des Papiers* (Munich, 2013).

31 Peter Tschudin, 'Paper comes to Italy' in *International Paper History* 12 (1998), pp. 60–66 (see p. 61 for a transcript of the contract). Cf. Peter Rückert, 'Papiergeschichte und Papierherstellung im Mittelalter', in *Ochsenkopf und Meerjungfrau. Wasserzeichen des Mittelalters. Begleitheft zur Ausstellung des Landesarchivs Baden-Württemberg* (Stuttgart, 2006), pp. 12–15.

32 *Orbis sensualium pictus* is the world's oldest children's

encyclopaedia. Some regard it as an early example of a carefully thought-out set of didactic teaching materials, others as a precursor to comic books. See Meyer and Sauer, 'Papier', p. 362, and Tschudin, *Grundzüge der Papiergeschichte*, pp. 93–5.

33 At the beginning of the sixteenth century, for instance, there were no fewer than seven paper mills along a five-kilometre stretch along the Iller in Swabia, as well as a hammer mill with wire-drawing facilities (for the mesh moulds). Eleven 'masters' and more than thirty-five workmen were employed there. If we assume that each workman had an average of three to five apprentices, assistants and general dogsbodies, the seven mills will have boasted a substantial staff. Cf. Wolfgang Petz, 'Ein Handwerk zwischen Stadt und Land: Das Kemptener Papierergewerbe', in Birgit Kata, Volker Laube and Markus Naumann (eds), *Mehr als 1,000 Jahre. Das Stift Kempten zwischen Gründung und Auflösung 752–1802* (Friedberg, 2006), pp. 237–300.

34 Hermann Stern, *Die geschichtliche Entwicklung und die gegenwärtige Lage des Lumpenhandels in Deutschland* (Leipzig, 1914), p. 3f.

35 See e.g. Alfred H. Shorter and Richard L. Hills (eds), *Studies on the History of Papermaking in Britain* (Aldershot, 1993).

36 Johann Lindt, *The Paper-Mills of Berne and their Watermarks, 1465–1859* (Hiversum, 1964), pp. 119–22.

37 Wisso Weiss, 'Buchdrucker erhalten die Kontrolle über das Lumpensammeln' in *Gutenberg-Jahrbuch* 40 (1965), pp. 13–17 (13f). In Halberstadt, for instance, a man called Jakob Arnold Kote was issued a printing licence on 20 August 1612. However, he was unable to launch his operation because the regional mills were selling their paper to clients outside the region and could not increase production because of a shortage of rags. Ten years later, when Kote renewed his licence, he also obtained the right to collect rags – for a fee, of course. The permit gave him the authority to issue permits to rag-and-bone-men in the relevant territories, which bound them to deliver their hauls to him or his partners, the paper mills. The practice seems to have worked; at least, there is evidence that such 'right to collect' licences were issued on a regular basis.

38 See Arno Kapp, 'Leipzigs Lumpenhandel und der Papiermangel

am Ende des 18. Jahrhunderts in Kursachsen' in *Papier Geschichte* 1 (1951), pp. 56–7.

39 Wilhelm A. Bauer and Otto Deutsch (eds), *Mozart, Briefe und Aufzeichnungen. Gesamtausgabe*, Vol. 1 1755–76 (Munich, 2005), p. 8.

40 For what follows see Tschudin, *Grundzüge der Papiergeschichte*, p. 141.

41 Jacob Christian Schäffer, *Sr. Königl. Majest. zu Dännemark Rathes und Professors ... Empfehlung, Beschreibung und erweiterter Gebrauch des sogenannten und zur Erspahrung des Holzes höchstvortheilhaften Bockofens. Nebst 5. Kupfertafeln* (Regensburg, 1770). The oven is introduced in a chapter on saving energy; see https://reader.digitale-sammlungen.de/de/fs1/object/display/bsb10229123_00031.html?zoom=0.55.

42 Jacob Christian Schäffer, *Versuche und Muster ohne alle Lumpen oder doch mit einem geringen Zusatze derselben Papier zu machen* (Regensburg, 1765), p. 3, http://mdz-nbn-resolving.de/urn:nbn:de:bvb:12-bsb11217980-8 // https://reader.digitale-sammlungen.de/de/fs1/object/display/bsb11217980_00003.html.

43 Ibid., p. 8.

44 Ibid., p. 15.

45 Georg Christoph Keferstein, *Unterricht eines Papiermachers an seine Söhne, diese Kunst betreffend* (Leipzig, 1766; new edn Leipzig, 1936), p. 17.

46 'E. G.', review of Jacob Christian Schäffer, *Neue Versuche und Muster, das Pflanzenreich zum Papiermachen und andern Sachen wirthschaftlich zu gebrauchen*, Vols 1–3, Regensburg 1765–67, in *Allgemeine Deutsche Bibliothek* 11/1 (1770), pp. 283f, Zeitschriften der Aufklärung, Bielefeld, http://ds.ub.uni-bielefeld.de/viewer/image/2002572_021/294/LOG_0082/.

47 August Wilhelm Kazmeier, 'Historischer Streifzug durch die Rohstofffragen der Papierherstellung', in *Papiergeschichte* 1 (1951), p. 40. Kazmeier was in charge of publishing the Association of Pulp and Paper Chemists and Engineers' newsletter. In 1951, he declared that the US was currently the leading recycler of old paper – despite its extensive forests – and proposed that it should be considered more seriously as a raw material in future.

48 Tschudin, *Grundzüge der Papiergeschichte*, p. 142.

49 Kazmeier, 'Historischer Streifzug', p. 42.

50 The eight-page auction catalogue gives us a good idea of how extravagant the project had been: the site boasted several large storerooms, a handsome mansion, numerous factory buildings, a steam engine and a canal from the Thames to Bermondsey which had been dug especially for the plant at a cost of £7,000. Today the site is occupied by an 1860s Grade-II listed building that replaced the original paper mill, which was presumably demolished after the foreclosure sale in 1804. Koops's story reads like an adventure novel, and the reason we know so much about it is that the poet William Blake happened to be his neighbour. See Keri Davies, 'William Blake and the Straw Paper Manufactory at Millbank', in Karen Mulhallen (ed.), *Blake in Our Time: Essays in Honour of G. E. Bentley Jr.* (Toronto, 2010), p. 235ff.

51 From a 1951 newsletter of the Association of Pulp and Paper Chemists and Engineers – and it is difficult to suspect them of scaremongering – we learn that the shortage of wood pulp threatened to lead to a paper production crisis: 'The need for a suitable alternative material is once again preoccupying experts.' Interestingly, its author considers straw cellulose the most likely solution alongside used paper. Straw, he argues, offers a possible way out of the raw material shortage in the paper industry; and he concludes with the thought that 'for Germany, only the increased employment of straw in the production of paper and pulp can make up for the lack of pulpwood'. Cited in Kazmeier, 'Historischer Streifzug', p. 45.

52 'E. G.', 'Review of Jacob Christian Schäffer, *Neue Versuche und Muster*', p. 283f.

53 Caroline Wahnbeck, 'Graspapier. Diese Kartons bestehen aus Gras' in *Utopia*, 22 November 2018, https://utopia.de/ratgeber/graspapier-diese-kartonsibestehen-aus-gras/20191003.

54 Anna Jones, *A Modern Way to Eat: Over 200 Satisfying, Everyday Vegetarian Recipes* (London, 2014).

55 See e.g. (among many others) the 2013–14 Zurich Museum of Design exhibition entitled 'Design mit bewegter Vergangenheit' ('Designs with an eventful past'), https://

www.artoffer.com / Museum-fuer-Gestaltung-Zuerich / Vintagex2013-Design-mit-bewegter-Vergangenheit / 870.

56 Joseph Alchermes, 'Spolia in Roman Cities of the Late Empire: Legislative Rationales and Architectural Reuse' in *Dumbarton Oaks Papers* 48 (1994), pp. 167–78, especially p. 178; Lukas Clemens, *Tempore Romanorum constructa. Zur Nutzung und Wahrnehmung antiker Überreste nördlich der Alpen während des Mittelalters* (Stuttgart, 2003); Günther Binding, 'Antike Säulen als Spolien in Früh- und Hochmittelalterlichen Kirchen und Pfalzen – Materialspolie oder Bedeutungsträger?', in *Proceedings of the Academic Association of the Johann Wolfgang Goethe University in Frankfurt am Main* XLV / 1 (Stuttgart, 2007); Carola Jäggi, 'Spolia', in *Lexikon des Mittelalters*, Vol. 7 (Munich, 1994), pp. 2129–31. On the stores of building materials see Hugo Brandenburg, 'Magazinierte Baudekoration und ihre Verwendung in der spätantiken Architektur Roms des 4. und 5. Jh. Ein Beitrag zur Bewertung der Spolie' in *Boreas. Münstersche Beiträge zur Archäologie* 30 / 31 (2010), pp. 169–89.

57 Arnold Esch, 'Spolien: Zur Wiederverwendung antiker Baustücke und Skulpturen im mittelalterlichen Italien' in *Archiv für Kulturgeschichte* 51 (1969), pp. 1–64 (5, 42f). For examples from Ravenna see Carola Jäggi, 'Spolien aus Ravenna: Transformation einer Stadt von der Antike bis in die frühe Neuzeit', in Stefan Altekamp, Carmen Marcks-Jacobs and Peter Seiler (eds), *Perspektiven der Spolienforschung Vol. 1: Spoliierung und Transposition* (Berlin, 2013), pp. 287–330.

58 Karl Leo Noethlichs, 'Kaiserzeitliche und spätantike staatliche Regularien zur Spoliierung – ein Kommentar', in Altekamp, Marcks-Jacobs and Seiler (eds), *Perspektiven der Spolienforschung*, pp. 11–21 (13f).

59 See Esch, *Spolien*, p. 6f and notes.

60 Ibid., p. 11f, citing Karl Noehles, 'Zur Wiederverwendung antiken Spolienmaterials in der Kathedrale von Sessa Aurunca', in *Festschrift für M. Wegner zum 60. Geburtstag* (Münster, 1962), p. 91.

61 Matthias Untermann, 'Vom Schicksal der Dinge aus archäologischer Sicht', in Ulrich Klein (ed.), *Vom Schicksal der Dinge. Spolie – Wiederverwendung – Recycling* (Paderborn, 2014), pp. 9–16 (10) citing Ruth Meyer, *Frühmittelalterliche Kapitelle und Kämpfer in*

Deutschland. Typus, Technik, Stil, rev. by Daniel Herrmann (Berlin, 1997); for Lucca see Esch, *Spolien*, p. 15, n. 54.

62 Esch, *Spolien*, pp. 25–7.

63 Ibid., p. 36.

64 Veronica Biermann, 'Ortswechsel: Überlegungen zur Bedeutung der Bewegung schwerer Lasten für die Wirkung und Rezeption monumentaler Architektur am Beispiel des Vatikanischen Obelisken', in Altekamp, Marcks-Jacobs and Seiler (eds), *Perspektiven der Spolienforschung*, pp. 123–56; see p. 133, image 5.

65 Walter Kaemmerer (ed.), *Albrecht Dürer, Reisetagebuch, Aachener Quellentexte* (Aachen, 1980), p. 294, citing Binding, 'Antike Säulen', p. 20.

66 Binding, 'Antike Säulen', p. 18f. Cf. Bruno Reudenbach (ed.), *Karolingische und Ottonische Kunst* (Darmstadt, 2009), p. 217.

67 Bruno Reudenbach, *Geschichte der Bildenden Kunst in Deutschland* (Munich, 2009); for the coffin see Vol. 6, p. 196f; for the statue of the horseman see ibid., p. 196; for the she-bear see Vol. 4, p. 218.

68 As the famous cartographer and cosmographer Sebastian Münster described it in 1544: 'In Aachen, the admirable Charles then also built a pretty and exquisite minster, decorating it in silver and gold. He also had great columns and marble blocks taken there from Rome, Ravenna and Trier, and one can still see them there.' Sebastian Münster, *Cosmographey* (Basel, 1588), p. 721, cited by Binding in 'Antike Säulen', pp. 18 and 21.

69 Reinhold Rau (ed.), 'Einhard, Das Leben Karls des Großen, Einhardi Vita Karoli Kap. 22', in *Quellen zur karolingischen Reichsgeschichte Teil 1*, trans. O. Abel and J. v. Jasmund (AQdGM 5) (Darmstadt, 1955), pp. 192–5.

70 Jan Pieper, 'Der Karlsthron im Architektursystem der Pfalzkapelle zu Aachen. Eine architektonische Miniatur', in Jan Pieper and Bruno Schindler, *Thron und Altar, Oktogon und Sechzehneck. Die Herrschaftsikonographie der karolingischen Pfalzkapelle zu Aachen (Scriptorium Carolinum 5)* (Aachen/Berlin, 2017), pp. 47–124 (especially pp. 91–120); Sven Schütte, 'Der Aachener Thron', in Mario Kramp (ed.), *Krönungen, Könige in Aachen. Geschichte und Mythos* (Mainz, 1999), pp. 213–22; Katharina Corsepius, 'Der Aachener "Karlsthron" zwischen Zeremoniell und

Herrschermemoria', in Marion Steinicke and Stefan Weinfurter (eds), *Investitur- und Krönungsrituale. Herrschaftseinsetzungen im kulturellen Vergleich* (Cologne, 2005), pp. 359–75 – for the nine men's morris board see image 6.

71 Bruno Klein, introduction to 'Spolien' (MA seminar session, 3 April 2017), https://tu-dresden.de/gsw/phil/ikm/studium/lehrveranstaltungen/kunstgeschichte/archiv/studienjahr-2016/ss_17/hauptseminare-1/hs-jahn. See also Hans-Rudolf Meier, 'Rückführungen. Spolien in der zeitgenössischen Architektur', in Stefan Altekamp et al., *Perspektiven der Spolienforschung 1*, pp. 333–49 (pp. 334f).

4. Microfinance

1 For corporate responsibility, including the example of the Fuggerei almshouses in Augsburg, see Marion Tietz-Strödel, *Die Fuggerei in Augsburg. Studien zur Entwicklung des sozialen Stiftungsbaus im 15. und 16. Jahrhundert* (Tübingen, 1982); C. Stutz and S. Sachs, 'Facing the normative challenges: The potential of reflexive historical research' in *Business & Society* 57.1 (2018), pp. 98–130; and R. Phillips, J. Schrempf-Stirling and C. Stutz, 'The past, history, and corporate social responsibility' in *Journal of Business Ethics* 166 (2020), pp. 203–13, https://doi.org/10.1007/s10551-019-04319-0.

2 Christiane Laudage, *Das Geschäft mit der Sünde* (Vienna, 2016); Andreas Rehberg (ed.), *Ablasskampagnen des Spätmittelalters. Luthers Thesen von 1517 im Kontext* (Berlin/Boston, 2017); and Robert Swanson, *Indulgences in Late Medieval England: Passport to Paradise* (Cambridge, 2007).

3 For more on indulgences see e.g. Nikolaus Paulus, *Der Ablass im Mittelalter als Kulturfaktor* (Cologne, 1920); Laudage, *Das Geschäft mit der Sünde*; Rehberg, *Ablasskampagnen des Spätmittelalters*; Swanson, *Indulgences in Late Medieval England*; Christiane Schuchard, 'Was ist ein Ablasskommissar?', in Hartmut Kühne, Enno Bünz and Peter Wiegand (eds), *Johann Tetzel und der Ablass* (Berlin, 2017), pp. 111–23; and Marilynn Dunn, 'Paradigms of Penance' in *Journal of Medieval Monastic Studies* 1 (2012), pp. 17–39. For more on philanthropy see Michael Borgolte (ed.), *Enzyklopädie des Stiftungswesens in mittelalterlichen Gesellschaften*, Vol. 1–2

(Berlin/New York, 2014); *idem*, 'Stiftungen für das Seelenheil' in *Zeitschrift für Geschichtswissenschaft* 63(12) (2015), pp. 1037–56; Karl Schmid, 'Stiftungen für das Seelenheil' in *idem* (ed.), *Gedächtnis, das Gemeinschaft stiftet* (Munich, 1985), pp. 52–73; Joachim Wollasch, 'Konventsstärke und Armensorge in mittelalterlichen Klöstern. Zeugnisse und Fragen' in *Saeculum* 39(2) (1988), pp. 184–99; Annette Kehnel, 'Neue Kommunikationsformen im Bettelordenskonvent und der Aufstieg der Universitäten', in Mirko Breitenstein and Gert Melville (eds), *Die Wirkmacht klösterlichen Lebens im Mittelalter. Modelle, Ordnungen, Kompetenzen, Konzepte* (Regensburg, 2020), pp. 177–200; Andrew G. Little, 'Chronicles of the Mendicant Friars', in *idem*, *Franciscan Papers, Lists, and Documents* (Manchester, 1943), pp. 25–41; Herbert Edward Salter (ed.), *The Oxford Deeds of Balliol College* (Oxford, 1913); Hans-Jörg Gilomen, 'Renten und Grundbesitz in der Toten Hand: Realwirtschaftliche Probleme der Jenseitsökonomie', in Peter Jetzler (ed.), *Himmel, Hölle, Fegefeuer. Das Jenseits im Mittelalter. Eine Ausstellung des Schweizerischen Landesmuseums in Zusammenarbeit mit dem Schnütgen-Museum und der Mittelalterabteilung des Wallraf-Richartz-Museums der Stadt Köln* (Zürich, 1994), pp. 135–48; Heiko Ernst, *Weitergeben! Anstiften zum generativen Leben* (Hamburg, 2008), p. 193; and Vera King, 'Generativität und die Zukunft der Nachkommen', in Ingrid Moeslein-Teising, Georg Schäfer and Rupert Martin (eds), *Generativität* (Giessen, 2020), pp. 13–28.

4 Nobel Peace Prize press release, 13 October 2006, https://www.nobelprize.org/prizes/peace/2006/summary/.

5 Aristotle, *Nicomachean Ethics*, Book V. 5, trans. David Ross (Oxford, 2009), p. 90.

6 Ibid., p. 89.

7 Cf. Thomas Piketty, *Capital and Ideology* (London, 2020), and Jochen Streb's review in *Vierteljahrschrift für Sozial- und Wirtschaftsgeschichte* 107 (2020).

8 Using a Tyrolean case study, Stephan Nicolussi-Köhler shows that these banks were also created in rural areas. See 'Money lending and settling debts in and around Meran (South Tirol) in the 14th century' in *Mannheim Working Papers in Premodern Economic History* 2020, pp. 13–45 https://doi.org/10.25521/mwppeh.2020.139; and

cf. Nicolussi-Köhler (ed.), *Change and Transformation of Premodern Credit Markets: The Importance of Small-Scale Credits* (Heidelberg, 2021).

9 For more on the *monti di pietà* see Maria Giuseppina Muzzarelli, *Il denaro e la salvezza. L'invenzione del Monte di Pietà* (Bologna, 2001); Giacomo Todeschini, *I mercanti e il tempio. La società cristiana e il circolo virtuoso della ricchezza fra Medioevo ed Età Moderna* (Bologna, 2002), pp. 449–86; Daniele Montanari, *Il credito e la carità. Monti di Pietà delle città lombarde in età moderna* (Milan, 2001); Vittorino Meneghin, *I Monti di Pietà in Italia. Dal 1462 al 1562* (Vicenza, 1986), p. 14. Hardly anyone has heard of the *monti di pietà*; although many survived until the end of the twentieth century, others disappeared from Italian towns and cities before that. See Mauro Carboni, 'Converting Goods into Cash: An Ethical Approach to Pawnbroking in Early Modern Bologna', in Nicholas Terpstra and Mauro Carboni, *The Material Culture of Debt*, Centre for Reformation and Renaissance Studies (Toronto, 2012), pp. 63–83 (64). Carboni adopts the phrase 'socially responsible consumer credit' used by Herman van der Wee, *The Low Countries and the Early Modern World* (Aldershot, 1993), p. 184. Tanja Skambraks, *Karitativer Kredit. Die Monti di Pietà, franziskanische Wirtschaftsethik und städtische Sozialpolitik in Italien (15. und 16. Jahrhundert)* (Stuttgart, 2023); Tanja Skambraks, 'Strategies of Survival: Pawnbroking and Credit Relations in Rome and Perugia (15th and 16th Centuries)', in Stephan Köhler (ed.), *Change and Transformation of Premodern Credit Markets* (Heidelberg, 2021), p. 293–331; Tanja Skambraks, 'Credit for the poor. Trust, regulation and charity in the Roman Monte di Pietà', in *RiMe. Rivista dell'Istituto di Storia dell'Europa Mediterranea* Ser. NS, 8 (2) (2021), pp. 137–58.

10 Jacques Heers, 'Montes pietatis', in *Lexikon des Mittelalters*, Vol. 6 (Stuttgart, 2000), cols 795f. See also Heribert Holzapfel, *Die Anfänge der Montes Pietatis (1462–1515)* (Munich, 1903), pp. 15–21. *Montes pietatis*, synonymous with *deposita pietatis*, was a term used for alms or donations to impoverished monks; other names are *monte della carità, mamma pauperum Christi* and *mare di pietà*. Originally there were also *montes gratuiti* alongside those demanding the reimbursement of expenses. Another kind were the *montes profani*

– the oldest of these was founded in Venice between 1164 and 1178 to cover an acute municipal cash shortage: to raise capital, citizens were ordered to deposit money in the city's *mons* (or *imprestita*), in return for which the city promised to pay an annual interest rate of 2–5 per cent until the capital was repaid; similar institutions existed also in Genoa and Florence. For the *monti frumentari* see Ippolita Checcoli, *I Monti frumentari e le forme di credito non monetario tra Medioevo ed Età moderna* (Bologna, 2016).

11 Lawrin Armstrong, 'Usury, Conscience and Public Debt: Angelo Corbinelli's Testament of 1419', in John A. Munor and Thomas Kuehn (eds), *A Renaissance of Conflicts: Visions and Revisions of Law and Society in Italy and Spain* (Toronto, 2004), pp. 173–240 (230f), cited by Katherine Jansen, Joanne Drell and Frances Andrews (eds), *Medieval Italy: Texts in Translation* (Philadelphia, 2009), p. 108. On Florence's Monte Commune see also Richard Lindholm, *Quantitative Studies of the Renaissance Florentine Economy and Society* (New York, 2017), pp. 35–58.

12 Muzzarelli, *Il denaro e la salvezza*; Paola Avallone (ed.), *Il 'povero' va in Banca. I Monti di Pietà negli antichi stati Italiani* (Naples, 2001); Carol Bresnahan Menning, *Charity and State in Late Renaissance Italy. The Monte di Pietà of Florence* (Ithaca, NY, 1993); Meneghin, *I Monti di Pietà*; Holzapfel, *Die Anfänge des Montes Pietatis*.

13 For an overview of the history of microfinance scholarship see Nicola Lorenzo Barile, 'Renaissance Monti di Pietà in Modern Scholarship: Themes, Studies, and Historiographic Trends', in Terpstra and Carboni, *The Material Culture of Debt*, pp. 85–114. On the *monti*'s bookkeeping see Mauro Carboni and Maria Giuseppina Muzzarelli (eds), *I Conti dei Monti. Teoria e Pratica amministrativa nei Monti di Pietà fra Medioevo ed Età Moderna* (Venice, 2008).

14 Meneghin, *I Monti di Pietà*, p.14. 'La diminuzione della povertà, l'evoluzione sociale, il sorgere di nuovi enti creditizi, le varie forme di assistenza estese dallo Stato ad ogni.' Cf. Skambraks, *Karitativer Kredit*.

15 Robert S. Lopez, *The Commercial Revolution of the Middle Ages, 950–1350* (Cambridge, 1976), p. 87. Bindo Piaciti's letter is addressed to Francesco di Marco Datini (2 and 5 November 1400; Archivio di Stato Prato, Datini 712, Carteggio Bologna), trans. Eleanor A.

Congdon, 'A run on a Bank (1400)', in Katherine Jansen, Joanne Drell and Frances Andrews (eds), *Medieval Italy: Texts in Translation* (Philadelphia, 2009), p. 98f.

16 See Carboni, 'Converting Goods into Cash', p. 64.

17 S. Lodi and Maria Teresa Sambin De Norcen, 'Il complesso del Monte di pietà al Duomo (XIV sec.–1619)', in *Il palazzo del Monte di pietà a Padova* (Padua, 1996), pp. 25–101, https://www.fondazionedelmonte.it/centro-studi-monti-di-pieta/storia/padova-1491/.

18 Skambraks, *Karitativer Kredit*, p. 172.

19 For more on this see Chapter 5 of the present book.

20 Meneghin, *I Monti di Pietà*, p. 14, and see pp. 117–25 for the list of more than 140 missionaries.

21 For more on the Jewish pawnbrokers see Tanja Skambraks, 'Zwischen Kooperation und Konkurrenz. Jüdische Pfandleihe und Monti di Pietà in Italien', in Gerhard Fouquet and Sven Rabeler (eds), *Ökonomische Glaubensfragen. Strukturen und Praktiken jüdischen und christlichen Kleinkredits im Spätmittelalter* (Stuttgart, 2018), pp. 99–120; Maristella Botticini, 'A tale of "benevolent" governments: Private credit markets, public finance, and the role of the Jewish lenders in Medieval and Renaissance Italy' in *Journal of Economic History* 60(1) (2000), pp. 164–89.

22 For a taste of what the sermons could be like see Muzzarelli's study of Bernardino da Feltre's antisemitic diatribes in 'The effect of Bernardino da Feltre's preaching on the Jews', in Jonathan Adams and Jussi Hanska (eds), *The Jewish Christian Encounter in Medieval Preaching* (New York, 2014), pp. 170–94; Ariel Toaff, 'Jews, Franciscans and the First Monti di Pietà in Italy', in Steven J. McMichael and Susan E. Meyers (eds), *Friars and Jews in the Middle Ages and Renaissance* (Leiden/Boston, 2004), pp. 239–53 (245). Cf. also Toaff, *The Jews in Umbria*, Vols 1–3 (Leiden, 1993–4).

23 For more on Perugia see Toaff, 'Jews, Franciscans and the First Monti', pp. 241–6; and cf. Skambraks, 'Zwischen Kooperation und Konkurrenz', p. 105f.

24 'Silent partner' is the term used by Toaff in 'Jews, Franciscans and the First Monti', p. 247.

25 In 'Zwischen Kooperation und Konkurrenz' Skambraks

describes how the towns wanted to continue the tried and tested cooperation between Jewish and Christian businessmen because these benefited both the *bonum commune* and the municipal economy; see p. 100, citing Alfred Haverkamp, 'Juden in Italien und Deutschland während des Spätmittelalters. Ansätze zum Vergleich', in Alfred Haverkamp, Christoph Cluse and Jörg R. Müller (eds), *Neue Forschungen zur mittelalterlichen Geschichte (2000–2011). Festgabe zum 75. Geburtstag* (Hanover, 2012), pp. 59–102 (75).

26 René Girard, *The Scapegoat* (Baltimore, 1986).

27 Muzzarelli, 'The effect of Bernardino da Feltre's preaching on the Jews'.

28 See Skambraks, *Karitativer Kredit*, the chapter on 'A Trustworthy Institution?'.

29 Maria Giuseppina Muzzarelli, 'From the Closet to the Wallet: Pawning Clothes in Renaissance Italy', in *Renaissance and Reformation* 35 (3) (2012), pp. 23–38 (25f); Carboni, 'Converting Goods into Cash', p. 71f.

30 Skambraks, *Karitativer Kredit*.

31 Michel Mollat (ed.), *Études sur l'histoire de la pauvreté*, Vol. 1–2, Paris 1974; Franz J. Felten, 'Zusammenfassung. Mit zwei Exkursen zu den 'Starken Armen' im frühen und hohen Mittelalter und zur Erforschung der pauperes der Karolingerzeit', in Otto Gerhard Oexle (ed.), *Armut im Mittelalter*, Ostfildern 2004, pp. 349–401. Herbert Uerlings, Nina Trauth and Lukas Clemens (eds), *Armut. Perspektiven in Kunst und Gesellschaft. Katalog zur Ausstellung*, Darmstadt 2011. Cf. also Gabriela Signori, *Schuldenwirtschaft: Konsumenten-und Hypothekenkredite im spätmittelalterlichen Basel*, Konstanz/Munich 2015, pp. 26f; Signori prefers to speak of 'little' people only when the subject is the disenfranchised poor, rather than people who merely fall outside the taxpayer bracket. For urban alms networks, see e.g. Rubin, Miri, *Charity and Community in Medieval Cambridge* (Cambridge, 1987).

32 Valentin Groebner, 'Mobile Werte, informelle Ökonomie. Zur "Kultur" der Armut in der spätmittelalterlichen Stadt', in Oexle (ed.), *Armut im Mittelalter*, pp. 165–87. Historians also talk of objects as 'bearers' of capital in the context of medieval commodity-based economies, where, in societies where credit was common, objects

replaced money as stores of value. This is also reflected in the broad palette of goods that the *monti* accepted by way of collateral, to give their clients a degree of financial flexibility.

33 Carboni, 'Converting Goods into Cash', p. 65.

34 Mauro Carboni and Maria Giuseppina Muzzarelli, *In pegno. Oggetti in transito tra valore d'uso e valore di scambio (secoli XIII–XX)* (Bologna, 2012); for the value of everyday objects, cf. Daniel L. Smail, *Legal plunder. Households and Debt Collections in Late Medieval Europe*, Harvard 2016, especially pp. 31–88 ('The value of things').

35 Muzzarelli, 'From the Closet to the Wallet'. Cf. Skambraks, *Karitativer Kredit*, for a detailed examination of the Perugian list.

36 For Maddalena see Muzzarelli, 'From the Closet to the Wallet', p. 32.

37 Skambraks, *Karitativer Kredit*, Chapter 4.1. Interestingly, it appears that clients could redeem any unredeemed pledges at a later date even if they had been sold off in the meantime: a collection of black velvet dresses pledged by a wool weaver called Nucenzio who had defaulted on his loan was bought at auction by a certain Permatheus de Cavaceppis for twelve florins each – but a note added later says that Permatheus agreed to let another wool weaver redeem them on Nucenzio's behalf. It was evidently possible for a debtor to belatedly reacquire forfeited collateral, something which Skambraks interprets as a sign of considerable flexibility among the system's participants, and that this was a business which allowed participants to informally come to an amicable settlement.

38 Muzzarelli interprets this differently, and points to the data from Pistoia and Urbino: in Pistoia, just 5 per cent of creditors were women; in Urbino the percentage stood a little higher, at 12.5 per cent (Muzzarrelli, 'From the Closet to the Wallet', p. 28).

39 For some vivid examples see Jansen, *Medieval Italy*, pp. 104–9. On the problem of interest earnings in the urban *monti*, specifically the Monte Commune in Florence, see Julius Kirshner, 'Storm over the Monte Commune. Genesis of the moral controversy over the public debts of Florence' in *Archivum Fratrum Praedicatorum* 53 (1983), pp. 219–76.

40 Rosa Maria Dessi, 'Usura, Caritas e Monti di Pietà. Le prediche

antiusurarie e antiebraiche di Marco da Bologna e di Michele Carcano', in *I fratri osservanti e la società in Italia nel secolo XV, Atti del XL Convegno internazionale in occasione del 550 ° anniversario della fondazione del Monte di pietà di Perugia, 1462, Assisi – Perugia, 11–13 Oct 2012* (Spoleto, 2013), pp. 169–226 (202).

41 Cf. Laurence Fontaine, *The Moral Economy: Poverty, Credit, and Trust in Early Modern Europe* (Cambridge, 2014); Maria Giuseppina Muzzarelli, 'Il Monte, la pietà e la misericordia. Parole e immagini', in Pietro Delcorno (ed.), *Politiche di misericordia tra teoria e prassi. Confraternite, ospedali e monti di pietà (XIII–XVI secolo)* (Bologna, 2018), pp. 229–42.

42 Meneghin, *I Monti di Pietà*, p. 9f, n. 2.

43 Key texts here are Simon Teuscher, 'Schulden, Abhängigkeiten und politische Kultur. Das Beispiel der Kleinstadt Thun im Spätmittelalter', in Gabriela Signori (ed.), *Prekäre Ökonomien. Schulden in Spätmittelalter und Früher Neuzeit* (Konstanz / Munich, 2014), pp. 243–62 (243, n. 1); Mark Häberlein, 'Kreditbeziehung und Kapitalmärkte vom 16. bis 19. Jahrhundert', in Jürgen Schlumbohm (ed.), *Soziale Praxis des Kredits 16.–20. Jahrhundert* (Hanover, 2007), pp. 37–51; and cf. Signori, *Schuldenwirtschaft*, p. 10.

44 Signori, *Schuldenwirtschaft*, p. 11, referring to the much-cited article by Bruno Kuske, 'Die Entstehung der Kreditwirtschaft und des Kapitalverkehrs', in *idem* (ed.), *Köln, der Rhein und das Reich. Beiträge aus fünf Jahrzehnten wirtschaftsgeschichtlicher Forschung* (Cologne / Graz, 1956), pp. 48–138: 'The credit systems of the past show evidence of considerable loan activity, in the narrower sense of consumer credit activity, and one cannot stress enough how astonishingly widespread it was across the whole of society, so long as you were in some small degree creditworthy.'

45 Teuscher, *Schulden*, p. 248.

46 Ibid., p. 249; cf. also *idem, Bekannte, Klienten, Verwandte. Soziabilität und Politik in der Stadt Bern um 1500* (Cologne, 1998).

47 Signori, *Schuldenwirtschaft*, p. 16f. I am very grateful to Gabriela Signori for sending me the digital file. This so-called 'little catalogue', the '*Beschreibbuch*', is located in Basel's city archive, StABS ÄNA GA K 2 (1475–1478), p. 74. On the part played by hospitals see Julia Mandry's study *Armenfürsorge, Hospitäler und*

Bettel in Thüringen in Spätmittelalter und Reformation (1300–1600) (Vienna, 2018); Brigitte Pohl-Resl, *Rechnen mit der Ewigkeit. Das Wiener Bürgerspital im Mittelalter* (Vienna, 1996).

48 Signori, *Schuldenwirtschaft*, p. 20.

49 Signori takes a different view: in her opinion, the *Vergichtbücher* are proof that there was growing mistrust among people in Basel ('These books are proof of [a] lack of trust', *Schuldenwirtschaft*, p. 46). She disagrees with, among others, Craig Muldrew's thesis in *The Economy of Obligation: The Culture of Credit and Social Relations in Early Modern England* (London, 1998), that England's early modern economy was based on relationships of trust and the good reputation of those involved – and asks, 'If there is trust, do you really need that many books?' (*Schuldenwirtschaft*, p. 19).

50 Signori, *Schuldenwirtschaft*, p. 35ff.

51 According to a 1428 council decision, ibid., p. 30.

52 Ibid., p. 43f.

53 Ibid., pp. 54f and 77, referencing Katharina Simon-Muscheid, *Die Dinge im Schnittpunkt sozialer Beziehungsnetze* (Göttingen, 2004), pp. 91–7.

54 Signori, *Schuldenwirtschaft*, p. 76, nn. 85–8, and pp. 49, 54 and 75.

55 Ibid., p. 138f.

56 Fontaine, *Moral Economy*, p. 96, n. 2, referencing Daniel Roche, who (in *Le Peuple de Paris* [Paris, 1981], p. 84) rejects the term 'day labourer' as misleading and replaces it with 'wage worker' instead.

57 Fontaine, *Moral Economy*, pp. 95–9, citing Anne Montenach, 'Une économie de l'infime. Espace et pratiques du commerce alimentaire à Lyon au XVII siecle', PhD thesis, Institut Universitaire Européen de Florence, 2003, pp. 387–94.

58 Gaël Chantepie and Mathias Latina, *La réforme du droit des obligations. Commentaire théorique et pratique dans l'ordre du Code civil* (Dalloz, 2016). *Code civil. Livre III: Des différentes manières dont on acquiert la propriété*, 'Titre III: Des contrats ou des obligations conventionnelles en général. Chapitre VI: De la preuve des obligations et de celle du paiement. Section 1: De la preuve littérale. Paragraphe 1: Dispositions générales. Article 1316 La preuve littérale, ou preuve par écrit, résulte d'une suite de lettres, de caractères, de chiffres ou de tous autres signes ou symboles

dotés d'une signification intelligible, quels que soient leur support et leurs modalités de transmission. […] Paragraphe 4: Des tailles [archive], Article 1333 Les tailles corrélatives à leurs échantillons font foi entre les personnes qui sont dans l'usage de constater ainsi les fournitures qu'elles font ou reçoivent en détail.' Tanja Skambraks (University of Graz) is currently preparing a cross-cultural survey of the use and function of tally sticks. For a first overview see her paper 'Tally sticks as media of knowledge in the contexts of medieval economic and administrative history', in *L'economia della conoscenza. Innovazione, produttività e crescita economica nei secoli XIII–XVIII* (2023), pp. 137–58.

59 Karl-Heinz Ludwig, 'Kerbholz', in *Lexikon des Mittelalters*, Vol. 5 (Stuttgart, 1993), col. 1115.

60 Ludolf Kuchenbuch, 'Pragmatische Rechenhaftigkeit? Kerbhölzer in Bild, Gestalt und Schrift', in *Frühmittelalterliche Studien* 36 (2002), pp. 469–90; *idem*, 'Kerbhölzer in Alteuropa – zwischen Dorfschmiede und Schatzamt', in Nagy Balázs and Marcell Sebök (eds), *The Man of Many Devices Who Wandered Full Many Ways: Festschrift in Honor of János M. Bak* (Budapest, 1999), pp. 303–25; *idem*, 'Les baguettes de taille au Moyen Âge. Un moyen de calcul sans écriture?', in Natacha Coquery, François Menant and Florence Weber (eds), *Écrire, compter, mesurer. Vers une histoire des rationalités pratiques* (Paris, 2006), pp. 113–42; Ulla Kypta, *Die Autonomie der Routine: Wie im 12. Jahrhundert das englische Schatzamt entstand* (Göttingen, 2014); Moritz Wedell, *Zählen: Semantische und praxeologische Studien zum numerischen Wissen im Mittelalter* (Göttingen, 2011); Roman Kovalev and Thomas S. Noonan, 'What can archaeology tell us about how debts were documented and collected in Kievan Rus'?' in *Russian History* 27 (2000) pp. 119–54.

61 Ludolf Kuchenbuch, 'Am Nerv des Geldes. Die Verbankung der deutschen Verbraucher 1945–2005' in *Historische Anthropologie* 17(2) (2009), pp. 260–75.

62 Jacob Wackernagel, *Die Viehverstellung. Eine Sonderbildung der spätmittelalterlichen Gesellschaft, dargestellt auf Grund italienischer, französischer und deutscher Quellen* (Weimar, 1923), p. 1f. See also Nikolaus Grass, 'Viehverstellung', in Adalbert Erler and Ekkehard Kaufmann (eds), *Handwörterbuch zur Deutschen Rechtsgeschichte*, Vol.

5 (Berlin, 1998), cols 912–13; Dorothee Rippmann, 'Viehverstellung', in Friedrich Jäeger (ed.), *Enzyklopädie der Neuzeit*, Vol. 14 (Stuttgart, 2011), pp. 312–14.

63 Stephan Nicolussi-Köhler, *Marseille, Montpellier und das Mittelmeer. Die Entstehung des südfranz.sischen Fernhandels im 12. und 13. Jahrhundert (Pariser Historische Schriften 121)* (Heidelberg, 2021); Wackernagel, *Viehverstellung*, p. 12f, where Wackernagel wonders whether there was a direct link between livestock lease and *commenda* contracts; however, despite a thorough investigation, he was unable to find any evidence of such a link, and concludes that the maritime trade and agricultural production were wholly separate business sectors – notwithstanding the fact that some French sources refer to livestock leasing as *commande*.

64 In Switzerland you occasionally find provision for such agreements (called *Offnungen*, 'declarations') included in village statutes. For instance, the late fifteenth-century *Offnung* of Magdenau in the Canton of St Gall stipulates that every 11 November (St Martin's day), lessees must give their lessors a calf for every two cows; or, on the same day every two years, give them one calf for every one cow. See Stefan Sonderegger, *Landwirtschaftliche Entwicklung in der spätmittelalterlichen Nordostschweiz. Eine Untersuchung ausgehend von den wirtschaftlichen Aktivitäten des Heiliggeist-Spitals* (St Gall, 1994), p. 252.

65 Grass, 'Viehverstellung', cols 912f.

66 Wackernagel, *Viehverstellung*, p. 68f.

67 Sonderegger, *Landwirtschaftliche Entwicklung*, pp. 251–9 (255, n. 675).

68 Ibid., pp. 252–4.

69 Matthias Steinbrink, *Ulrich Meltinger. Ein Basler Kaufmann am Ende des 15. Jahrhunderts* (Stuttgart, 2007), p. 33f. Meltinger died in 1504.

70 Ibid., pp. 169–72.

71 Ibid., pp. 345 and 170.

72 Dorothee Rippmann, *Bauern und Städter: Stadt-Land-Beziehungen im 15. Jahrhundert: Das Beispiel Basel, unter besonderer Berücksichtigung der Nahmarktbeziehungen und der sozialen Verhältnisse im Umland* (Basel/Frankfurt, 1990), p. 203.

73 Wackernagel, *Viehverstellung*, p. 109.

74 The sustained impact of the Renaissance on European history

involved more than merely its artistic output; the MFIs were also a cultural product of the Renaissance, and (almost) as long-lived, with many continuing to exist well into the twentieth century. At the start of the nineteenth century, under Napoleon, they were subsumed by the new 'congregations of charity' (*congregazioni di carità*) set up in 1807. They quickly regained their autonomy almost everywhere, however, which very much seems to reflect the crucial role they played in urban society. Then, in the mid-nineteenth century, new and powerful rivals showed up: the savings banks. These also took on an important welfare role, and covered similar sectors of the urban credit market. The dual nature of the *monti* (as both welfare and credit institutions) was subsequently dealt with in the 1920s and 1930s, when two laws were passed that, respectively, separated the *monti* into two categories – those that were exclusively credit institutions and thus equivalent to savings banks, and those that would carry on their business as institutional pawnbrokers – and renamed the latter *monti di credito su pegno* and introduced relevant regulation. These developments enabled the *monti* to adjust to Italy's changing economic and social conditions. (See Massimo Fornasari, 'I Monti di Pietà tra Otto e Novecento', at the Fondazione del Monte, https://www.fondazionedelmonte.it/centro-studi-monti-di-pieta/storia/.)

5. Minimalism

1 Manfred Folkers and Niko Paech, *All you need is less. Eine Kultur des Genug aus ökonomischer und ökologischer Sicht* (Munich, 2020).

2 Theresa Bäuerlein, 'Freiwillig einfacher Leben', *Krautreporter*, 2018, https://krautreporter.de/1252-freiwillig-einfacher-leben?shared=ecb28325-a096-4f62-b1f5-407a62702f8c.

3 Note the subtitle of E. F. Schumacher's *Small Is Beautiful: A Study of Economics As If People Mattered* (London, 1973); Wolfgang Sachs, 'Ernst Friedrich Schumacher im Zeitalter der grenzenlosen Mega-Ökonomie' in *Politische Ökologie* 24 (2006), pp. 24–6, referencing Lewis Mumford, André Gorz and Ivan Illich, contemporaries of Schumacher's who wrote about the same issues. Others, too, demanded a return to a more human scale, including Schumacher's friend, the political economist Alfred Kohr, who

coined the term 'overdeveloped nations' and championed the dissolution of nation states in favour of smaller autonomous units in his 1978 work *The Breakdown of Nations*. Schumacher spent some time in Burma, where he encountered the minimalist tenets of Buddhism and wondered whether they could help shape an economic model based on something other than the principle of the maximisation of utility, which would better suit both mankind and nature; see Gábor Kóvacs, 'Buddhist Economics', in Hendrik Opdebeeck, *Responsible Economics: E. F. Schumacher and His Legacy for the 21st Century* (Oxford, 2013), pp. 33–52. John Seymour's *The Complete Book of Self-Sufficiency* (1978) also became a bestseller.

4 Georg Luck (ed.), *Die Weisheit der Hunde. Texte der antiken Kyniker in deutscher Übersetzung mit Erläuterungen* (Stuttgart, 1997), p. 76f.

5 Ibid., p. 139, n. 338.

6 Ibid., p. 101f, n. 170.

7 Ibid., p. 117, n. 211.

8 Luis E. Navia, *Diogenes of Sinope: The Man in the Tub* (Westport/London, 1998), p. 62f.

9 Luck, *Die Weisheit der Hunde*, p. 3f.

10 Ibid., p. 134, n. 305; p. 135, n. 310.

11 Luck, *Die Weisheit der Hunde*, p. 185, n. 510.

12 Ibid., p. 196, on Crates of Thebes; Léonce Paquet (ed.), *Lex Cyniques Grecs. Fragments et témoignages* (Ottawa, 1975), p. 130, on Bion.

13 Luck, *Die Weisheit der Hunde*, p. 197, n. 529, and for what follows see also pp. 104 and 197.

14 Ibid., p. 205.

15 Ibid., p. 212.

16 Donald R. Dudley, *A History of Cynicism: From Diogenes to the 6th Century A.D.* (London, 1937), p. 51.

17 Luck, *Die Weisheit der Hunde*, p. 10f.

18 R. Bracht Branham and Marie-Odile Goulet-Cazé (eds), *The Cynics: The Cynic Movement in Antiquity and Its Legacy* (Berkeley, CA, 1996), p. 24.

19 Marie-Odile Goulet-Cazé, 'A Comprehensive Catalogue of Known Cynic Philosophers', in ibid., pp. 389–413, and see also the Introduction, ibid., p. 16.

20 Luck, *Die Weisheit der Hunde*, pp. 430–65.
21 See Thomas of Celano, *Leben und Wunder des Heiligen Franziskus von Assisi*; introduced, trans. and ed. with notes by Engelbert Grau (5th edn, Werl/Westfalen, 1994), pp. 128f (1 Cel 55); and ibid., p. 118 (1 Cel 43) on refusing to meet the emperor. The Latin sources concerning the life of St Francis are edited and summarised in Enrico Menestò and Stefano Brufani (eds), *Fontes Franciscani* (Assisi, 1995).
22 Celano, *Leben und Wunder*, pp. 73–216 (114) (1 Cel 39), which mentions that bakers' ovens were commonly used as sleeping quarters; and ibid., pp. 128f (1 Cel 55) on the sea voyage.
23 Sophronius Clasen and Engelbert Grau (eds), *Die Dreigefährtenlegende des Heiligen Franziskus. Die Brüder Leo, Rufin und Angelus erzählen vom Anfang seines Ordens* (Werl, 1993), Chapter 1.2. Cf. Helmut Feld, *Franziskus von Assisi und seine Bewegung* (Darmstadt, 1994), p. 107.
24 Cf. Cristina Andenna, 'Familiäre Nähe und Distanz in der franziskanischen Welt des 13. Jahrhunderts' in *Saeculum* 2 (2018), pp. 321–42 (340).
25 Celano, *Leben und Wunder*, p. 97f (1 Cel 22): *Hoc est, inquit, quod volo, hoc est quod quaero, hoc totis medullis cordis facere concupisco*.
26 Celano, 'The First Life of St Francis', § 23, in M. L. Cameron, *The Inquiring Pilgrim's Guide to Assisi*, trans. A. G. Ferrers Howell (London, 1926), ed. and rev. by Deborah Mauskopf Deliyannis, https://dmdhist.sitehost.iu.edu/francis.htm#1.10.
27 See 1 Cel 22 for his restoration of the churches of San Damiano and Santa Maria degli Angeli (Portiuncula) and 'That is what I want' (1208); his journey to Rome with eleven companions to meet Innocent III (1209), Francis in the Holy Land (1219/20), *Regula non bullata* (1221), *Regula bullata* (1223), Christmas celebration in Greccio (1223), he receives the stigmata (1224), death (4 October 1226), canonisation (16 July 1228).
28 See Celano, *Leben und Wunder*; for his dislike of superfluous domestic equipment see p. 276f (2 Cel 60); concerning superfluous books see p. 278 (2 Cel 62); feather pillows, p. 279f (2 Cel 64); too many clothes p. 284 (2 Cel 69). Fascinating ideas concerning the Marie Kondo phenomenon can be found in Haringke Fugmann,

Aufräumen als heilige Handlung. Zum weltanschaulichen Hintergrund des Bestsellers 'Magic Cleaning' von Marie Kondo (Berlin, 2017).

29 Celano, *Leben und Wunder*, pp. 281–4 (2 Cel 65–68).

30 Thomas of Celano, *St. Francis of Assisi: First and Second Life of St. Francis, with selections from 'The Treatise on the Miracles of Blessed Francis'*, trans. Placid Hermann (Chicago, 1988), pp. 187–8. For a definitive translation of Franciscan writings see R. J. Armstrong, J. A. W. Hellmann and W. J. Short (eds), *Francis of Assisi: Early Documents* (4 vols, New York, 1999–2002), with a historical introduction and commentary to precede each text, https://digitalcollections.franciscantradition.org/collection/francis_of_assisi:_early_documents_-_the_founder?view=true&sort=label&page=1&searchOption=transcriptions&searchType=all_words&collection=Francis%20of%20Assisi:%20Early%20Documents%20-%20The%20Founder

31 The figure comes from Richard Southern, *Western Society and the Church* (London, 1970), p. 285; see also John B. Freed's *The Friars in German Society in the Thirteenth Century* (Cambridge, 1977), pp. 173–223, for a list of Dominican and Franciscan houses in Germany; cf. also Schwaiger, *Mönchtum, Orden, Klöster* (Munich, 1993).

32 The name 'straw mat chapter' is used for both the 1217 and the 1221 Whitsun chapters. Helmut Feld, *Franz von Assisi und seine Bewegung*, p. 512.

33 Celano, *Leben und Wunder*, p. 129, 1 Cel 55.

34 For the Franciscans' stance on Islam see Anne Müller, 'Die frühe Franziskanermission im muslimischen Orient: Ideen, normative Grundlagen und Praxis', in Giancarlo Collet and Johannes Meier (eds), *Geschichte der Sächsischen Franziskaner-Provinz von der Gründung bis zum Anfang des 21. Jahrhunderts*, Vol. 4 (*Missionen*) (Paderborn, 2013), pp. 33–56; Anne Müller, 'Bettelmönche und Islam. Beobachtungen zur symbolischen Darstellung von Missionsprinzipien der Mendikanten in Text, Handlung und Bildkunst des 13. Jahrhunderts', in Margit Mersch and Ulrike Ritzerfeld (eds), *Lateinisch-griechisch-arabische Begegnungen: Kulturelle Diversität im Mittelmeerraum des Spätmittelalters* (Berlin, 2009), pp. 285–308; Anne Müller, 'Dominikaner und Islam. Begegnung, Mission, Wahrnehmung', in Susanne Biber and Elias H. Füllenbach

(eds), *Mehr als Schwarz und Weiß. 800 Jahre Dominikanerorden* (Regensburg, 2016), pp. 307–18.

35 Jordan von Giano, 'Chronik', in *Nach Deutschland und England. Die Chroniken der Minderbrüder Jordan von Giano und Thomas von Eccleston*, ed. Lothar Hardick (Werl/Westfalen, 1957), pp. 54–65.

36 Thomas of Eccleston, *Chronicle*, pp. 14–25.

37 Ibid., p. 26.

38 Ibid., pp. xiv–xv and 29. See also Celano, *Leben und Wunder*, p. 274 (2 Cel 56), re Francis demanding simple huts built of wood rather than stone. When the brothers explained to him that in some places wood was considerably more expensive than stone, Francis decided not to argue the point and in his will merely states that the dwellings should meet the requirements of poverty (Celano, *Leben und Wunder*, 1, 96, 3–7).

39 See Felicitas Schmieder, *Johannes von Plano Carpini. Kunde von den Mongolen 1245–1247* (Sigmaringen, 1997), p. 16f; Thomas Ertl, 'Ihr irrt viel umher, ihr jungen Leute. Der mittelalterliche Franziskanerorden zwischen europäischer Entgrenzung und regionaler Beschränkung', in Uwe Israel (ed.), *Vita communis und ethnische Vielfalt. Multinational zusammengesetzte Klöster im Mittelalter* (Rome/Berlin, 2006), pp. 1–34.

40 Penn R. Szittya, *The Antifraternal Tradition in Medieval Literature* (Princeton, 1986); the cleric and University of Paris professor William of St-Amour (d. 1271) compiled a catalogue of fifty accusations against the Franciscans (*Tractatus Brevis De Periculis Novissimorum Temporum*). In the fourteenth century, Geoffrey Chaucer bundled every single contemporary prejudice and criticism of the Franciscans into his *Canterbury Tales*. Cf. Thomas Ertl, 'Franziskanische Armut in der Kritik. Anti-mendikantische Wahrnehmungsmuster im Wandel (13.–15. Jahrhundert)', in Heinz-Dieter Heimann et al. (eds), *Gelobte Armut. Armutskonzepte der franziskanischen Ordensfamilie* (Paderborn, 2012), pp. 369–92.

41 On towns and cities providing mendicant orders with convents see Leonie Silberer, *Klosterbaukunst der Konventualen Franziskaner vom 13. Jahrhundert bis zur Reformation* (Petersberg, 2016), pp. 37–9; Matthias Untermann, 'Fehlbenennungen von Klosterräumen und ihr Effekt auf die Forschung', in Gert Melville, Leonie Silberer and Bernd

Schmies (eds), *Die Klöster der Franziskaner im Mittelalter. Räume. Nutzungen. Symbolik* (Münster, 2015), pp. 19–44.

42 These medieval allegations affected scholarship over the centuries and into the present day, including the question of whether the Franciscans betrayed their founder's ideals. See, for example, Paul Sabatier, *Leben des heiligen Franz von Assisi*, trans. Margarete Lisco (La Vergne, TN, 2010) – in Sabatier's view (writing in 1897), the Church ruthlessly bastardised St Francis's theories: he has examined different versions of The Rule of St Francis from 1209, 1221 and 1223 and argues that only the first expresses the saint's true intentions, while the later versions, particularly that of 1223 (confirmed by papal bull and known as the *Regula bullata*), are purely the work of the Church and share nothing with the first version except its name. Cf. Raoul Manselli, *Franziskus der solidarische Bruder* (Freiburg, 1989).

43 Johannes Schlageter, 'Die Anfänge der Franziskaner in Thüringen', in Thomas T. Müller, Bernd Schmies and Christian Loefke (eds), *Für Gott und die Welt. Franziskaner in Thüringen* (Paderborn, 2008), pp. 32–7 (34–6).

44 Werner Malecek, '"Nackt dem nackten Christus folgen". Die freiwillig Armen in der religiösen Bewegung der mittelalterlichen Gesellschaft', in Heinz-Dieter Heimann et al., *Gelobte Armut*, pp. 17–34; Malecek emphasises the seriousness with which Christian poverty was posited, particularly during the thirteenth and fourteenth centuries.

45 Stefan Weinfurter, *Canossa. Die Entzauberung der Welt* (Munich, 2006).

46 Thomas Ertl, 'Netzwerke des Wissens. Die Bettelorden, ihre Mobilität und ihre Schulen', in Matthias Puhle (ed.), *Aufbruch in die Gotik. Der Madgeburger Dom und die späte Stauferzeit*, Vol. 1 (Madgeburg, 2009), pp. 312–23.

47 Simon Somerville Laurie, *The Rise and Early Constitution of Universities, with a Survey of Mediaeval Education* (New York, 1907), p. 175f.

48 On the creation of the first universities see Martin Kintzinger, *Wissen wird Macht. Bildung im Mittelalter* (Ostfildern, 2003). Bologna has been able to claim the title of oldest university in the world

thanks to a statement by a commission convened in 1888 to oversee Bologna's 800th anniversary celebrations. The commission consisted entirely of University of Bologna professors. See also Winfried Stelzer, 'Zum Scholarenprivileg Friedrich Barbarossas (*Authentica habita*)', in *DA* 34 (1978), pp. 123–65. The translation is by Wolfgang Lautemann, *Geschichte in Quellen*, Vol. 2: *Mittelalter* (Munich, 1978), p. 411.

49 Celano, *Leben und Wunder*, p. 150f, 1 Cel 77–79.

50 See Achim Wesjohann, 'Simplicitas als franziskanisches Ideal und der Prozess der Institutionalisierung', in Gert Melville and Jörg Oberste (eds), *Die Bettelorden im Aufbau. Beiträge zu Institutionalisierungsprozessen im mittelalterlichen Religiosentum* (Münster, 1999), pp. 107–68 (134) for 'Brother Simpleton'; see p. 137f for Juniper, a member of the order, who is reported to have enjoyed strolling naked, with his pants on his head and carrying his habit on his back, through the streets of Viterbo and, once, Assisi.

51 Celano, *Leben und Wunder*, p. 262 (2 Cel 44), p. 269 (2 Cel 50).

52 *Sacrum Commercium, Der Bund des Heiligen Franziskus mit der Herrin Armut*, trans. with notes by Kajetan Esser and Engelbert Grau (eds) (Werl/Westfalen, 1966); for Lady Poverty eating with the brothers see ibid., pp. 154–9: *'Ostenderunt ei totum orbem. Hoc est claustrum nostrum, Domina.'*

53 Lynn White, 'The Historical Roots of our Ecological Crisis' in *Science* 155(3767) (1967), pp. 1203–07.

54 Kenneth Pomeranz, *The Great Divergence: China, Europe and the Making of the Modern World* (Princeton, 2000).

55 Helmut Feld, *Beseelte Natur. Franziskanische Naturerzählungen* (Tübingen, 1993), p. 26f.

56 Pope John Paul II, *Litterae Apostolicae: Inter Sanctos* (29 November 1979), http://www.vatican.va/holy_father/john_paul_ii/apost_letters/1979/documents/hf_jp-ii_apl_19791129_inter-sanctos_lt.html.

57 Elspeth Whitney, 'Lynn White Jr.'s "The Historical Roots of Our Ecologic Crisis" After 50 Years' in *History Compass* 13 (2015), pp. 396–410. Doi: 10.1111/hic3.12254.

58 Axel Michaels, 'Sakralisierung als Naturschutz? Heilige Bäume und Wälder in Nepal', in Rolf Sieferle and Helga Breuninger (eds),

Natur-Bilder: Wahrnehmungen von Natur und Umwelt in der Geschichte (Frankfurt, 1999), pp. 117–36 (132); Mark Elvin, 'Three thousand years of unsustainable growth: China's environment from archaic times to the present' in *East Asian History* 6 (1993), pp. 7–46.

59 Christian F. Feest, *Beseelte Welten – Die Religionen der Indianer Nordamerikas* (Freiburg, 1998).

60 Joachim Radkau, 'Religion and Environmentalism', in John R. McNeill and Erin S. Mauldin (eds), *A Companion to Global Environmental History* (London, 2012), pp. 493–512. Cf. also the latest theories in palaeobiology and palaeoanthropology, as packaged by the Role of Culture in Early Expansions of Humans research centre (Heidelberg Academy of Sciences and Humanities and the Senckenberg Institute in Frankfurt); see Miriam N. Haidle, Niclas J. Conard and M. Bolus (eds), *The Nature of Culture – Based on an Interdisciplinary Symposium 'The Nature of Culture'* (Tübingen, 2016).

61 Grahame Thompson, 'Early Double-Entry Bookkeeping and the Rhetoric of Accounting Calculation', in Anthony G. Hopwood and Peter Miller (eds), *Accounting as a Social and Institutional Practice* (Cambridge, 1994), pp. 40–66.

62 Jörg Oberste, *Zwischen Heiligkeit und Häresie*, Vol. 1 (Cologne/Weimar/Vienna, 2003), pp. 235–81.

63 Giacomo Todeschini, *Franciscan Wealth* (New York, 2009), p. 107.

64 See Joel Kaye, *Economy and Nature in the Fourteenth Century: Money, Market Exchange, and the Emergence of Scientific Thought* (New York, 1998), p. 15, with reference to Nicholas Mayhew, 'Modelling Medieval Monetisation', in Richard H. Britnell and Bruce M. S. Campbell (eds), *A Commercialising Economy: England 1086–1300* (Manchester, 1995), pp. 55–77 (63f), and Peter Spufford, *Money and Its Use in Medieval Europe* (Cambridge, 1988), pp. 245–63.

65 Joel Kaye, *A History of Balance, 1250–1375: The Emergence of a New Model of Equilibrium and Its Impact on Thought* (Cambridge, 2014), p. 27, citing the *Summae confessorum* of Thomas of Chobham (1215–16) and Raymond of Penyafort (1225–27); see also Todeschini, 'La riflessione etica sulle attività economiche', in Roberto Creci (ed.), *Economie urbane ed etica economica nell'Italia medievale* (Rome, 2005), pp. 151–228.

66 Kaye, *A History of Balance*, p. 26.

67 Todeschini coined the term *economia franciscana* in 'Oeconomica franciscana. Proposte di una nuova lettura delle fonti dell'etica economica medievale' in *Rivista di Storia e Letteratura Religiosa* 12 (1976), pp. 15–77; see also *idem*, 'Oeconomica Franciscana II. Pietro di Giovanni Olivi come fonte per la storia dell'etica economica medievale' in *Rivista di Storia e Letteratura Religiosa* 13 (1977), pp. 461–94; Odd Langholm, *Economics in the Medieval Schools* (Leiden, 1992); Raymond De Roover, *San Bernardino of Siena and Sant' Antonino of Florence: The Two Great Economic Thinkers of the Middle Ages* (Boston, 1967), p. 19; and Martín Carbajo Núñez, *A Free and Fraternal Economy: The Franciscan Perspective* (Delhi, 2018).

68 Sylvain Piron, 'The formation of Olivi's intellectual project' in *Oliviana* (2003), http://journals.openedition.org/oliviana/8).

69 David Burr, 'Olivi and the limits of intellectual freedom', in George H. Shriver (ed.), *Contemporary Reflections on the Medieval Christian Tradition: Essays in Honor of Ray C. Petry* (Durham, 1974), pp. 185–99 (195).

70 Theo Kobusch, 'Petrus Johannis Olivi: ein franziskanischer Querkopf', in Markus Knapp and Theo Kobusch (eds), *Querdenker. Visionäre und Außenseiter in Philosophie und Theologie* (Darmstadt, 2005), pp. 106–16 (108); and Burr, *Olivi*, pp. 194–6.

71 Frank Rexroth, *Fröhliche Scholastik. Die Wissenschaftsrevolution des Mittelalters* (Munich, 2018), p. 34f.

72 For a reconstruction of the controversy, whose outline I have sketched here, see David Burr, *Olivi and Franciscan Poverty. The Origins of the Usus Pauper Controversy* (Philadelphia, 1989), and more recently Sylvain Piron, 'Censures et condamnation de Pierre de Jean Olivi. Enquête dans les marges du Vatican', in *Mélanges de l'École française de Rome – Moyen Âge* (Rome, 2006), pp. 118–22 and 313–73.

73 Burr, *Olivi and Franciscan Poverty*, p. 40.

74 Burr, 'The Persecution of Peter Olivi' in *Transactions of the American Philosophical Society* 66(5) (1976), pp. 1–98; Piron, 'Censures et condemnation', pp. 313–73.

75 Sylvain Piron, *Pierre de Jean Olivi. Traité des Contrats* (Paris, 2012), pp. 94–109. Cf. De Roover, *San Bernardino of Siena*, pp. 16–23. De Roover at the time still assumed that Bernardino di Siena

(1389–1444) was the author of the *Treatise*, because he drew on the text for his sermons and copied it word for word. De Roover thought the theses truly revolutionary for the fifteenth century, and saw in them an early version of a Renaissance theory of economics. He declared Bernardino the greatest economist of all time, and was fascinated by the fact that the *Treatise* contained some of the ideas familiar to us from 'modern' economic theories. He only learnt years later that the text was not by Bernardino, and had in fact been written more than a century earlier.

76 Piron, *Traité*, p. 96. *Tantum valet res quantum vendi potest* was a principle in Roman law. It has been attributed among others to Publilius Syrus, but there is no concrete evidence that he said it (see Hermann Beckby, *Die Sprüche des Publilius Syrus* [Munich, 1969]). It appears in French in a fifteenth-century MS – cf. Joseph Morawski, *Proverbes français antérieurs au XVe siècle* (Paris, 1925), p. 83, no. 2303: 'Tant vault la chose comme elle peut estre vendue' (Paris, Bibliothèque National MS lat. 10360, 15. Jh.). Re Olivi's approach see also Kaye, *A History of Balance*, pp. 107–17.

77 Piron, *Traité*, p. 96; Samuel Singer (ed.), *Thesaurus proverbiorum medii aevi*, Vol. 12 (Berlin, 2001), pp. 42–8.

78 Piron, *Traité*, p. 98; Hans Walther, *Proverbia sententiaeque latinitatis medii aevi*, Vol. 2 (2) (Göttingen, 1964), p. 661.

79 Piron, *Traité*, p. 98, § 8.

80 Juhana Toivanen, 'Voluntarist Anthropology in Peter of John Olivi's *De Contractibus*' in *Franciscan Studies* 74 (2016), pp. 41–65 (56).

81 Ibid., pp. 100–103, § 9–11.

82 Ibid., p. 100.

83 Todeschini, 'Pietro di Giovanni Olivi come fonte per la storia dell'etica-economica medievale', in Ovidio Capitani (ed.), *Una economia politica nel medioevo* (Bologna, 1987), pp. 59–91 (87); in *Economy and Nature in the Fourteenth Century*, p. 148, Kaye discusses the relationship between goods and buyer as a factor involved in setting prices – but Odd Landholm disagrees: see 'Olivi to Hutcheson: Tracing an early tradition in value theory' in *Journal of the History of Economic Thought* 31 (2009) pp. 131–41 (133).

84 Langholm, *Economics*, p. 354.

85 Piron, *Traité*, p. 102, § 12.

86 *Pretium iustum* means the prevalent market price – no more, no less. The older, misleading interpretation of it as a 'fair price' is no longer considered valid. Ever since John Baldwin's 1959 study of the topic, historians have come to believe that the concept of a 'fair price' may never have existed, whether in reality or in theory, as a measure separate from what was actually happening on the markets. Cf. De Roover, 'The concept of the just price: Theory and economic policy' in *Journal of Economic History* 18 (1958), pp. 418–38 (420) and John Baldwin, 'The medieval theories of the just price: Romanists, canonists, and theologians in the twelfth and thirteenth centuries' in *Transactions of the American Philosophical Society* 49(4) (1959), pp. 1–92.

87 Piron, *Traité*, p. 120, § 43.

88 Langholm, *Economics*, p. 361.

89 Piron, *Traité*, p. 114, § 30; cf. also Langholm, *Economics*, p. 363.

90 Langholm, *Economics*, p. 363f.

91 Ibid., pp. 228–33, pp. 59–64; Langholm, *Economics*, pp. 369–72.

92 Ibid., p. 233, n. 21.

93 Kaye, *A History of Balance*, p. 70; cf. also Christian Rode, 'Die Geburt des Kapitalismus aus dem Geist der franziskanischen Armutsbewegung. Der Kapitalbegriff bei Petrus Johannis Olivi', in Günther Mensching and Alia Mensching-Estakhr (eds), *Geistige und körperliche Arbeit im Mittelalter* (Würzburg, 2016), pp. 107–22.

94 Ibid., p. 52.

95 Langholm, *Economics*, p. 22; cf. Kaye, *A History of Balance*, pp. 63 and 107.

6. A Tailwind from the Past

1 Donella H. Meadows et al., *The Limits to Growth: A Report for the Club of Rome's Project on the Predicament of Mankind* (New York, 1972), p. 17.

2 Maja Göpel, *Unsere Welt neu denken: Eine Einladung* (Berlin, 2020).

3 See Mark Häberlein, *Die Fugger. Geschichte einer Augsburger Familie (1367–1660)* (Stuttgart, 2006), p. 26, citing Martha Schad, *Die Frauen des Hauses Fugger von der Lilie (15.–17. Jahrhundert)* (Augsburg, 1989), p. 12.

4 Peter Unfried and Harald Welzer, 'Maja Göpel im Interview:

Verbote können Menschen befreien' in *Taz Futurzwei* 10 (2019), pp. 36–41, https://taz.de/Maja-Goepel-im-Interview/!169655/.

5 Kate Raworth, 'What on Earth is the Doughnut?', https://www.kateraworth.com/doughnut/.

6 Lothario dei Segni (Pope Innocent III), *On the Misery of the Human Condition*, trans. Margaret Mary Dietz (New York, 1969).

7 Kobusch, 'Petrus Johannis Olivi', pp. 111–14.

INDEX

Numbers in italic refer to illustrations

Index

R

S

Index